SEVEN INTERPRETIVE ESSAYS ON PERUVIAN REALITY

THE TEXAS PAN AMERICAN SERIES

seven interpretive essays on
PERUVIAN REALITY

BY JOSÉ CARLOS MARIÁTEGUI

TRANSLATED BY MARJORY URQUIDI

INTRODUCTION BY JORGE BASADRE

UNIVERSITY OF TEXAS PRESS AUSTIN

International Standard Book Number 0-292-77611-x
Library of Congress Catalog Card Number 73-156346
Copyright © 1971 by the University of Texas Press
Printed in the United States of America

Third Paperback Printing, 1990

Requests for permission to reproduce material
from this work should be sent to:
Permissions
University of Texas Press
Box 7819
Austin, Texas 78713-7819

⊗ The paper used in this publication meets the minimum require-
ments of American National Standard for Information Sciences—
Permanence of Paper for Printed Library Materials, ANSI
Z39.48-1984.

The Texas Pan American Series is published with the assistance
of a revolving publication fund established by the Pan American
Sulphur Company and other friends of Latin America in Texas.
Publication of this book was also assisted by a grant from the
Rockefeller Foundation through the Latin American translation
program of the Association of American University Presses.

CONTENTS

INTRODUCTION

Until a short time ago, it was believed that José Carlos Mariátegui was born on June 14, 1895, in Lima. Recently, Guillermo
Rouillón uncovered the fact that he was actually born in Moquegua in 1894.[1] His family belonged to the lower middle class. His
father, Francisco Javier Mariátegui, was a minor employee of
the General Court of Accounts; his mother, María Amalia La-
chira, was a mestiza from the countryside near Huacho. Of their
four children, one girl, Amanda, died in infancy, so that José
Carlos was left with a sister, Guillermina, and a brother, Julio
César, who later became a bookseller and publisher. His boyhood
was spent in poverty. Perhaps for this reason (his father disappeared and his mother worked as a seamstress), or because of
his health (always a sickly child, in 1902 he became hopelessly
crippled in one leg), the Mariátegui family moved to the village
of Huacho. There, José Carlos entered a small school, but he
never managed to go beyond a primary education. In 1909, at
the age of fourteen, he began to work as a humble linotypist's
assistant and proofreader for the Lima newspaper *La Prensa*.[2]

Mariátegui at first went unnoticed in the printing room of the
newspaper. He often had to go to the editors' homes to pick up

---

[1] Guillermo Rouillón, *Bio-bibliografía de José Carlos Mariátegui* (Lima:
Universidad Nacional Mayor de San Marcos, 1963), p. 9.

[2] See Alberto Ulloa Sotomayor, "José Carlos Mariátegui," *Nueva Revista
Peruana*, 1 June 1930.

their manuscripts. During this period he walked a great deal around the city, in spite of his lame leg. Sometimes he went by streetcar and was able to use those trips to read. He also wrote, having begun with the patriotic and religious poetry he composed at school. Little by little he rose in *La Prensa*. For a while he was assigned to classifying telegrams from the provinces, writing police and fire reports, and other secondary jobs. In 1914 the new journalist became known. He popularized his pen name, "Juan Croniqueur," by writing verses, theater, art, and book reviews, stories, local news items, and occasional commentaries on national and international events. He also contributed in 1914 to the journal *Mundo Limeño*, which was intended for an aristocratic public. He soon made many friends among his colleagues, of whom the best known at that time was Abraham Valdelomar. Also in this group was César Falcón, who was long to accompany Mariátegui in his life and ideas. All these writers and others of his contemporaries approached journalism from an aesthetic point of view.

In 1915 Mariátegui became co-director of the journal *El Turf*. Here he tried to create a new type of "literature," not only by means of light and ironic reports and social news, but also through poems and stories about horses. He stayed with *El Turf* until 1917. In 1915 and 1916 he also contributed to the journal *Lulu*, which was aimed mainly at a public of society girls and young intellectuals. In 1915 he was one of the initiators and founders of the Circle of Journalists, the first attempt made in Lima to gather together the men of his profession as a group.

Mariátegui's literary personality also found expression in the theater. January 12, 1916, marked the opening in Lima's Colón Theater of the scenic poem *Las Tapadas*, which he wrote in collaboration with Julio Baudouin (Julio de la Paz), with music by La Rosa. "Its theme is derived from the classic Spanish theater, its music is mediocre, it has no value as theater, its scenery is taken from a puppet show; but it has unquestionable literary merit," wrote an independent critic, Alfredo González Prada, in *Colónida*. "The polished, elegant, flowing, graceful verse of Juan Croniqueur," he added, "is delicately modern in style within a classic 'savoir-faire.' " Actually, the author was not trying to revive a classic style, but to imitate the poetic theater in verse cultivated in Spain in the first two decades of the twentieth century by Eduardo Marquina and Francisco Villaespesa, which was characterized by sonorous poetry, high-flown sentiments, and a pseudohistoric setting.

Las Tapadas (parodied as *Las Patadas* by Florentino Alcorta in his newspaper, *El Mosquito*) was not Mariátegui's only theatrical venture. Toward the end of 1916, in collaboration with Abraham Valdelomar, he finished writing the scenic poem *La Mariscala*. This work was never produced and only fragments of it, which appeared in *El Tiempo*, are known. Also in 1916, Mariátegui announced his completion of a book of poetry, *Tristeza*, which was never published. His sonnets "Los salmos del dolor," printed in the literary journal *Colónida*, were taken from that collection. The three sonnets were "Plegaria del cansancio," "Coloquio sentimental," and "Insomnio." In one of them he describes himself as "a child both somewhat mystic and somewhat sensual." In another, in reference to an unhappy love affair, he speaks of "another shadow of sorrow in my life."[3] At that time an Ecuadorian writing on new Peruvian literature said that Mariátegui was "pagan and mystic," more poet than "goldsmith," more "ideologist" than "stylist."[4]

A new daily newspaper, *El Tiempo*, published its first numbers in Lima on July 17, 1916, and it was dedicated to firmly opposing the conservative government of José Pardo. Some of its writers, among them Mariátegui, had voluntarily left *La Prensa*,

[3] "Los salmos del dolor," *Colónida*, 1, no. 3 (March 1916). Reprinted in Edmundo Cornejo Ubillús, *Páginas literarias* (Lima: Talleres Cumbre, 1955), pp. 69–71.
[4] Medardo Ángel Silva, "Un juicio sobre la actual generación literaria del Perú," *El Tiempo* (Lima), 27 March 1917.

a newspaper supporting the Pardo regime.[5] He was extremely
active on *El Tiempo* between 1916 and 1919. He wrote a daily
section of humorous political comments entitled "Voces," in
which he went over the events of each day, parliamentary affairs, and current gossip and rumors, real or imagined. It is very
possible that his experience as author of "Voces" contributed to
his skeptical attitude toward Peru's political life. His pseudonyms also appeared on other pages of *El Tiempo* under such sec-
tions as "Lunes Literarios," where he printed some of his stories
about horses. In "Ecos Sociales," "Juan Croniqueur" occasionally signed a gallant tale or commentary alluding to ladies of the
aristocracy. Any incident, however painful or deplorable, could
suggest a story to him, as with his "Teoría del incendio." In one
of his "Cartas a X" he praised Manuel Ugarte for his anti-
imperialism, adding that our race is not one of apostles, that we
are too apathetic, and that although contemporary champions of
the Indians are not drawn and quartered like Tupac Amaru,
they are ignored. And when in February, 1916, a jealous rival
shot to death the poet Leonidas Yerovi, Mariátegui published in
El Tiempo his "Oración al espíritu inmortal de Leonidas Yerovi," which began with these words: "I, who am your brother
in pain and laughter, in faith and disbelief, in toil and reverie,
in apathy and violence, in love and egotism, in sentiment and
intellect, in the human and the divine, I invoke you, Yerovi, in
this hour of anguish."

When the Pardo Government founded the newspaper *El Día*
in 1917, Mariátegui tried to create a humorous counterpoint, *La
Noche*, but it lasted only a short time.

Also in 1917 he received the "Municipalidad de Lima" prize
from the Circle of Journalists for his article "La procesión tradi-
cional," which appeared in *El Tiempo* on April 12 and described
Lima's popular religious procession in honor of Our Lord of

---

[5] Jorge Basadre, *Historia de la República del Perú*, VIII, 3812–3813, 3934–
3935.

Miracles. Always respectful of religion, he was inspired by a brief retreat in the monastery of the discalced friars to compose the sonnet "Elogio de la celda ascética."

Nevertheless, Mariátegui and other writer friends provoked an uproar when they went to the cemetery on the night of November 4 to watch Norka Rouskaya, an Argentine dancer, perform to the strains of Chopin's "Funeral March." The principals of this incident were jailed for a short period. Mariátegui and his friends, in various Lima newspapers and before congress, vehemently claimed that they had not meant any irreverence by their action, that the cemetery had been used for much more reprehensible purposes, that they were being attacked through ignorance, superstition, or narrowmindedness by critics who were themselves no models of moral rectitude, and that it had been simply an artistic performance.

But Mariátegui was gradually changing in spirit. On June 22, 1918, under the influence of Luis Araquistain's militant journal *España*, he joined César Falcón and Felix del Valle to publish in Lima a newspaper devoted to social criticism, *Nuestra Epoca*. The serious objectives of *Nuestra Epoca* made it very different from *La Noche*, just as its intention to be more than a literary journal set it apart from *Colónida*. The following text appeared in *Nuestra Epoca*: "Our colleague José Carlos Mariátegui has completely renounced the pseudonym Juan Croniqueur by which he is known, and he has decided to ask forgiveness from God and the Public for the many sins he has committed while writing under that pen name."

The first number of *Nuestra Epoca* included an article signed by Mariátegui attacking the social composition and the character of the Peruvian army. This brought down on his head the wrath of a group of officers, and *Nuestra Epoca* expired after only two issues.[6]

A short time later, Mariátegui and Falcón formed part of a

[6] Ibid., VIII, 3829–3830, and IX, 4198.

group that tried to organize a committee of socialist propaganda; but they withdrew from this movement when, under the influence of Luis Ulloa and Carlos del Barzo, it was agreed to immediately establish a party with this name. The dissidents believed that this decision was premature and subsequent events seemed to bear them out, for the party did not last very long.

In January, 1919, the two journalists and another colleague abruptly left *El Tiempo*. Apparently they were not in agreement with the newspaper's policy in the election of that year. They published a letter announcing the formation of a new newspaper that "truly represents the ideals, trends, and orientation that inspire our work." This promise was fulfilled on May 14, 1919, with *La Razón*, a small newspaper of four pages. In the presidential campaign, *La Razón* showed its independence and its extreme hostility to the candidacy of Augusto B. Leguía. It became well known as a spokesman for students, laborers, and the common people. *La Razón* supported the demands of business employees and workers when they struck in May of 1919 to protest high food prices. After the leaders of their strike were freed, the workers held a mass demonstration in honor of Mariátegui on July 8, 1919. He advised them to join together in a stable organization, and that very night they established the Peruvian Regional Labor Federation. In addition, a group of students used *La Razón* to initiate their campaign for university reforms, which led to a strike that same year at the University of San Marcos.

On July 4, 1919, Augusto B. Leguía became president through a revolution, and *La Razón* began to oppose him vigorously. On August 8, 1919, Mariátegui and Falcón announced that their newspaper would no longer appear. Because of a very strong editorial, the printing house refused to continue publishing it.[7]

---

[7] On *La Razón* and its campaigns, see the articles by Humberto del Águila, under the pseudonym "Rinconete," in *La Prensa* (Lima), 25 and 30 August 1949, 1 and 16 October 1949.

A little later, so it was said, a high government official who was a friend of the two journalists presented them with the choice of going to jail or traveling to Europe at government expense. Mariátegui and Falcón chose the second alternative and quietly departed on October 8, 1919, with modest official allowances. Although their trip was severely criticized, they never eulogized or supported the government. No traces of them remained in Lima; but between 1920 and 1923, *El Tiempo*, then a government newspaper, published "Cartas de Italia" and "Aspectos de Europa," signed with the old pseudonyms that Mariátegui himself had repudiated earlier. Falcón began to appear as a contributor to the Madrid newspaper *El Sol* with his famous letters from London. Mariátegui did not write for any European publications. He was in France, Italy, Germany, and Switzerland, and also briefly in Austria and Czechoslovakia. He learned to read and speak fluently Italian and French and to understand German; he clearly defined his beliefs and loyalties; and in Italy he married Ana Chiappe, who was an exemplary wife, attending him faithfully through the illness that ended in his death. "Tolerant of her ideas," he had their son, Sandro, who was born in Rome, baptized a Catholic; and on March 23, 1923, he returned to Lima.

On March 31, *Variedades*, a Lima journal, interviewed Mariátegui for a series it was publishing. Mariátegui refused to define art or his concept of life "because metaphysics is not in style and the world is more interested in the physicist Einstein than in the metaphysicist Bergson"; and he stated that his ideal in life "is always to have a high ideal." In his opinion, journalism, the daily episodic history of mankind, had been created by the capitalist civilization as a great material, but not moral, instrument. He confessed that six or seven years earlier his preferred poets had been Rubén Darío, later Mallarmé and Apollinaire, then Pascoli, Heine, and Aleksandr Blok, and that at the moment he preferred Walt Whitman. His favorite prose writers were Andreyev and Gorki. He considered the theater still too realist and analytic and hoped it would become impressionist and synthetic. "There exist, however, signs of evolution. The Russian genius has created the 'grotesque' and the musical setting. In Berlin, in 'Der Blaue Vogel,' I saw ten-minute musical scenes that had more substance and emotion than many dramas of three hours." Eleanora Duse, by then tired and fading, was the actress who had most impressed him. Among composers he preferred Beethoven, and his favorite painters were Leonardo da Vinci, Sandro Botticelli, and Piero della Francesca, together with Degas, Cezanne, and Matisse and the German expressionist Franz Marc. He judged the contemporary epoch to be revolutionary, but more destructive than creative. As the men most representative of the times, he chose Lenin, Einstein, and Hugo Stinnes, in that order. From the past he admired Christopher Columbus and from the present "the anonymous hero of factory, mine, and fields, the unknown soldier of the social revolution." He enjoyed travel because he thought of himself as essentially a wanderer, inquisitive and restless. When asked which of his writings he liked best and was most satisfied with, he replied that they were still to be written. Regarding the so-called decadence of the Old World, he said: "Europe's decadence is this civilization's decadence. The future of New York and Buenos Aires is tied up with the future of London, Berlin, and Paris. The new civilization is being forged in Europe. America has a secondary role in this stage of human history."[8]

When he stated in the interview that he still had not written his best work, he only expressed once again his constant wish to repudiate his "literary adolescence" nourished (as he wrote in his article on Alcides Spelucín) in a "decadent, modernist, aesthetic, individualist, and skeptical attitude." At that time, he referred disparagingly to his "stone age" of journalism from 1909 to 1919. Actually, that period had two stages: one purely liter-

[8] *Variedades*, 23 March 1923.

ary from 1914 to 1917, when he wrote under the pen name "Juan Croniqueur," and a second from 1918 to 1919, when he began to be concerned with social problems.[9]

In July, 1923, he gave a series of lectures to a working-class public at the González Prada Popular University on the history of the world crisis.[10] In September of the same year he began to publish stories in *Variedades* under the title "Figuras y aspectos de la escena mundial." The lectures are a better expression of his social and political philosophy than the stories.

When Haya de la Torre was exiled in 1924, Mariátegui succeeded him as director of the Popular University and of the journal *Claridad*, which he guided through two or three issues.

In the same year, Mariátegui's life was threatened by a serious illness. A malignant tumor in his left thigh suppurated and had to be drained; as the disease continued its course, he appeared to be near death. An operation, with little likelihood of success, was the only alternative. In their biographies of Mariátegui, both María Wiesse and Armando Bazán relate that his mother opposed the operation but that his wife dramatically insisted on its being performed. Mariátegui survived the operation and for several days thought that his amputated leg, which was the one he had used for walking, was asleep. He was, therefore, condemned to live immobilized or carried by others.

After a rapid recovery, he returned to his intellectual activities with renewed energy. His contributions to *Mundial* and *Variedades* later formed part of his book *Seven Interpretive Essays on Peruvian Reality*. Despite his limited means, he was always careful to obtain, especially from France and Italy, the latest publications, which sometimes could not be found in the bookstores and libraries of Lima. His home contained not only

[9] The best study thus far of Mariátegui's "stone age" is Genaro Carnero Checa, *La acción escrita. José Carlos Mariátegui, periodista* (Lima: Torres Aguirre, 1964), pp. 51–113.

[10] Published as vol. 8 in José Carlos Mariátegui, *Obras completas* (Lima: Biblioteca Amauta, 1959).

Marxist bibliographical information but also the works of independent progressive authors like Romain Rolland and even of authors like Raymond Radiguet, of purely literary prestige. He had broken publicly with his aesthetic past; nonetheless, he appeared to return occasionally to his former predilections. For example, he revered and found inspiration in the Italian critic Piero Gobetti, who was not a Marxist and who died prematurely, assassinated by the Fascists. These paradoxes, unacceptable to the rigid Stalinist doctrine, abounded in Mariátegui's reading and literary and artistic criticisms. They also led him to admire the Peruvian poet of symbolism, José María Eguren, to esteem writers like Waldo Frank, and to preface his essays on Peruvian reality with an epigraph in German taken from Friedrich Nietzsche's *Der Wanderer und sein Schatten.*

In September, 1926, he founded the journal *Amauta*, which he directed until just before his death in 1930. A typical issue of this journal offered interesting characteristics. On the one hand there was its indigenous orientation, beginning with its name and its title page, a prehispanic design in two colors by José Sabogal. This also accounted for its articles by anti-Spanish authors like Luis E. Valcárcel, some of its poems, its enthusiasm for the literary or artistic expressions of American Indians, and its revival of contemporary popular art, encouraged by Sabogal. On the other hand, it was easy to see the doctrinaire line, not only in articles by Marx, Lenin, or Lunacharsky, but also in some by Mariátegui himself (for example, his "Defensa del marxismo"). A similar line was followed by the Peruvian Marxist writer Ricardo Martínez de la Torre in his interpretations of social reality, and by César Antonio Ugarte and Abelardo Solís, among others with different ideas. But this doctrinaire trend was expressed in various ways and included articles on university reform and progress in education. In addition, *Amauta* always or almost always published in its final section the critical notes by María Wiesse on records and other musical events; and it took particular interest in modern European and American art, with a few pages of reproductions of paintings or sculptures. From a literary standpoint, its young contributors became well-known writers, dealing with a great variety of subjects. *Amauta* discovered new values, some as far removed from this journal's "affiliation and faith" as Martín Adán and José Diez Canseco. Later on, it published an increasing number of articles by American and European figures like Waldo Frank. Of the generation of Peruvian writers then considered outstanding, only José María Eguren and Enrique López Albujar were accepted into the pages of *Amauta*. Number 21 of February–March, 1929, was an homage to the poet of *Simbólicas*; but in that same issue appeared articles by Eudocio Ravines on the instruments of finance capital, César Antonio Ugarte on the Socialist regime of Russia, and Ricardo Martínez de la Torre on aspects of capitalist stabilization.[11]

At first, intellectual groups and the general public took little notice of Mariátegui's ideology. He had always been considered a journalist and professional writer. It seemed quite logical that on his return from Europe he should write for the journals of Lima. *Variedades* gave wide circulation to his comments on world politics. At that time, the only other political commentaries were those of Luis Varela y Orbegoso ("Clovis") in the afternoon edition of the newspaper *El Comercio*; they were pleasant and clearly written, although bland and superficial, with no attempt at interpretation and orientation. Mariátegui's quick mind and his precision and skill gave his articles an intrinsic value quite apart from their ultimate purpose, which sometimes was not immediately discernible. Furthermore, by not intervening in matters that directly affected Leguía's policies, he avoided difficulties, at least for a while.

If Mariátegui had defended liberal democracy or the citizen against the state, he would have annoyed the Leguía govern-

---

[11] Carnero Checa, *La acción escrita*, p. 183.

ment and placed it in a difficult position; supporters of the dictatorship believed that to fight those ideas or mention them with scorn or sarcasm was indirectly to help the regime. Since Mariátegui's Marxist theories—he called them "Socialist"—were not expressed in pedantic doctrinaire terms, but emerged as the tacit consequence of his analysis of concrete situations, cases, or persons, they caused no alarm (except later, when the spreading influence of his newpaper *Labor* led to his arrest in 1927 and a raid on his house in 1929, without, however, interfering with his continued publication of *Amauta*). The Leguía era was, paradoxically, more favorable to Mariátegui than a truly doctrinaire regime would have been, because it had no appeal for young intellectuals. With his book on Peruvian reality, in which he criticized the educational ideas of Manuel Vicente Villarán, the literary history of José de la Riva-Agüero, and the value of writers like Felipe Pardo y Aliaga; with his controversy with Víctor Andrés Belaúnde, living in exile in the United States; and with his opposition to the election of José Matías Manzanilla as rector of the university, Mariátegui helped to undermine the prestige of the intellectual leaders of the *civilismo* opposition, who had been exiled, silenced, and humiliated by Leguía. On the other hand, his attitude of political independence was exemplary, for he never sought to profit from the regime's long years of prosperity. Nevertheless, he maintained friendly relations with some political figures, who were not, in any event, very highly placed in the Leguía government.

In June, 1927, there seemed to be a change in the course of events. The government announced its discovery of a "Communist" conspiracy. This scandal probably grew out of a number of circumstances: a determination to block the labor union movement of the Workers Congress currently in session; opposition to the development of a working-class publishing house sponsored by Mariátegui; and the reaction (presumably spurred by the United States Embassy) to a strongly anti-imperialist issue of

Amauta (this was at the time of the fighting in Nicaragua). It has also been said that the decisive factor was the handing over of a letter sent from Haya de la Torre to Mariátegui concerning the organization of the APRA (Alianza Popular Revolucionaria Americana) either to the Minister of State or to President Leguía. Mariátegui was arrested and put into a military hospital, where he spent six days. Many students and workers were also imprisoned. *Amauta* was temporarily shut down, but reopened six months later.

From the military hospital, Mariátegui sent a letter to the Lima newspapers, which they published.[12] He accepted all responsibility for the ideas he had expressed in various newspaper articles, but rejected accusations that he was involved in a subversive plot or intrigue. He declared himself to be a convinced and avowed Marxist and, by that token, far from utopianism, in theory or practice, or absurd conspiracies. "I categorically deny," he added, "my presumed connection with the Communist party in Russia or with any other in Europe or America, and I assert that there is no authentic document that proves such a connection. In this respect, I would like to remind you that when the Russian office in London was searched, it was announced that nothing relative to Peru was found among the addresses of and information about correspondents in America." He mentioned the names of great intellectual figures who, without being Communist, had applauded the work of *Amauta*. He acknowledged his opinions, but added that "under the law, they are not subject to the control, much less the penalties, of the police and the courts." "The word 'revolution,'" he continued, "has acquired a new meaning that is very different from its traditional association with conspiracies."

By the end of 1927, the question being discussed among exile student groups in various cities in America and Europe and

[12] *El Comercio* and *La Prensa* (Lima), 11 June 1927; reprinted in Carnero Checa, *La acción escrita*, pp. 198–199.

among certain circles in Lima was: "Is the APRA an alliance or
a party?" With the appearance of the Nationalist Liberation
Party, founded in Mexico and directed by Víctor Raúl Haya de
la Torre, this question seemed to be answered. On April 16,
1928, Mariátegui wrote a letter to the Mexican group in which
he expressed his disagreement with Haya de la Torre. He criticized the transformation of the APRA from an "alliance" into a
"party"; the organization of the nationalist liberation movement
without consulting "the members of the vanguard who work in
Lima and the provinces"; the party's political literature, reminiscent of "the old regime"; its recourse to "bluff" and lies; its
failure to use the word "socialism"; its similarity to Italian fascism. "An ideological movement which, because of its historical
justification, the intelligence and abnegation of its partisans, and
the lofty purpose and nobility of its doctrine, will gain the support of the better part of the country unless we ourselves ruin
it, must not be permitted to degenerate into a vulgar electoral
struggle."[13]

Haya de la Torre replied from Mexico on May 20, 1928. He
accused Mariátegui of having fallen into "tropical illusions and
absurd sentimentalism," of an excess of Europeanism, and of
personal hostility revealing a hidden obsession. "You will see
that the APRA is a party, an alliance, and a movement. What
does not exist in Europe can exist in America. There were no
skyscrapers and there are no cannibals in Europe." He charged
his opponent with being unreasonable and with having let himself be influenced by the reactionary mentality and pseudo-revo-
lutionary demagogues of the hysterical continent. He denied
that he was an offshoot of Mussolini. He condemned Mariátegui for not having proclaimed the anti-imperialist revolution,
"the only possible and immediate revolution of this era," when

[13] Published in Ricardo Martínez de la Torre, *Apuntes de una interpretación marxista de historia social del Perú* (Lima: Empresa Editora Peruana,
1948), II, 296–298.

he addressed the workers of Vitarte. He added, "Be realistic and try to take your discipline not from revolutionary Europe but from revolutionary America. You are doing a great deal of damage because of your lack of calm and your eagerness always to appear European within the terminology of Europe. In that way, you rupture the APRA. I know that you are against us, and I am not surprised. Nevertheless, we shall accomplish the revolution without mentioning socialism, and by distributing land and fighting imperialism."[14]

After receiving this message, Mariátegui broke off his correspondence with Haya de la Torre. He and his group drafted and sent to all groups residing abroad a "collective letter" with the following conclusions: 1) The APRA should be officially and categorically defined as an alliance or common front and not as a party; 2) We who represent the elements of the Left in Peru now establish in fact and shall organize formally a Socialist group or party with a precise affiliation and orientation. Within the movement, we shall collaborate with the liberal and revolutionary elements of the middle class that accept our point of view, and we shall work to direct the masses toward Socialist ideas.[15] To commemorate the second anniversary of *Amauta* (Number 17 of September) Mariátegui wrote an editorial entitled "Aniversario y balance," in which he developed these same ideas on a high level and without personal allusions.

Bitter quarrels arose in Lima and among the exiles. In the APRA cell in Paris, a group including Eudocio Ravines, César Vallejo, and Armando Bazán advocated, in a document dated December 29, 1928, the formation of a proletarian party as a worker-peasant bloc. This was a much more radical position than Mariátegui's. A column called "Curso nuevo del APRA" appeared in Number 25 of *Amauta* (July–August, 1929) with a letter dated May 1, 1929, from Armando Bazán, secretary of the

---

14 Ibid., pp. 298–299.
15 Ibid., pp. 299–302.

propaganda committee of this organization's cell in Paris. This document announced that the members of the APRA cell and the Center of Anti-Imperialist Studies of Paris had decided to dissolve those bodies because "there exists a profound disagreement among their members concerning the orientation and conduct of the movement." At the same time, it invited the comrades to join anti-imperialist leagues or proletarian revolutionary parties. This attitude coincided with the strictly class rules established by the Second World Congress of the Anti-Imperialist League held in Frankfort, which *Amauta* published in its Number 27 (November–December, 1929).

Luis E. Heysen, the new secretary of the APRA's Paris section, protested the *Amauta* news item in a letter published in the Lima journal *La Sierra*. *Amauta* commented on this letter in its Number 28 (January, 1930): "The only too notorious truth is that the APRA never was more than a plan, a project, an idea for an 'alliance' or a 'common front' which a few groups of Peruvian students tried unsuccessfully to organize. . . . Any attempt, therefore, to take advantage of Latin American credulity with somewhat pompous letterheads is inopportune." The text of Heysen's communication, for which there was not enough space in that issue, appeared in the following issue (Number 29, February–March). It was accompanied by a new note insisting on the need for the proletariat to have an independent program and action and denying the objective existence of the APRA. "It does exist as a trend toward confusion and demagoguery, which must be confronted by a clearly defined proletarian position." It concluded with: "*Amauta* is not a publicity agent for any pretentious performer." This was the last issue directed by Mariátegui; two more were then published under the direction of Ricardo Martínez de la Torre.

Mariátegui, apart from his intellectual work and his political interests, was directly connected with the Peruvian trade union movement. After the general strike of May, 1919, the Regional

Federation of Peruvian Workers was established in Lima, as previously mentioned. In April, 1921, the First Local Congress of Workers met in Lima. It dealt with broad problems such as the organization and orientation of the proletariat, fighting tactics, the eight-hour working day, opposition to compulsory arbitration, the right to strike, solidarity of the organized trade unions, the association of miners, the Indian, popular culture, and affiliation with international organizations. It also discussed the following question: "Should organized labor take political action or not?" After a lively debate, it was agreed to postpone the vote until the next congress "because the proletariat would be better organized and oriented, more experienced, and with a greater grasp of the ideologies of workers everywhere; therefore, fully aware and profoundly convinced of the cause, it would vote for anarchist communism." Supporters of anarchist syndicalism dominated the congress, but they were not sufficiently strong to carry the confused masses.

The Popular University, founded in 1921, did not try to give doctrinaire guidance. According to a widely circulated statement, its only dogma was social justice. But Mariátegui, in his lectures on the world crisis, defended the Russian Revolution and interpreted current events in a way that was favorable to that revolution.

The First Workers Congress led to the creation of the Local Federation of Workers in Lima and Callao. During that period, Mariátegui advocated a syndicalist common front. In 1927, the Federation called a meeting of the Second Workers Congress. After long and heated discussions, the only important conclusion reached was that the sole purpose of syndicalism was the proletarian labor union. Political repression abruptly ended the meetings. With its leaders imprisoned and the Local Federation of Workers dissolved, the labor movement entered a serious crisis.

Parallel to the formation of the Socialist party, mentioned further on, Julio Portocarrero, Avelino Navarro, and others, under the direction of Mariátegui, worked hard from the end of 1928 to reorganize syndicalism. In early 1929, a Committee for the General Confederation of Workers of Peru was set up. On May 17, 1929, a provisional committee began work and was warmly welcomed by Mariátegui in the June issue of *Amauta*. The Peruvian labor movement moved politically from anarchist syndicalism to communism. A delegation led by Julio Porto-carrero participated in the Communist-oriented Latin American Syndicalist Congress, which took place in Montevideo in May, 1929.

On the occasion of the Fifth Congress of the Red Syndicalist International held in Moscow in 1927, Julio Portocarrero jour-neyed secretly to that city as a delegate of Peruvian labor un-ions. On his return, he brought a message from the Third Inter-national urging Peru's association with that movement and blaming Haya de la Torre and his adherents for the delay in the formation of a Communist party in Peru; it offered severe criti-cism and called for action.

Persuaded by this message and by his own convictions, and in the light of his experience with the APRA, Mariátegui and a very select group of friends decided on September 16, 1928, to set up the first cell of a broadly based party to be called the Socialist party of Peru and to be directed by declared Marxists. "The secret cell of seven" was comprised of Mariátegui, Ricardo Martínez de la Torre, who was an insurance company em-ployee, the workers Julio Portocarrero, Avelino Navarro, Hino-josa, and Borja, and the street peddler Bernardo Regman. Later meetings included Luciano Castillo, Fernando Chávez León, Hugo Pesce, and others. Mariátegui wrote the program of the new party. The committee received invitations to attend the Congress of the Latin American Syndicalist Central held in Montevideo in May, 1929, and the first Latin American Com-munist Conference, which met in Buenos Aires in June of the same year. It sent five delegates under Julio Portocarrero to the first meeting and it was represented by Hugo Pesce and Julio Portocarrero in the second. Mariátegui drafted documents on "The Problem of Races in Latin America," "Background and Development of the Class Struggle," and "The Imperialist Point of View." Martínez de la Torre prepared "A Report on Peru" in collaboration with Julio Portocarrero.[16]

There is a record of the debates that took place in the Communist conference in Buenos Aires.[17] Here the Peruvian workers were officially censured for their passive acceptance of the 1929 settlement on Tacna and Arica. They were told to take action against Leguía and Yankee imperialism and to militate for the self-determination of those populations, that is, for a plebiscite under worker and peasant supervision. Mariátegui and his friends were sharply attacked for their decision to create in Peru a Socialist party with a reform program which, although directed by a secret group reserved for initiates, was open to the middle class and the masses. It was argued that a monolithic Communist party had to be formed immediately. Opinions were also divided about the problem of races, and the prevailing thesis was that present boundaries should no longer be considered sacred and that the Indians should be given the right to self-determination, with the possibility of establishing Quechua and Aymara republics.

The discussions in Buenos Aires, which influenced the rules adopted by the organizing committee of the Socialist party, together with personal frictions (Eudocio Ravines arrived secretly in February, 1930, with specific instructions), led to the resignation of some of the leaders (March 16, 1930). After his newspaper, *Labor*, was closed down in September, 1929, and his home raided by the police, Mariátegui planned a trip to Buenos Aires,

[16] Ibid., pp. 392–519.
[17] *El movimiento revolucionario latinoamericano. Versiones de la Primera Conferencia Comunista Sud Americana* (Buenos Aires: *La Correspondencia Sud Americana*, 1929).

where he hoped to publish *Amauta* and several books,[18] and to Santiago. This trip, which was arranged by Samuel Glusberg (who was not a Communist) in Buenos Aires and by Luis Alberto Sánchez (who was also not a Communist) in Santiago, indicated a personal attitude independent of any party directive. Mariátegui never took this trip. He died on April 16, at the age of thirty-five. He left ready for publication the works *Defensa del marxismo*[19] and *El alma matinal*,[20] and he had sent to Spain the original manuscript of a book on the political and ideological evolution of Peru, which was lost.

A few days after Mariátegui's funeral, a long communication reached Lima from the Third International, which referred to the debate begun in Buenos Aires on the necessity of founding a Communist instead of a Socialist party. The latter, during the illness of Mariátegui, already had discussed affiliation with the Communist party. On May 20, 1930, the Peruvian Communist party was born. The only negative vote was cast by Martínez de la Torre, who defended the beliefs of his friend and teacher.[21] The Communist party, therefore, appeared later in Peru than in other countries: Uruguay (1920), Argentina (1921), Mexico and Chile (1922), Ecuador and Cuba (1925). Nevertheless, there were already Moscow-trained national leaders like Eudocio Ravines and a few students, as well as workers, who traveled secretly. It is interesting to note that, although Mariátegui died soon after his political line had been sternly criticized, Ravines, Portocarrero, Armando Bazán, and other convinced and declared Communists of that time later left the party.

Whether or not Mariátegui was the founder of the Communist party is a question that is and will continue to be widely

---

[18] Samuel Glusberg ["Enrique Espinoza"], *Trinchera* (Buenos Aires: Babel, 1931), pp. 40–69.

[19] Published with *Polémica revolucionaria* as vol. 5 of *Obras completas*.

[20] Published as vol. 3 of *Obras completas*.

[21] Martínez de la Torre, *Apuntes de una interpretación marxista*, II, 497–510.

debated in Peru. Actually, it is a pointless controversy. Mariátegui was not basically in disagreement with the leaders of the
Communist International; the nature of his objections was tacti-
cal, immediate, and incidental. Among his last writings, published shortly before his death, were his reply to a questionnaire
about contemporary problems and his comments on Panait
Istrati's book on the Soviet Union.[22] In the first article, Mariátegui examined once more "the death of the principles and dogmas
that made up the bourgeois Absolute" and "the loss of bourgeois morale"; in the second, he made clear his sympathies by
trying to disparage Istrati's censure of Soviet society. Mariátegui,
then, did not change shortly before his death.

It is not certain whether Mariátegui intended to use his trip
to Buenos Aires to intensify his activities as a writer over his
activities as a political and social organizer. The latter had
brought him into painful conflict with the Communist party line
of that time and with the interests, plans, and undertakings of
other, more powerful, men.

Mariátegui may be studied on different levels: the human and
biographical, the literary, the ideological, the political, and the
social. Often his interpreters and critics do not cover all these
aspects. It is not unusual for some of his disciples, as well as
diverse elements of both the extreme Right and the extreme
Left, to emphasize only one dimension of this man, who did not
hide his affiliation and faith—the social agitator, the organizer,
the anti-intellectual Mariátegui who continues and will continue to be involved in elections, labor unions, and political
tracts and controversies. On the other hand, there is the historical image of another Mariátegui seen from a perspective that
embraces his whole life and not just a part of it, that seeks to
reach the man himself and not merely the ideas or things he
loyally supported, and, finally, that shows him as the promoter

22 *Mundial* (Lima), 20 March 1930, and *Variedades* (Lima), 12 March
1930; both are included in *Obras completas*, VI, 29–31, 150–153.

of a great cultural and social renaissance and as a hero in a cripple's chair. This image appeals to persons of different positions —liberal, moderate, Socialist—provided they have a progressive spirit. In the same way, González Prada is not simply one more author in the anarchist pages of his time, but above all a great literary figure, a great thinker, and, in spite of all his imprecations against Peru, a great Peruvian.

There should be a place in these pages for Mariátegui as he appeared in his house on Washington Street. He received his friends at the end of the afternoon, for he jealously guarded for his own work or special interviews the hours other people spent in offices. His visitors found him seated on a sofa with a blanket covering the lower part of his body. He received them quietly, with a smile on his delicate lips that was neither conventional nor affected. His black eyes, gleaming in his wasted, pale brown face, commanded attention. His features were sharp and his thick, black hair was always carefully groomed, but with a bohemian lock sometimes falling onto his forehead. He dressed in a plain, spotlessly clean suit and he invariably wore a black bow tie. His conversation was free of vanity and expansive autobiography, rhetoric, and vague banalities. On the contrary, he was objective in his judgment and always ready to listen and ask questions, reluctant to discuss himself, and immune to commonplaces. His past experience as the humorous columnist of "Voces" in *El Tiempo* and as a veteran of criollo life behind the scenes was expressed in witty, nimble remarks on men and events. His room was without decoration except for books set at random on modest shelves along the walls. His visitors arrived informally until there would be a group of fifteen or twenty persons. Apart from many other writers and artists, he saw an increasing number of students and workers and, in his last years, visitors from abroad. Mariátegui's wife occasionally appeared on her return from shopping or the post office. His children were not exhibited with the relentless complacency typical of so many homes that want to show off their private life. Following the foundation of the publishing house and journal *Amauta*, Julio César Mariátegui joined the group. There was nothing about these gatherings that was deliberate or compulsory or that would imply a commitment. People were free to go every day or just once and never return, or to disappear for a while and then reappear. No attempt was made to proselytize. Current events were commented on, especially those relating to books, paintings, or music. There was no sign of the heavy atmosphere, charged with gossip and backbiting, of political cliques.

The year 1923–1924 marked the beginning of Mariátegui's intellectual activities. In spite of his uncertain health, he managed to overcome initial doubts, distrusts, and hostilities in order to make his ideas known. From 1925 to 1927, his position became more secure as people became more accustomed to it. In 1925, he published his book *La escena contemporánea*, made up of many of his articles for *Variedades* on the contemporary world. Toward 1927, he entered his period of political action: he organized and guided labor unions; he joined the APRA movement and then left it; he founded the newspaper *Labor* (1928) in order to be in closer contact with the workers; and, finally, he tried to form the Socialist party of Peru. In 1928, he published the book *Seven Interpretive Essays on Peruvian Reality*, in which he collected articles he had written since 1925 for the journal *Mundial* under the heading "Peruanicemos el Perú," together with other articles from *Amauta*.

Mariátegui's spiritual homeland was not the university but journalism. If the latter miraculously produced the distinguished author of aesthetic essays, Valdelomar, it also produced the great social essayist of Peru, who was almost his contemporary. He himself said: "I have raised myself from journalism to doctrine." It is amazing that a man who barely finished primary school and who began as a linotypist's assistant, messenger, and proofreader should later be able to expound "the contemporary scene"; "figures and aspects of world life"; Marxism; art; Italian, French, Spanish and other literature of our time; and seven of Peru's most vital problems.

The official Marxist position on Mariátegui appears to have varied. At one time he was considered a "populist" and was so qualified somewhat contemptuously by V. Miroshevsky in an article called "Mariátegui's Role in the History of Latin American Social Thought," published in 1942 (May–June issue) in the Havana journal *Dialéctica*. But, in more recent years, an apparently irresistible movement has arisen to make the author of *Seven Essays* the father of Peruvian and even South American communism. A Soviet edition of that book came out in 1963; and in 1957 S. Semionov and A. Shalgovski extolled "the role of Mariátegui in the formation of the Communist party in Peru" in the Moscow journal *Modern and Contemporary History*.[23] It would seem that we are witnessing the birth of a myth, strengthened by the memory of the premature death, the heroically endured illness, the stubborn loyalty to ideas, and the brilliant talent that sometimes approached genius.

The independent critic must here fulfill his mission of serenity, precision, and high purpose. With his *Seven Essays*, Mariátegui introduced to Peru a serious and methodical approach to national affairs that disdained pedantry, excessive details, and rhetoric. He linked history to the drama of the present and the imponderables of the future. He pointed out problems that, unsolved in the past, still weigh on present generations, along with other problems that have appeared in the latter's time. He drew attention to lacerating and pathetic realities that many did not or would not see. He was exempt from the dislike or contempt of study that fills the soul of every demagogue, whether of the Right or Left. On attempting a diagnosis of his own country, which has so much in common with other countries of Andean

[23] Published in translation in *Problemas peruanas*, no. 1, 1960.

America, Mariátegui replaced in those years others who could have done similar work from the standpoint of different ideologies, but who did not because they were traveling abroad or because they had dispersed their energies or dedicated themselves to erudition, light literature, or the many activities of a political, bureaucratic, or social life.

His observations were often astute and provocative, although at times one-sided and sketchy. They also suffered from his personal prejudices (especially evident in the essay on literature), the tendentious nature of his political sympathies, or simply insufficient information.

He himself stated in his preface: "I am not an impartial, objective critic. My judgments are nourished by my ideals, my sentiments, my passions. I have an avowed and resolute ambition: to assist in the creation of Peruvian socialism. I am far removed from the academic techniques of the university." The reader should never forget these frank words.

On the other hand, it requires a great deal of basic preparation to study, present, and resolve from an invalid's chair, over a few years, the problem of the Indian, the problem of land, the problem of public education, the religious factor, regionalism and centralism, and the process of literature. This actually was a much more difficult undertaking than to comment on contemporary European politics or on the literary and other artistic products of the time, because of the lack or scarcity of specialized studies and, in many cases, because of the need for background materials consisting of monographs, statistics, surveys, and the like.

But the example and significance of Mariátegui's work will always remain, in spite of all the amendments that may be made to it and even assuming that it becomes outdated in some respects. This work will never deserve "the silence reserved for superficial, malicious hacks, or the bold flattery thrust on incompetents in high positions, or the empty words of praise accorded to second-rate but agreeable writers." Instead, it will be worthy of "the keen, harsh analysis" given to work that lives and vibrates in spite of the passage of time (*Seven Essays* was written more than forty years ago), that examines subjects of permanent interest, and that aims at the public good. No one can deny that Mariátegui initiated social studies in Peru. No one can help but admire his devotion to culture and social justice in a hostile and poisoned atmosphere. And if at the beginning he led a bohemian and even dissolute life, his later discipline—only intensified by his physical suffering—demonstrates that grandeur derives from the free selection of a chastened soul and not from the facile exercise of an innate gift.

Mariátegui's great value lies, not in his prescriptions and formulas, but in his whole personality, which must be interpreted without making use of the clichés and conventional adjectives that he disliked so intensely. It should not be forgotten, moreover, that he died at the age of thirty-five.

Jorge Basadre

AUTHOR'S NOTE

I bring together in this book, organized and annotated in seven essays, the articles that I published in *Mundial* and *Amauta* concerning some essential aspects of Peruvian reality. Like *La escena contemporánea*, therefore, this was not conceived of as a book. Better this way. My work has developed as Nietzsche would have wished, for he did not love authors who strained after the intentional, deliberate production of a book, but rather those whose thoughts formed a book spontaneously and without premeditation. Many projects for books occur to me as I lie awake, but I know beforehand that I shall carry out only those to which I am summoned by an imperious force. My thought and my life are one process. And if I hope to have some merit recognized, it is that—following another of Nietzsche's precepts —I have written with my blood.

I intended to include in this collection an essay on the political and ideological evolution of Peru. But as I advance in it, I realize that I must develop it separately in another book. I find that the seven essays are already too long, so much so that they do not permit me to complete other work as I would like to and ought to; nevertheless, they should be published before my new study appears. In this way, my reading public will already be familiar with the materials and ideas of my political and ideological views.

I shall return to these topics as often as shall be indicated by the course of my research and arguments. Perhaps in each of these essays there is the outline, the plan, of an independent book. None is finished; they never will be as long as I live and think and have something to add to what I have written, lived, and thought.

All this work is but a contribution to Socialist criticism of the problems and history of Peru. There are many who think that I am tied to European culture and alien to the facts and issues of my country. Let my book defend me against this cheap and biased assumption. I have served my best apprenticeship in Europe and I believe the only salvation for Indo-America lies in European and Western science and thought. Sarmiento, who is still one of the creators of *argentinidad* [Argentine-ness], at one time turned his eyes toward Europe. He found no better way to be an Argentine.

Once again I repeat that I am not an impartial, objective critic. My judgments are nourished by my ideals, my sentiments, my passions. I have an avowed and resolute ambition: to assist in the creation of Peruvian socialism. I am far removed from the academic techniques of the university.

This is all that I feel honestly bound to tell the reader before he begins my book.

Lima, 1928   *José Carlos Mariátegui*

SEVEN INTERPRETIVE ESSAYS ON PERUVIAN REALITY

Ich will keinen Autor mehr lesen,
dem man anmerkt, er wollte ein
Buch machen; sondern nur jene,
deren Gedanken unversehens ein
Buch werden.

Nietzsche, *Der Wanderer und
sein Schatten*

Outline of the Economic Evolution

The Colonial Economy

THE DEGREE TO WHICH the history of Peru was severed by the conquest can be seen better on an economic than on any other level. Here the conquest most clearly appears to be a break in continuity. Until the conquest, an economy developed in Peru that sprang spontaneously and freely from the Peruvian soil and people. The most interesting aspect of the empire of the Incas, which was a grouping of agricultural and sedentary communities, was its economy. All historical evidence agrees that the Inca people—industrious, disciplined, pantheist, and simple—lived in material comfort. With abundant food their population increased. The Malthusian problem was completely unknown to the empire. Although the collectivist organization directed by the Incas had weakened the Indians' individual initiative, it had instilled in them the habit of a humble and religious obedience to social duty, which benefitted the economic system. The Incas derived as much social utility as possible from this trait. They improved the vast Inca territory by constructing roads, canals, et cetera, and they extended its borders by conquering nearby tribes. Collective work and common effort were employed fruit-fully for social purposes.

The Spanish conquistadors destroyed this impressive productive machine without being able to replace it. The indigenous society and the Inca economy were wholly disrupted and anni-hilated by the shock of the conquest. Once the bonds that had united it were broken, the nation dissolved into scattered com-munities. Indigenous labor ceased to function as a concerted and integrated effort. The conquistadors were mainly concerned with distributing and wrangling over their rich booty. They plundered the treasures of temples and palaces; they allotted land and men with no thought of their future use as forces and means of production.

The viceroyalty marks the beginning of the difficult and com-plex process of forming a new economy. During this period, Spain tried to organize its immense colony politically and eco-nomically. The Spaniards began to till the soil and mine the gold and silver. On the ruins and remnants of a socialist econo-my, they established the bases of a feudal economy.

But Spain did not send to Peru, nor for that matter to any of its other possessions, throngs of colonizers. The weakness of the Spanish Empire lay precisely in its character and structure as a military and ecclesiastic rather than a political and economic power. No large bands of pioneers, like those who disembarked on the shores of New England, arrived in the Spanish colonies. Viceroys, courtesans, adventurers, priests, lawyers, and soldiers were almost the only ones to come to Spanish America. There-fore, no real colonizing force developed in Peru. The population of Lima was made up of a small court, a bureaucracy, a few monasteries, officials of the Inquisition, merchants, domestic servants, and slaves.[1] Furthermore, the Spanish pioneer had no

[1] Commenting on Donoso Cortés, the late Italian critic Piero Gobetti de-scribed Spain as "a race of colonizers, of seekers after gold, known to take

talent for creating working groups. Instead of making use of the Indian, he seemed to be intent on exterminating him. And the colonizers could not create a solid and integrated economy by themselves. The very foundation of colonial organization was defective because it lacked demographic cement. There were not enough Spaniards and mestizos to develop the territorial wealth on a large scale. And since Negro slaves were imported to work on the coastal plantations, the elements and characteristics of a slave society were mixed into those of a feudal society.

Only the Jesuits, with their systematic positivism, showed in Peru, as in other countries of America, some aptitude for economic creation. The latifundia assigned to them prospered and traces of their organization still survive. Remembering how skillfully the Jesuits in Paraguay made use of the natives' natural inclination to communal work, it is not surprising that this congregation of the sons of Saint Ignatius of Loyola, as Unamuno called them, created centers of work and production on Peruvian soil, while nobles, lawyers, and priests enjoyed a luxurious and worldly life in Lima.

Almost the sole interest of the colonizers was the mining of Peruvian gold and silver. I have referred more than once to the tendency of the Spaniards to settle in the lowlands and to how they feared and distrusted the Andes, of which they never really felt themselves masters. Undoubtedly, the criollo towns that formed in the sierra were the result of mining activities. The conquest of the sierra would have been even more incom-

---

slaves in case of hardship." Gobetti was mistaken in considering mere conquistadors to be colonizers. But his next observation merits reflection: "The cult of the bullfight is an aspect of this love of entertainment and of this catholicism of spectacle and form; it is natural that an emphasis on the purely decorative should be the ideal of the man in rags who puts on lordly airs and cannot follow either the Anglo-Saxon teachings of resolute and stubborn heroism or the French tradition of subtle skill. The Spanish ideal of an arrogant nobility borders on indolence and, therefore, finds its proper expression and symbol in the court."

plete had it not been for the Spaniards' greed for the precious metals buried deep within the Andes.

These were the historical bases of the new Peruvian economy, of the colonial economy, colonial to its roots—a process that is still evolving. Let us now examine the outlines of a second stage, the stage in which a feudal economy gradually became a bourgeois economy, but without losing its colonial character within the world picture.

The Economic Foundations of the Republic

Like the first, the second stage of this economy derives from a political and military event. The first stage arose from the conquest. The second stage began with independence. But whereas the conquest was entirely responsible for the formation of our colonial economy, independence appears to have been determined and dominated by the latter process.

I have already had occasion, since my first Marxist attempt to ground Peruvian history in the study of economic events, to concern myself with the economic aspect of the War of Independence, and my reasoning was as follows:

The ideas of the French Revolution and of the North American Constitution were favorably received in South America, where there already existed an emerging bourgeoisie which, because of its economic needs and interests, could and should have been infected by the revolutionary spirit of the European bourgeoisie. Spanish America could not have achieved its independence had it not commanded a heroic generation, sensitive to the emotional tenor of its time, able and willing to carry out a genuine revolution. From this point of view, independence takes on the appearance of a romantic adventure. But this does not contradict my thesis of an economic pattern underlying the revolution of liberation. The directors, caudillos, and ideologists of this revolution did not precede or transcend the economic premises and causes of this event. Intellectual and emotional circumstances did not precede economic circumstances.

Spain's policy totally obstructed and thwarted the economic development of its colonies by not permitting them to trade with any other nation and by reserving to itself the privileges of the mother country to monopolize all commerce and business carried on in its dominions.

The producing forces of the colonies naturally fought to shake off these fetters. If the emerging economy of the embryonic nations of America was to develop, it needed above all to be free of the rigid authority and medieval mentality of the king of Spain. The student of this period cannot help but see here that South America's independence movement was only too obviously inspired by the interests of the criollo and even the Spanish population, rather than by the interests of the indigenous population.

From the standpoint of world history, South America's independence was determined by the needs of the development of Western or, more precisely, capitalist civilization. The rise of capitalism had a much more decisive and profound, if less apparent and recognizable, influence on the evolution of independence than the philosophy and literature of the Encyclopedists. The British Empire, fated to become the real and unsurpassed representative of the interests of capitalist civilization, was taking shape. In England, center of liberalism and Protestantism, it was industry and machinery that prepared the way for capitalism, rather than that country's traditionally cited political philosophy and religious belief. Therefore, England—with the clear sense of destiny and historic mission that was to gain it hegemony in capitalist civilization—played a leading role in South America's independence. Whereas the prime minister of France, the nation that some years earlier had given the world a great revolution, refused to recognize these young South American republics that could export "not only their products but their revolutionary ideas,"[2] Mr. Canning, faithful inter-

[2] "If Europe is obliged to recognize the de facto governments of Ameri-

preter and agent of England's interests, recognized them and thereby justified their right to separate from Spain and, in addition, to organize themselves democratically. And even before Mr. Canning, the bankers of London—no less timely and effective for being usurers—had financed the formation of the new republic.

The Spanish Empire sank into oblivion because it did not rest on military and political foundations and, especially, because it represented an outdated economy. Spain could supply its colonies only with priests, lawyers, and nobles. Its colonies craved more practical and modern instruments and, consequently, turned to England's industrialists and bankers. Acting as agents of an empire created by a manufacturing and free trade economy, the new-style colonizers wanted, in turn, to dominate these markets.

The economic interests of the Spanish colonies and of the capitalist West coincided exactly, although, as often happens in history, neither of the parties concerned was aware of this fact.

The new nations, following the same natural impulse that had led them to independence, dealt with the capital and industry of the West in order to obtain the elements and relations necessary to expand their economies. They began to send to the capitalist West the products of their soil and subsoil and to receive from it cloth, machinery, and a thousand industrial products. In this way, a continual and increasing trade was established between South America and Western civilization. The countries on the Atlantic naturally benefited most from this trade because of their proximity to Europe. Argentina and Brazil, especially, attracted great quantities of European capital and immigrants; and the floods from the West left rich and homogeneous deposits that accelerated the changes by which the economy and culture

---

ca," said Viscount Chateaubriand, "its entire policy should be aimed at establishing monarchies instead of these republics that will send us their principles along with the products of their soil."

of these countries gradually acquired the function and structure of the European economy and culture. There, liberal, bourgeois democracy could take root, whereas in the rest of South America it was blocked by extensive and tenacious remains of feudalism.

In this period, the general historical process in Peru entered a stage that differentiated and separated it from the historical process of other countries in South America. Because of geography, some countries would advance more rapidly than others. The independence that had united them in a common cause decreed that they should part to follow their individual destinies. Since European ships could reach Peru's ports only after a very long voyage, that country found itself closer geographically to the Orient, and its trade with Asia became substantial. The Peruvian coast received contingents of Chinese immigrants who replaced the Negro slaves imported during the viceroyalty and emancipated partly as a result of the transformation from a feudal to a more or less bourgeois economy. But trade with Asia could not contribute effectively to the formation of a new Peruvian economy. Peru, having emerged from the conquest and confirmed its independence, required the machinery, techniques, and ideas of the Europeans, the Westerners.

The Period of Guano and Nitrates

There is a chapter in the evolution of the Peruvian economy that opens with the discovery of guano and nitrates and closes with the loss of this wealth. Here is found a full explanation of a series of political phenomena in our historical process that have been distorted and falsified by a superficial approach to Peruvian history based on anecdotes and rhetoric. However, my rapid interpretation does not propose to explore or closely examine these phenomena, but to point out and define the essential characteristics of the formation of our economy, in order to make clearer its colonial cast. Let us consider only the economic facts.

It is interesting that in the story of the republic such coarse and humble substances as guano and nitrates should have taken over the role that had been reserved to gold and silver in a more romantic and less positivist era. Spain wanted and kept Peru as a producer of precious metals. England preferred Peru as a producer of guano and nitrates. But the motive remained the same; only the times changed. The attraction of Peru's gold diminished with the discovery of gold in California. On the other hand, guano and nitrates—found almost exclusively in Peru—had been worthless to previous civilizations but were extremely valuable to an industrial civilization. These materials, on a remote coast in the South Pacific, were essential to the development of European or Western industrialism. In addition, unlike other Peruvian products they were not hampered by the rudimentary and primitive state of land transport. Whereas gold, silver, copper, and coal mined from the Andes had to be conveyed great distances over rugged mountain ranges, guano and nitrate deposits lay on the coast within easy reach of the cargo ships.

These natural resources were so easily exploited that they became the center of the country's economic life and occupied a disproportionately large place in the Peruvian economy. The treasury derived its principal revenue from their export and the country felt wealthy. The government made lavish use of its credit, mortgaging its future to English finance.

This is in broad outline the entire history of guano and nitrates from a purely economic standpoint. The rest, at first glance, belongs to the historian. But as in all such cases, the economics of the situation is much more complex and far-reaching than it appears.

Guano and nitrates, first and foremost, generated a lively trade with the Western world during a period when Peru, in its unfavorable geographical location, had little hope of attracting the colonizing and civilizing currents that were sweeping through other Latin American countries. This trade placed its economy under the control of British capital. Later, as a result of debts guaranteed by both products, Peru was forced to hand over to England the administration of its railroads, that is, the very key to the exploitation of its resources.

The profits earned from the export of guano and nitrates created in Peru, where property always had preserved its aristocratic and feudal character, the first solid elements of commercial and banking capital. Those who profited directly and indirectly from the wealth on the coast began to constitute a capitalist class. The bourgeoisie that developed in Peru was related in its origin and structure to the aristocracy, which, though composed chiefly of the descendants of colonial land-holders, had been obliged by its role to adopt the basic principles of liberal economics and politics. This circumstance, which will be referred to in later essays, is pertinent to the following statements: "In the first period of independence, the struggle between military factions and leaders appeared to be a consequence of the lack of an integrated bourgeoisie. Peru had lagged behind other Spanish American countries in defining the elements of a liberal bourgeoisie; to enable the latter to function, it needed to establish a strong capitalist class. Meanwhile, power remained in the hands of the military caudillos. The Castilla regime marked the consolidation of the capitalist class. Government concessions and profits from guano and nitrates created capitalism and a bourgeoisie which, once organized into *civilismo*, soon took over all power."

Another aspect of this chapter in the economic history of Peru was the shifting of the economy to the coast. The search for gold and silver had compelled the Spaniards—against their inclination to settle on the coast—to maintain advanced posts in the sierra. Mining was the mainspring of the economic system imposed by Spain and required that the colonial regime be based in the sierra, an area which previously had supported a genuinely and typically agrarian society. Guano and nitrates corrected this situation by strengthening the power of the coast. The new Peru moved to the lowlands, thereby intensifying its social dualism and conflict, which to this day remain its greatest historical problem.

The period of guano and nitrates, therefore, cannot be isolated from the subsequent development of Peru's economy, because it contains the roots and elements of the period that follows. One consequence of guano and nitrates, the War of the Pacific, did not cancel out the other consequences of their discovery and exploitation. With the loss of these resources came the tragic realization of the danger of an economic prosperity supported or held together almost solely by the possession of natural wealth at the mercy of the greed or aggression of foreign imperialism or vulnerable to the continual changes in industrial needs arising from scientific invention. Caillaux speaks with obvious capitalist realism of the economic and industrial instability produced by scientific progress.[3]

During the period dominated and characterized by trade in guano and nitrates, the transformation of Peru's economy from feudal to bourgeois received its first powerful stimulus. If, instead of a mediocre metamorphosis of the ruling class, there had emerged a new class with vigor and purpose, unquestionably that transformation would have progressed more evenly and firmly. Peru's postwar history is evidence of this. Its defeat and loss of nitrate territory initiated a prolonged decline in productive drive, unfortunately not compensated for by a liquidation of the past.

The Character of Peru's Present Economy

The last chapter in the evolution of the Peruvian economy is its postwar period. This chapter begins with the almost complete collapse of the country's productive energy.

[3] J. Caillaux, *Whither France? Whither Europe?*, trans. H. B. Armstrong (New York: Alfred A. Knopf, 1923).

Defeat not only meant that the national economy lost its principal resources, nitrates and guano; it also meant the paralysis of economic initative, a general depression in production and commerce, the depreciation of national currency, and the loss of foreign credit. Bleeding and mutilated, the country suffered from a terrible anemia.

Again, as after independence, military leaders took charge; but they were spiritually and organically incapable of directing the task of economic reconstruction. Very soon the capitalist group that had formed during the period of guano and nitrates resumed its activity and returned to power. The solution they found for the monetary problem, for example, was typical of the mentality of *latifundistas* or large landowners. They were indifferent not only to the interests of the proletariat but also to those of the bourgeoisie, the only social groups that would be ruined by the abrupt demonetization of paper currency.

This measure and the Grace Contract were undoubtedly the most significant and characteristic actions taken by a landholding plutocracy to eliminate the economic consequences of the war.

The Grace Contract ratified British domination in Peru by delivering the state railways to the English bankers who until then had financed the republic and its extravagances. At the same time, it gave the London financial market the guarantees necessary to make new investments in Peruvian business. No immediate results were obtained with the restoration of the government's credit; but prudent and safe investments again began to attract British capital. The Peruvian economy, by means of a practical examination of its condition as a colonial economy, secured some aid for its convalescence. With the completion of the railway to Oroya, traffic was opened to the industrial products of the department of Junín, permitting large-scale exploitation of its mining wealth.

Piérola fully adapted his economic policy to the same interests. The democratic caudillo, who for so long had thunderously aroused the masses against the wealthy, now took pains to carry out a *civilismo* administration. His tax system and fiscal measures removed any possible doubts that might have been raised by his phraseology and metaphysics. This confirms the principle that the meaning and shape of men, their policy and deeds, are more clearly revealed on an economic than on a political level.

The fundamental aspects of this chapter, in which our economy, recuperating from its postwar crisis, slowly organized itself on less lucrative but more solid bases than those of guano and nitrates, can be outlined by the following facts:

1. The appearance of modern industry. The establishment of factories, plants, transport, et cetera, which has transformed life on the coast. The formation of an industrial proletariat with a growing natural tendency to adopt a class ideology, thereby blocking one of the traditional paths of caudillo proselytism and changing the terms of the political struggle.

2. The role of finance capital. The emergence of national banks which finance various industrial and commercial enterprises but which are very limited in scope because of their subservience to foreign capital and large agricultural properties; and the establishment of branches of foreign banks serving the interests of North American and English finance.

3. The shorter distance and increased traffic between Peru and the United States and Europe. As a result of the opening of the Panama Canal, Peru's geographical position has notably improved and its incorporation into Western civilization has accelerated.

4. The gradual substitution of North American for British ascendancy. The Panama Canal seems to have brought Peru closer to the United States than to Europe. The participation of North American capital in the exploitation of Peru's copper and petroleum, which have become two of its most important products, furnishes a broad and enduring base for the growing influ-

ence of the United States. Exports to England, which in 1898 made up 56.7 percent of total exports, by 1923 came only to 33.2 percent. In the same period, exports to the United States rose from 9.5 percent to 39.7 percent. And this trend was even more striking in imports: whereas in that twenty-five year period, imports from the United States went up from 10.0 percent to 38.9 percent, those from Great Britain dropped from 44.7 percent to 19.6 percent.[4]

5. The development of a capitalist class no longer dominated by the old aristocracy. Although agricultural property owners retain their power, the authority of families with viceregal names has declined. The bourgeoisie has grown stronger.

6. The rubber illusion. In its halcyon days, Peru thought it had found El Dorado in its tropical forests, which temporarily acquired enormous value in the economy. They especially caught the imagination of the country and attracted hordes of "hardy adventurers." This illusion—tropical in origin and tone —faded with the fall in the price of rubber.[5]

7. The excess profits of the European period. The boom in Peruvian products caused a rapid increase in domestic private wealth. The hegemony of the coast in the Peruvian economy was reinforced.

8. The policy on borrowing. The reestablishment of Peruvian credit abroad has enabled the government once again to use loans to carry out its public works program.[6] North America

---

[4] *Extracto estadístico del Perú.* From 1924 to 1926, trade with Great Britain fell farther and farther behind trade with the United States. By 1926, Peru's imports from Great Britain had declined to 15.6 percent of total imports and its exports to Great Britain represented only 28.5 percent. On the other hand, imports from the United States had reached 46.2 percent, which more than offset the drop in exports to 34.5 percent.

[5] See the sixth essay, "Regionalism and Centralism," footnote no. 4.

[6] Peru's foreign debt, according to the *Extracto estadístico* of 1926, went up to *Lp.* [*libras peruanas*] 10,341,906 by December 31 of this year. Since then, under the law that authorizes the president to place government bonds abroad at a price no lower than 86 percent and with interest no higher than

also has replaced Great Britain as creditor. Overflowing with gold, the New York market offers the best terms. North American bankers study the possibilities of lending capital to Latin American governments. And they are careful, of course, that such investments benefit North American industry and commerce.

These would appear to be the principal aspects of the economic evolution of Peru in its postwar period. This series of comments does not permit a thorough study of the foregoing statements or propositions. I have sought only to sketch some of the essential characteristics of the formation and development of the Peruvian economy.

I shall make a final observation: the elements of three different economies coexist in Peru today. Underneath the feudal economy inherited from the colonial period, vestiges of the indigenous communal economy can still be found in the sierra. On the coast, a bourgeois economy is growing in feudal soil; it gives every indication of being backward, at least in its mental outlook.

The Agrarian Economy and the Feudal Latifundium System

Peru, despite its expanded mining industry, remains an agricultural country. The great majority of the population is rural, with the Indian, who is usually and by tradition a farmer, making up four-fifths of the population. Since 1925, as a result of price declines in sugar and cotton and of diminishing yields, mining exports have greatly exceeded agricultural. The rapid rise in exports of petroleum and derivatives from *Lp.* [*libras peruanas*] 1,387,778 in 1916 to *Lp.* 7,421,128 in 1926 has been a significant factor. But farm production is only partially represented by export products: cotton, sugar and derivatives, wool,

---

6 per cent, a loan of 50 million dollars has been floated in New York in order to refinance previous loans contracted with interest at 7½ to 8 per cent.

and rubber. Agriculture and livestock supply domestic consumption, whereas mining products are almost entirely exported. Imports of food and beverages reached *Lp.* 4,148,311 in 1925. The largest item in these imports is wheat, which the country still does not produce in sufficient quantities. There are no complete statistics on domestic production and consumption. Estimating a daily per capita consumption of 50 centavos on agricultural and livestock products, more than *Lp.* 84,000,000 was spent by the population of 4,609,999 counted in 1896. If it is assumed that there are now 5,000,000 inhabitants, domestic consumption reaches a total of *Lp.* 91,250,000. These figures show the enormous importance of agricultural and livestock production in the country's economy.

Mining, on the other hand, employs a small number of workers—28,592 in 1926, according to the *Extracto estadístico.* The manufacturing industry also uses little labor.[7] Sugar cane haciendas alone employed 22,367 men and 1,173 women in their fields in 1926; cotton haciendas used 40,557 laborers in 1922–1923, the last period for which there are published statistics; and rice haciendas used 11,332 laborers in 1924–1925.

Most agricultural and livestock products consumed in the country come from the valleys and tablelands of the sierra. On the coastal haciendas, food crops amount to less than the minimum set by a law passed when food became very expensive because landholders were growing almost nothing but sugar and cotton in order to take advantage of the soaring prices of these two products.

The landowning class has not been transformed into a capitalist middle class, ally of the national economy.[8] Mining, commerce, and transport are in the hands of foreign capital. The

[7] The *Extracto estadístico del Perú* furnishes no data on this, nor does the *Estadística industrial del Perú* (1922), of Carlos P. Jiménez give any overall figure.

[8] The conditions in which the country's agricultural life develops are studied in the third essay, "The Problem of Land."

latifundistas have been satisfied to serve as the latter's intermediaries in the production of sugar and cotton. This economic
system has kept agriculture to a semi-feudal organization that
constitutes the heaviest burden on the country's development.

The survival of feudalism on the coast is reflected in the stagnation and poverty of urban life. There are few towns and
cities on the coast, and the village as such hardly exists except
for the occasional cluster of plots that still adorns the countryside in the midst of a feudalized agrarian structure.

In Europe, the village is descended from the fief.[9] On the
Peruvian coast, the village does not exist because the fief is still
preserved virtually intact. The hacienda with its more or less
classic manor house and usually wretched workers' compound
[*ranchería*], and the sugar mill with its outbuildings [*colcas*],
are the typical rural community. This lack of villages and
scarcity of towns prolongs the desert into the cultivated and fertile land of the valley.

Cities, according to a law of economic geography, are formed
regularly in valleys where roads intersect. The rich and broad
valleys of the Peruvian coast, which head the statistics of national production, have not yet produced a city. At their crossroads or railway stations may be found scattered towns—torpid,
malaria-ridden and feeble, lacking either rural health or urban
attire. And in some cases, as in the Chicama Valley, the latifundium has begun to suffocate the city. Capitalist enterprise,
more than the castle or the feudal domain, opposed the preroga-

---

[9] Lucien Romier writes: "The village is not the result of a grouping together, as is the town or city; it is produced by the breaking up of an old
feudal domain, of an estate, or of the lay or church property surrounding a
bell tower. The unitary origin of the village has come down to us in such
current expressions as 'the spirit of the bell tower' and in the traditional
rivalries between parishes. It also explains the striking fact that old roads
skirt villages as though they were private properties rather than go through
them." *Explication de Notre Temps* (Paris: Bernard Grasset, 1925), pp. 37–
38.

tives of the city by competing for its business and robbing it of its function.

Within European feudalism, the elements of growth—the factors of town life—were, in spite of the rural economy, much greater than within criollo semi-feudalism. The countryside, however secluded, needed the town. It had, above all, a surplus of food crops to dispose of. Instead, the coastal hacienda grows cotton or sugar cane for distant markets. Assured of the transport of these products, it has little interest in relations with its surroundings. Food crops, when not completely eliminated by the cultivation of cotton or sugar cane, are raised only for consumption on the hacienda. In many valleys, the town receives nothing from and possesses nothing in the countryside. Therefore, it lives in poverty from a few urban trades, from the men it sends to work at the hacienda, and from its wearisome employment as a way station for the many thousands of tons of agricultural products that pass through it annually. The rare stretch of farmland supporting an independent and industrious community is an oasis in a succession of fiefs that, defaced by machinery and rails, have lost the stamp of a noble tradition.

In many cases, the hacienda completely closes its doors to outside trade: only its company stores are allowed to supply its workers. On the one hand, this practice indicates that the peasant is treated as a thing and not as a person; on the other, it prevents the town from fulfilling the role that would maintain it and guarantee its development within the rural economy of the valleys. The hacienda, by taking over the trade and transport as well as land and dependent industries, deprives the town of a livelihood and condemns it to a sordid and meager existence.

The industries and commerce of cities are subject to supervision, regulations, municipal taxes. Community life and services are sustained by their activity. The latifundium, however, escapes these rules and levies. It can compete unfairly with urban industry and commerce and is in a position to ruin them.

The favorite legal argument for large estates is that they are essential to the creation of great production centers. Modern agriculture, it is claimed, requires expensive machinery, huge investments, and expert management. Small properties cannot meet these needs. Exports of sugar and cotton safeguard Peru's balance of payments.

But the crops, the machinery, and the exports that the *latifundistas* boast of are far from being their own achievement. Production of cotton and sugar has flourished thanks to the stimulus of credits obtained for that purpose and on the basis of appropriated lands and cheap labor. The financial organization of these crops, which depend for development and profit on the world market, is not the result of either the foresight or the cooperation of landowners. The latifundium simply has adapted itself to outside incentives. Foreign capital, in its perennial search for land, labor, and markets, has financed and directed the work of landowners by lending them money secured by the latters' products and properties. Many mortgaged estates already are being directly administered by exporting firms.

The country's landowning aristocracy has most clearly shown its incompetence in the department of La Libertad, where it owned large valley haciendas. Many years of capitalist development brought the following results: the concentration of the sugar industry in the region of two huge sugar mills, Cartavio and Casa Grande, both foreign-owned; the absorption of domestic business by these two enterprises, especially the second, which also monopolized import trade; and the commercial decline of the city of Trujillo and the bankruptcy of most of its import firms.[10]

The old landowners of La Libertad, with their provincialism

---

[10] Alcides Spelucín recently has published in a Lima newspaper a very objective and thoughtful discussion of the causes and the stages of this crisis. Although his criticism stresses the invasive action of foreign capital, he concludes by placing the primary responsibility on local capitalism for its absenteeism and its lack of vision and energy.

and feudal customs, have not been able to resist the expansion of foreign capital enterprise, with its scientific methods, discipline, and determination. In general, all this has been lacking in local landholders, some of whom could have accomplished as much as the German industrialists if they had had the same entrepreneurial temperament.

The criollo landowner is handicapped by his Spanish heritage and education, which keeps him from clearly perceiving and understanding all that distinguishes capitalism from feudalism. The moral, political, and psychological elements of capitalism apparently have not found a favorable climate here.[11] The capitalist, or rather the criollo landowner, believes in income before production. The love of adventure, the drive to create, and the organizing ability that characterize the authentic capitalist are almost unknown in Peru.

Capitalist concentration has been preceded by a stage of free competition. Great modern property does not arise, therefore, from great feudal property, as the criollo landowner probably imagines; all to the contrary, it could only emerge after the great feudal property had been broken up and dissolved. Capitalism is an urban phenomenon; it has the spirit of the industrial, manufacturing, mercantile town. Therefore, one of its first acts was the liberation of land and the destruction of the fief. The development of the city had to be sustained by the free activity of the peasant.

In Peru, the meaning of republican emancipation has been violated by entrusting the creation of a capitalist economy to the spirit of the fief—the antithesis and negation of the spirit of the town.

[11] Capitalism is not just a technique; it is also a spirit. This spirit, which reaches its height in the Anglo-Saxon countries, is weak, incipient, and rudimentary in Peru.

The Problem of the Indian

A New Approach

ANY TREATMENT OF THE PROBLEM of the Indian—
written or verbal—that fails or refuses to recognize it as a socio-
economic problem is but a sterile, theoretical exercise destined
to be completely discredited. Good faith is no justification. Almost all such treatments have served merely to mask or distort
the reality of the problem. The socialist critic exposes and defines the problem because he looks for its causes in the country's
economy and not in its administrative, legal, or ecclesiastic
machinery, its racial dualism or pluralism, or its cultural or
moral conditions. The problem of the Indian is rooted in the
land tenure system of our economy. Any attempt to solve it with
administrative or police measures, through education or by a
road building program, is superficial and secondary as long as
the feudalism of the *gamonales* continues to exist.[1]

Gamonalismo necessarily invalidates any law or regulation

---

[1] Because of the length of this note, it has been placed at the end of the
chapter. *Ed.*

for the protection of the Indian. The hacienda owner, the *lati-fundista*, is a feudal lord. The written law is powerless against his authority, which is supported by custom and habit. Unpaid labor is illegal, yet unpaid and even forced labor survive in the latifundium. The judge, the subprefect, the commissary, the teacher, the tax collector, all are in bondage to the landed estate. The law cannot prevail against the *gamonales*. Any official who insisted on applying it would be abandoned and sacrificed by the central government; here, the influences of *gamonalismo* are all-powerful, acting directly or through parliament with equal effectiveness.

A fresh approach to the problem of the Indian, therefore, ought to be much more concerned with the consequences of the land tenure system than with drawing up protective legislation. The new trend was started in 1918 by Dr. José A. Encinas in his *Contribución a una legislación tutelar indígena*, and it has steadily gained strength.[2] But by the very nature of his study, Dr. Encinas could not frame a socio-economic program. Since his proposals were designed to protect Indian property, they had to be limited to legal objectives. Outlining an indigenous home-stead act, Dr. Encinas recommended the distribution of state and church lands. Although he did not mention expropriating the land of the latifundium *gamonales*, he repeatedly and con-clusively denounced the effects of the latifundium system[3] and,

[2] González Prada had already said in one of his early speeches as an in-tellectual agitator that the real Peru was made up of the millions of Indians living in the Andean valleys. The most recent edition of *Horas de lucha* in-cludes a chapter called "Nuestros indios" that shows him to be the forerunner of a new social conscience: "Nothing changes a man's psychology more swiftly and radically than the acquisition of property; once his viscera are purged of slavery, he grows by leaps and bounds. By simply owning some-thing, a man climbs a few rungs in the social ladder, because classes are divided into groups classified by wealth. Contrary to the law of aerostatics, what weighs the most goes up the most. To those who say schools the reply is schools and bread. The Indian question is economic and social, rather than pedagogic."

[3] "Improving the economic condition of the Indian," writes Encinas, "is

thereby, to some extent ushered in the present socio-economic approach to the Indian question.

This approach rejects and disqualifies any thesis that confines the question to one or another of the following unilateral criteria: administrative, legal, ethnic, moral, educational, ecclesiastic.

The oldest and most obvious mistake is, unquestionably, that of reducing the protection of the Indian to an ordinary administrative matter. From the days of Spanish colonial legislation, wise and detailed ordinances, worked out after conscientious study, have been quite useless. The republic, since independence, has been prodigal in its decrees, laws, and provisions intended to protect the Indian against exaction and abuse. The *gamonal* of today, like the *encomendero* of yesterday, however, has little to fear from administrative theory; he knows that its practice is altogether different.

The individualistic character of the republic's legislation has favored the absorption of Indian property by the latifundium system. The situation of the Indian, in this respect, was viewed more realistically by Spanish legislation. But legal reform has no more practical value than administrative reform when confronted by feudalism intact within the economic structure. The appropriation of most communal and individual Indian property is an accomplished fact. The experience of all countries that have evolved from their feudal stage shows us, on the other

---

the best way to raise his social condition. His economic strength and all his activity are found in the land. To take him away from the land is to alter profoundly and dangerously the ancestral tendency of his race. In no other place and in no other way can he find a better source of wealth than in the land." *Contribución a una legislación tutelar indígena*, p. 39. Encina says elsewhere (p. 13): "Legal institutions related to property are derived from economic necessities. Our civil code is not in harmony with economic principles because it is individualistic. Unrestricted property rights have created the latifundium to the detriment of Indian property. Ownership of unproductive land has condemned a race to serfdom and misery."

hand, that liberal rights have not been able to operate without the dissolution of feudalism.

The assumption that the Indian problem is ethnic is sustained by the most outmoded repertory of imperialist ideas. The concept of inferior races was useful to the white man's West for purposes of expansion and conquest. To expect that the Indian will be emancipated through a steady crossing of the aboriginal race with white immigrants is an anti-sociological naiveté that could only occur to the primitive mentality of an importer of merino sheep. The people of Asia, who are in no way superior to the Indians, have not needed any transfusion of European blood in order to assimilate the most dynamic and creative aspects of Western culture. The degeneration of the Peruvian Indian is a cheap invention of sophists who serve feudal interests.

The tendency to consider the Indian problem as a moral one embodies a liberal, humanitarian, enlightened nineteenth-century attitude that in the political sphere of the Western world inspires and motivates the "leagues of human rights." The anti-slavery conferences and societies in Europe that have denounced more or less futilely the crimes of the colonizing nations are born of this tendency, which always has trusted too much in its appeals to the conscience of civilization. González Prada was not immune to this hope when he wrote that "the condition of the Indian can improve in two ways: either the heart of the oppressor will be moved to take pity and recognize the rights of the oppressed, or the spirit of the oppressed will find the valor needed to turn on the oppressors."[4] The Pro-Indian Association (1900–1917) represented the same hope, although it owed its real effectiveness to the concrete and immediate measures taken by its directors in defense of the Indian. This policy was due in large measure to the practical, typically Saxon idealism of Dora Mayer,[5] and the work of the Association became well

[4] González Prada, "Nuestros indios," in *Horas de lucha*, 2nd ed.
[5] Dora Mayer de Zulen summarizes the character of the Pro-Indian Asso-

known in Peru and the rest of the world. Humanitarian teachings have not halted or hampered European imperialism, nor
have they reformed its methods. The struggle against imperialism now relies only on the solidarity and strength of the liberation movement of the colonial masses. This concept governs anti-
imperialist action in contemporary Europe, action that is
supported by liberals like Albert Einstein and Romain Rolland
and, therefore, cannot be considered exclusively Socialist.

On a moral and intellectual plane, the church took a more
energetic or at least a more authoritative stand centuries ago.
This crusade, however, achieved only very wise laws and provisions. The lot of the Indian remained substantially the same.
González Prada, whose point of view, as we know, was not
strictly Socialist, looked for the explanation of its failure in the
economic essentials: "It could not have happened otherwise;
exploitation was the official order; it was pretended that evils
were humanely perpetrated and injustices committed equitably.
To wipe out abuses, it would have been necessary to abolish
land appropriation and forced labor, in brief, to change the entire colonial regime. Without the toil of the American Indian,

---

ciation in this way: "In specific and practical terms, the Pro-Indian Association signifies for historians what Mariátegui assumes to be an experiment in
the redemption of the backward and enslaved indigenous race through an
outside protective body that without charge and by legal means has sought
to serve it as a lawyer in its claims against the government." But, as appears in the same interesting review of the Association's work, Dora Mayer
believes that it tried above all to create a sense of responsibility. "One hundred years after the republican emanciation of Peru, the conscience of the
governors, the *gamonales*, the clergy, and the educated and semi-educated
public continued to disregard its responsibilities to a people who not only
deserved philanthropic deliverance from inhuman treatment, but to whom
Peruvian patriotism owed a debt of national honor, because the Inca race
had lost the respect of its own and other countries." The best result of the
Pro-Indian Association, however, was, according to Dora Mayer's faithful
testimony, its influence in awakening the Indian. "What needed to happen
was happening; the Indians themselves were learning to do without the protection of outsiders and to find ways to redress their grievances."

the coffers of the Spanish treasury would have been emptied."[6] In any event, religious tenets were more likely to succeed than liberal tenets. The former appealed to a noble and active Spanish Catholicism, whereas the latter tried to make itself heard by a weak and formalist criollo liberalism.

But today a religious solution is unquestionably the most outdated and antihistoric of all. Its representatives—unlike their distant, how very distant, teachers—are not concerned with obtaining a new declaration of the rights of Indians, with adequate authority and ordinances; the missionary is merely assigned the role of mediator between the Indian and the *gamonal*.[7] If the church could not accomplish its task in a medieval era, when its spiritual and intellectual capacity could be measured by friars like Las Casas, how can it succeed with the elements it commands today? The Seventh-Day Adventists, in that respect, have taken the lead from the Catholic clergy, whose cloisters attract fewer and fewer evangelists.

The belief that the Indian problem is one of education does not seem to be supported by even a strictly and independently pedagogical criterion. Education is now more than ever aware of social and economic factors. The modern pedagogue knows perfectly well that education is not just a question of school and teaching methods. Economic and social circumstances necessarily condition the work of the teacher. *Gamonalismo* is fundamentally opposed to the education of the Indian; it has the same

6 González Prada, *Horas de lucha*.

7 "Only the missionary," writes José León y Bueno, one of the leaders of Acción Social de la Juventud, "can redeem and make restitution to the Indian. Only he can return to Peru its unity, dignity, and strength by acting as the tireless intermediary between the *gamonal* and the resident hacienda laborer and between the *latifundista* and the communal farmer; by preventing the arbitrary acts of the governor, who heeds solely the political interests of the criollo cacique; by explaining in simple terms the objective lessons of nature and interpreting life in its fatality and liberty; by condemning excesses during celebrations; by cutting off carnal appetites at their source; and by revealing to the Indian race its lofty mission." *Boletín de la A.S.J.*, May, 1928.

interest in keeping the Indian ignorant as it has in encouraging him to depend on alcohol.[8] The modern school—assuming that in the present situation it could be multiplied at the same rate as the rural school-age population—is incompatible with the feudal latifundium. The mechanics of the Indian's servitude would altogether cancel the action of the school if the latter, by a miracle that is inconceivable within social reality, should manage to preserve its pedagogical mission under a feudal regime. The most efficient and grandiose teaching system could not perform these prodigies. School and teacher are doomed to be debased under the pressure of the feudal regime, which cannot be reconciled with the most elementary concept of progress and evolution. When this truth becomes partially understood, the saving formula is thought to be discovered in boarding schools for Indians. But the glaring inadequacy of this formula is self-evident in view of the tiny percentage of the indigenous school population that can be boarded in these schools.

The pedagogical solution, advocated by many in good faith, has been discarded officially. Educators, I repeat, can least afford to ignore economic and social reality. At present, it only exists as a vague and formless suggestion which no body or doctrine wants to adopt.

The new approach locates the problem of the Indian in the land tenure system.

[8] It is well known that the production—and also the smuggling—of cane alcohol is a profitable business of the *hacendados* of the sierra. Even those on the coast exploit this market to some extent. The alcoholism of the peon and the resident laborer is indispensable to the prosperity of our great agricultural properties.

NOTE 1
In my prologue to *Tempestad en los Andes* by Valcárcel, an impassioned and militant champion of the Indian, I have explained my point of view as follows:
"Faith in the renaissance of the Indian is not pinned to the material process of 'Westernizing' the Quechua country. The soul of the Indian is

not raised by the white man's civilization or alphabet but by the myth, the idea, of the Socialist revolution. The hope of the Indian is absolutely revolutionary. That same myth, that same idea, are the decisive agents in the awakening of other ancient peoples or races in ruin: the Hindus, the Chinese, et cetera. Universal history today tends as never before to chart its course with a common quadrant. Why should the Inca people, who constructed the most highly-developed and harmonious communistic system, be the only ones unmoved by this worldwide emotion? The consanguinity of the Indian movement with world revolutionary currents is too evident to need documentation. I have said already that I reached an understanding and appreciation of the Indian through socialism. The case of Valcárcel proves the validity of my personal experience. Valcárcel, a man with a different intellectual background, influenced by traditionalist tastes and oriented by another type of guidance and studies, politically resolved his concern for the Indian in socialism. In this book, he tells us that 'the Indian proletariat awaits its Lenin.' A Marxist would not state it differently.

"As long as the vindication of the Indian is kept on a philosophical and cultural plane, it lacks a concrete historical base. To acquire such a base— that is, to acquire physical reality—it must be converted into an economic and political vindication. Socialism has taught us how to present the problem of the Indian in new terms. We have ceased to consider it abstractly as an ethnic or moral problem and we now recognize it concretely as a social, economic, and political problem. And, for the first time, we have felt it to be clearly defined.

"Those who have not yet broken free of the limitations of a liberal bourgeois education take an abstractionist and literary position. They idly discuss the racial aspects of the problem, disguising its reality under a pseudo-idealistic language and forgetting that it is essentially dominated by politics and, therefore, by economics. They counter revolutionary dialectics with a confused critical jargon, according to which a political reform or event cannot solve the Indian problem because its immediate effects would not reach a multitude of complicated customs and vices that can only be changed through a long and normal evolutionary process.

"History, fortunately, dispels all doubts and clears up all ambiguities. The conquest was a political event. Although it abruptly interrupted the autonomous evolution of the Quechua nation, it did not involve a sudden substitution of the conquerors' law and customs for those of the natives. Nevertheless, this political event opened up a new period in every aspect of their spiritual and material existence. The change in regime altered the life of the Quechua people to its very foundations. Independence was another political event. It, too, did not bring about a radical transformation in the economic and social structure of Peru; but it initiated, notwithstanding, another period of our history. Although it did not noticeably improve the condition of the Indian, having hardly touched the colonial economic infrastructure, it did change his legal situation and clear the way for his political and social emancipation. If the republic did not continue along this road, the fault lies entirely with the class that profited from independence, which was potentially very rich in values and creative principles.

"The problem of the Indian must no longer be obscured and confused by the perpetual arguments of the throng of lawyers and writers who are consciously or unconsciously in league with the *latifundistas*. The moral and material misery of the Indian is too clearly the result of the economic and social system that has oppressed him for centuries. This system, which succeeded colonial feudalism, is *gamonalismo*. While it rules supreme, there can be no question of redeeming the Indian.

"The term *gamonalismo* designates more than just a social and economic category: that of the *latifundistas* or large landowners. It signifies a whole phenomenon. *Gamonalismo* is represented not only by the *gamonales* but by a long hierarchy of officials, intermediaries, agents, parasites, et cetera. The literate Indian who enters the service of *gamonalismo* turns into an exploiter of his own race. The central factor of the phenomenon is the hegemony of the semi-feudal landed estate in the policy and mechanism of the government. Therefore, it is this factor that should be acted upon if the evil is to be attacked at its roots and not merely observed in its temporary or subsidiary manifestations.

"*Gamonalismo* or feudalism could have been eliminated by the republic within its liberal and capitalist principles. But for reasons I have already indicated, those principles have not effectively and fully directed our historic process. They were sabotaged by the very class charged with applying them and for more than a century they have been powerless to rescue the Indian from a servitude that was an integral part of the feudal system. It cannot be hoped that today, when those principles are in crisis all over the world, they can suddenly acquire in Peru an unwonted creative vitality.

"Revolutionary and even reformist thought can no longer be liberal; they must be Socialist. Socialism appears in our history not because of chance, imitation, or fashion, as some superficial minds would believe, but because it was historically inevitable. On the one hand, we who profess socialism struggle logically and consistently for the reorganization of our country on Socialist bases; proving that the economic and political regime that we oppose has turned into an instrument for colonizing the country on behalf of foreign imperialist capitalism, we declare that this is a moment in our history when it is impossible to be really nationalist and revolutionary without being Socialist. On the other hand, there does not exist and never has existed in Peru a progressive bourgeoisie, endowed with national feelings, that claims to be liberal and democratic and that derives its policy from the postulates of its doctrine."

The Problem of Land

The Agrarian Problem and the Indian Problem

THOSE OF US WHO APPROACH and define the Indian problem from a Socialist point of view must start out by declaring the complete obsolescence of the humanitarian and philanthropic points of view which, like a prolongation of the apostolic battle of Las Casas, continued to motivate the old pro-Indian campaign. We shall try to establish the basically economic character of the problem. First, we protest against the instinctive attempt of the criollo or mestizo to reduce it to an exclusively administrative, pedagogical, ethnic, or moral problem in order to avoid at all cost recognizing its economic aspect. Therefore, it would be absurd to accuse us of being romantic or literary. By identifying it as primarily a socio-economic problem, we are taking the least romantic and literary position possible. We are not satisfied to assert the Indian's right to education, culture, progress, love, and heaven. We begin by categorically asserting his right to land. This thoroughly materialistic claim should suffice to distinguish us from the heirs or imitators of the evangelical fervor of the great Spanish friar, whom, on the other hand, our materialism does not prevent us from admiring and esteeming.

The problem of land is obviously too bound up with the Indian problem to be conveniently mitigated or diminished. Quite the contrary. As for myself, I shall try to present it in unmistakable and clearcut terms.

The agrarian problem is first and foremost the problem of eliminating feudalism in Peru, which should have been done by the democratic-bourgeois regime that followed the War of Independence. But in its one hundred years as a republic, Peru has not had a genuine bourgeois class, a true capitalist class. The old feudal class—camouflaged or disguised as a republican bourgeoisie—has kept its position. The policy of disentailment, initiated by the War of Independence as a logical consequence of its ideology, did not lead to the development of small property. The old landholding class had not lost its surpremacy. The survival of the *latifundistas*, in practice, preserved the latifundium. Disentailment struck at the Indian community. During a century of Republican rule, great agricultural property actually has grown stronger and expanded, despite the theoretical liberalism of our constitution and the practical necessities of the development of our capitalist economy.

There are two expressions of feudalism that survive: the latifundium and servitude. Inseparable and of the same substance, their analysis leads us to the conclusion that the servitude oppressing the indigenous race cannot be abolished unless the latifundium is abolished.

When the agrarian problem is presented in these terms, it cannot be easily distorted. It appears in all its magnitude as a socio-economic, and therefore a political, problem, to be dealt with by men who move in this sphere of acts and ideas. And it is useless to try to convert it, for example, into a technical-agricultural problem for agronomists.

Everyone must know that according to individualist ideology, the liberal solution to this problem would be the breaking up of the latifundium to create small property. But there is so much ignorance of the elementary principles of socialism that it is worthwhile repeating that this formula—the breaking up of the latifundium in favor of small property—is neither utopian, nor heretical, nor revolutionary, nor Bolshevik, nor avant-garde, but orthodox, constitutional, democratic, capitalist, and bourgeois. It is based on the same liberal body of ideas that produced the constitutional laws of all democratic-bourgeois states. In the countries of Central and Eastern Europe—Czechoslovakia, Rumania, Poland, Bulgaria, et cetera—agrarian laws have been passed limiting land ownership, in principle, to a maximum of five hundred hectares. Here, the Great War razed the last ramparts of feudalism with the sanction of the capitalist West, which since then has used precisely this bloc of anti-Bolshevik countries as a bulwark against Russia.

In keeping with my ideological position, I believe that the moment for attempting the liberal, individualist method in Peru has already passed. Aside from reasons of doctrine, I consider that our agrarian problem has a special character due to an indisputable and concrete factor: the survival of the Indian "community" and of elements of practical socialism in indigenous agriculture and life.

If those who hold a democratic-liberal doctrine are truly seeking a solution to the problem of the Indian that, above all, will free him from servitude, they can turn to the Czechoslovakian or Rumanian experience rather than the Mexican example, which they may find dangerous given its inspiration and process. For them it is still time to advocate a liberal formula. They would at least ensure that discussion of the agrarian problem by the new generation would not altogether lack the liberal philosophy that, according to written history, has governed the life of Peru since the foundation of the republic.

Colonialism—Feudalism

The problem of land sheds light on the Socialist or vanguard-ist attitude toward the remains of the viceroyalty. Literary *perricholismo* does not interest us except as an indication or re-flection of economic colonialism. The colonial heritage that we want to do away with is not really the one of romantic damsels screened from sight behind shawls or shutters, but the one of a feudal system with its *gamonalismo*, latifundium, and servitude. Colonial literature—nostalgic evocation of the viceroyalty and its pomp—is for me only the mediocre product of a spirit en-gendered and nourished by that regime. The viceroyalty does not survive in the *perricholismo* of troubadors and storytellers. It survives in a feudalism that contains the germs of an unde-clared capitalism. We decry not our Spanish but our feudal legacy.

Spain brought us the Middle Ages: the Inquisition, feudal-ism, et cetera. Later it brought us the Counter Reformation: a reactionary spirit, a Jesuit method, a scholastic casuistry. We have painfully rid ourselves of most of these afflictions by assim-ilating Western culture, sometimes obtained through Spain it-self. But we are still burdened with their economic foundations embedded in the interests of a class whose hegemony was not destroyed by the War of Independence. The roots of feudalism are intact and they are responsible for the lag in our capitalist development.

The land tenure system determines the political and admin-istrative system of the nation. The agrarian problem, which the republic has not yet been able to solve, dominates all other problems. Democratic and liberal institutions cannot flourish or operate in a semi-feudal economy.

The subordination of the Indian problem to the problem of land is even more absolute, for special reasons. The indigenous race is a race of farmers. The Inca people were peasants, normally engaged in agriculture and shepherding. Their industries and arts were typically domestic and rural. The principle that life springs from the soil was truer in the Peru of the Incas than in any other country. The most notable public works and collective enterprises of Tawantinsuyo were for military, religious or agricultural purposes. The irrigation canals of the sierra and the coast and the agricultural terraces of the Andes remain the best evidence of the degree of economic organization reached by Inca Peru. Its civilization was agrarian in all its important aspects. Valcárcel, in his study of the economic life of Tawantinsuyo, writes that "the land, in native tradition, is the common mother; from her womb come not only food but man himself. Land provides all wealth. The cult of Mama Pacha is on a par with the worship of the sun and, like the sun, Mother Earth represents no one in particular. Joined in the aboriginal ideology, these two concepts gave birth to agrarianism, which combines communal ownership of land and the universal religion of the sun."[1]

Inca communism, which cannot be negated or disparaged for having developed under the autocratic regime of the Incas, is therefore designated as agrarian communism. The essential traits of the Inca economy, according to the careful definition of our historical process by César Ugarte, were the following:

Collective ownership of farmland by the *ayllu* or group of related families, although the property was divided into individual and non-transferable lots; collective ownership of waters, pasture, and woodlands by the *marca* or tribe, or the federation of *ayllus* settled around a village; cooperative labor; individual allotment of harvests and produce.[2]

Colonization unquestionably must bear the responsibility for the disappearance of this economy, together with the culture it

---

[1] Luis E. Valcárcel, *Del ayllu al imperio*, p. 166.
[2] César Antonio Ugarte, *Bosquejo de la historia económica del Perú*, p. 9.

nourished, not because it destroyed autochthonous forms but because it brought no superior substitutes. The colonial regime disrupted and demolished the Inca agrarian economy without replacing it with an economy of higher yields. Under the indigenous aristocracy, the natives made up a nation of ten million men, with an integrated government that efficiently ruled all its territory; under a foreign aristocracy, the natives became a scattered and anarchic mass of a million men reduced to servitude and peonage.

In this respect, demographic data are the most convincing and decisive. Although the Inca regime may be censured in the name of modern liberal concepts of liberty and justice, the positive and material historical fact is that it assured the subsistence and growth of a population that came to ten million when the conquistadors arrived in Peru, and that this population after three centuries of Spanish domination had fallen to one million. Colonization stands condemned not from any abstract, theoretical, or moral standpoint of justice, but from the practical, concrete, and material standpoint of utility.

Colonization, failing to organize even a feudal economy in Peru, introduced elements of a slave economy.

The Policy of Colonization: Depopulation and Slavery

It is easy to explain why the Spanish colonial regime was incapable of organizing a purely feudal economy in Peru. It is impossible to organize an economy without a clear understanding and sure appreciation, if not of its principles, at least of its needs. An indigenous, integrated economy develops alone. It spontaneously determines its own institutions. But a colonial economy is established on bases that are in part artificial and foreign, subordinate to the interests of the colonizer. Its normal development depends on the colonizer's ability either to adapt himself to local conditions or to change them.

The Spanish colonizer conspicuously lacked this ability. He

had an exaggerated idea of the economic value of natural wealth and absolutely no idea of the economic value of man.

With the practice of exterminating the indigenous population and destroying its institutions, the conquistadors impoverished and bled, more than they could realize, the fabulous country they had won for the king of Spain. Later, a nineteenth-century South American statesman, impressed by the spectacle of a semi-deserted continent, was to prescribe an economic principle for his epoch: "To govern is to populate." The Spanish colonizer, completely alien to this criterion, systematically depopulated Peru.

The persecution and enslavement of the Indian rapidly consumed resources that had been unbelievably underestimated by the colonizers: human capital. As the Spaniards found that they daily needed more labor for the exploitation of the wealth they had conquered, they resorted to the most antisocial and primitive system of colonization: the importation of slaves. The colonizer thereby renounced, on the other hand, an undertaking that the conquistador had thought feasible: the assimilation of the Indian. The Negro race he imported had to serve, among other things, to reduce the demographic imbalance between white and Indian.

The greed for precious metals—entirely logical in a century when distant lands could not send Europe any other product—drove the Spaniards to engage principally in mining. Therefore, they sought to convert to mining a people who had been essentially agricultural under the Inca and even before, and they ended by having to subject the Indian to the harsh law of slavery. Agricultural labor, under a naturally feudal system, would have made the Indian a serf bound to the land. Labor in mines and cities was to turn him into a slave. With the *mita*, the Spaniards established a system of forced labor and uprooted the Indian from his soil and his customs.

The importation of Negro slaves, which supplied laborers and domestic servants to the Spanish population on the coast, where the viceroyal court was located, helped mask its economic and political error from Spain. Slavery was injected into the regime, corrupting and weakening it.

In his study of the social situation in colonial Peru, Professor Javier Prado, whose premises I naturally do not share, reached conclusions that deal with an aspect of precisely this failure of colonization:

The Negro, considered as commercial merchandise and imported to America as a human labor machine, was to water the earth with the sweat of his brow, but without making it fruitful. It is the pattern of elimination followed by civilization in the history of all peoples. The slave is unproductive in his labor, as he was in the Roman Empire and as he has been in Peru. In the social organism he is a cancer that erodes national sentiments and ideals. In this way, the slave has disappeared from Peru, leaving behind barren fields and having taken revenge on the white race by mixing his blood with the latter's. By this vicious alliance, he debased the moral and intellectual judgment of those who were first his cruel masters and later his godfathers, companions, and brothers.[3]

The colonizer was not guilty of having brought an inferior race—this was the customary reproach of sociologists of fifty years ago—but of having brought slaves. Slavery was doomed to fail, both as a means of economic exploitation and organization of the colony and as a reinforcement of a regime based only on conquest and force.

Coastal agriculture still has not rid itself of its colonial defects, which derive largely from the slave system. The coastal *latifundista* never has asked for men, but for labor, to till his fields. Therefore, when he ran out of Negro slaves he found their successors in Chinese coolies. This other *encomendero* type of importation, like that of the Negroes, conflicted with the normal for-

[3] Javier Prado, "Estado social del Perú durante la dominación española," in *Anales universitarios del Perú*, XXII, 125–126.

mation of a liberal economy consistent with the political order established by the War of Independence. César Ugarte recognizes this in his study of the Peruvian economy when he states flatly that Peru needed "men," not "labor."[4]

The Spanish Colonizer

Colonization's inability to organize the Peruvian economy on its natural agricultural bases is explained by the kind of colonizer that came to Peru. Whereas in North America colonization planted the seeds of the spirit and economy then growing in Europe and representing the future, the Spaniard brought to America the effects and methods of an already declining spirit and economy that belonged to the past. This thesis may seem overly simplified to those who look only at its economic aspect and who are, unknowingly, the survivors of old-fashioned scholarly rhetoric. They share the common weakness of our historians: an incomprehension of economic reality. For this reason, I was glad to find in José Vasconcelos' recent book, *Indología*, an opinion that has the virtue of coming from a philosopher who cannot be accused of too much Marxism or too little Hispanism.

If there were not so many other causes of both a moral and physical order that amply explain the apparently reckless spectacle of the enormous progress of the Saxons in the North and the slow, aimless pace of the Latins in the South, a mere comparison of the two property systems would suffice to explain this contrast. In the North, there were no kings to dispose of another's land as though it were their own. Without any special favors from their monarchs and in a sort of moral rebellion against the king of England, the colonizers of the north proceeded to develop a system of private property under which each one paid the price of his land and occupied only as much as he could cultivate. In place of *encomiendas*, there were farms. In place of a military and landed

[4] Ugarte, *Historia económica del Perú*, p. 64.

aristocracy descended from a servile and murderous nobility,
there developed a democracy that at first followed only the French
precepts of liberty, equality, and fraternity. The men of the north
conquered virgin forest, but the general who led them to victory
against the Indians was not allowed to take possession, in our
tradition, "as far as the eye can see." The newly won lands were
not turned over to the king for him to give away at his discretion
and thereby create a nobility with double morals: a lackey of the
sovereign and an insolent oppressor of the weak masses. In the
north, the republic, which coincided with a great expansionist
movement, set aside a large part of the land and created vast reserves barred to private business. It did not use them to create
duchies or to reward patriotic services, but to promote popular
education. In that way, as the population increased, the rising
value of the land paid the rising costs of education. When new
cities arose in the middle of the desert, their lots were not distributed among favorites; they were put up for public sale, after
first being subdivided according to an overall plan for the new
city, with the condition that no one person could purchase many
lots at once. This wise and just social system is the source of North
America's strength. Because we did not act similarly, we have
fallen far behind.[5]

Feudalism is, as Vasconcelos implies, a blight inflicted upon
us by colonialism. Countries that were able to cure themselves
of it after independence have progressed; those that are still
afflicted are backward. We already have seen how feudalism
and slavery are related evils.

The Spaniard did not have the Anglo-Saxon's conditions of
colonization. The United States is considered to be the creation
of the pioneer. Spain, after the epic of the conquest, sent us
practically nothing but nobles, priests, and adventurers. The
conquistadors were of heroic stock; the colonizers were not.
Those who thought the wealth of Peru lay in its precious metals

[5] José Vasconcelos, *Indología* (Barcelona: Agencia Mundial de Librería,
1927).

converted mining into a factor in the liquidation of human resources and the decline of agriculture by using forced labor.
Accusations are even found in *civilismo* literature. Javier Prado
writes that "the state of agriculture in the viceroyal period
was absolutely deplorable, due to the absurd economic system
maintained by the Spaniards," and that the system of exploitation was responsible for depopulating the country.[6]

The colonizer who worked mines instead of fields had the
mentality of a gold prospector. He was not, consequently, a creator of wealth. An economy, a society, are the work of those
who colonize and bring to life the land, not of those who extract
treasures from its subsoil. The history of the flowering and
decay of many colonial populations in the sierra, determined
by the discovery and abandonment of mines quickly exhausted
or discarded, fully demonstrates this historical law in Peru.

Perhaps the only true colonizers sent to us by Spain were the
Jesuit and Dominican missionaries. Both orders, but especially
the Jesuits, created several interesting production centers in
Peru. The Jesuits introduced religious, political, and economic
elements into their enterprise, not to the same extent, but using
the same principles, as in Paraguay, where they carried out
their most famous and extensive experiment.

These religious activities were consistent not only with Jesuit
policy all over Spanish America but with the tradition of monasteries in the Middle Ages. One of the roles of the monastery
in medieval society was economic. In a warlike and mystic era,
they undertook to preserve the techniques of the arts and crafts,
refining and elaborating materials; this later served as a basis
for bourgeois industry. Georges Sorel is one of the modern
economists who best define the role of the monastery in the
European economy. In his study of the Benedictine order as the
prototype of the monastery-industrial enterprise he writes: "At

6 Prado, "Estado social del Perú," p. 37.

that time, it was very difficult to find capital; for the monks it was a simple matter. Donations from wealthy families rapidly furnished them with great quantities of precious metals, thereby facilitating primitive accumulation of capital. On the other hand, monasteries spent very little and their rules required them to practice a strict economy that recalls the frugal habits of the first capitalists. For a long time, monks were in a position to engage in operations that would increase their fortune." Sorel tells us how, 'after having rendered distinguished services to Europe that are universally recognized, these institutions swiftly declined," and how the Benedictines "stopped being workers gathered together in an almost capitalist workshop and became bourgeois retired businessmen who thought only of a life of pleasant leisure in the countryside."[7]

This aspect of colonization, like many others of our economy, has not yet been studied. It has fallen to me, a convinced and declared Marxist, to point it out. I believe this study is essential to the economic justification of any measures adopted by future agrarian policy concerning the properties of monasteries and religious orders, because it will conclusively establish that their right of ownership, along with the real titles on which it rested, has actually expired.

The "Community" Under the Colonial Regime

The Laws of the Indies protected indigenous property and recognized its communist organization. Legislation relative to Indian "communities" did not attack institutions or customs that were not opposed to the religious spirit and political character of colonization. The agrarian communism of the *ayllu*, once the Inca state was destroyed, was not incompatible with either one. To the contrary. The Jesuits took advantage of indigenous

[7] Georges Sorel, *Introduction à l'économie moderne* (Paris: Marcel Rivière, 1911), pp. 120, 130.

communism in Peru, in Mexico, and, on a still larger scale, in Paraguay, for purposes of religious instruction. The medieval regime, in theory and practice, reconciled feudal property with community property.

Recognition of the "communities" and of their economic customs by the Laws of the Indies not only shows the realistic wisdom of colonial policy but is absolutely adjusted to feudal theory and practice. The provisions of the colonial laws on "communities," which maintained the latters' economic mechanism with no trouble, reformed customs contrary to Catholic doctrine (trial marriage, et cetera) and tended to convert the "community" into a cog in the administrative and fiscal machinery. The "community" could and did exist for the greater glory and profit of king and church.

We know that this legislation was mostly on paper. Indian property could not be adequately protected because of colonial practices. All evidence agrees on this. Ugarte makes the following statements:

Neither the farsighted measures of Toledo nor other measures that were tried out on different occasions prevented a large part of indigenous property from falling legally or illegally into the hands of Spaniards or criollos. One of the institutions that facilitated this plunder was the *encomienda*. By law, the *encomendero* was in charge of collecting taxes and of the organization and conversion to Christianity of his tributaries. But in actual fact, he was a feudal lord, owner of lives and haciendas, for he disposed of Indians as if they were trees in a forest and, if they died or disappeared, he took possession by one means or another of their land. In brief, under the colonial agrarian regime, many indigenous agrarian communities were replaced by individually owned latifundia farmed by Indians within a feudal organization. These great feudal properties, far from being split up over the years, became concentrated and consolidated into few holdings, because real estate was subject to in-

numerable encumbrances and perpetual assessments that immobilized it, like primogeniture, religious bequests and payments, and
other entailments on the property.[8]

Feudalism similarly let rural communes continue in Russia, a
country that offers an interesting parallel because in its historical process it is much closer to these agricultural and semi-
feudal countries than are the capitalist countries of the West.
Eugene Schkaff, in his study of the evolution of the *mir* in
Russia, writes:

Since landlords were liable for the taxes, they wanted every peasant
to have approximately the same area of land so that each one would
contribute with his labor to pay the taxes; to make sure that these
taxes would be paid, they established joint responsibility, which
was extended by the government to the rest of the peasants. Land
was redistributed as the number of serfs varied. Feudalism and
absolutism gradually transformed the communal organization of
the peasants into an instrument of exploitation. In this respect, the
emancipation of the serfs brought no change.[9]

Under the system of landlords, the Russian *mir*, like the Peruvian community, was completely denaturalized. The area of
land available for community families became more and more
inadequate and its distribution increasingly faulty. The *mir* did
not guarantee the peasant enough land to support himself; on
the other hand, it guaranteed the landlord a labor supply for his
latifundium. When serfdom was abolished in 1861, the landlords found a way to replace it by making their peasants' lots so
small that they could not raise enough food to live on. Russian
agriculture thus kept its feudal character. The latifundium owner turned the reform to his advantage. He had already realized
that it was in his interest to assign lots to his peasants, provided
that they were less than subsistence size. There was no surer

[8] Ugarte, *Historia económica del Perú*, p. 24.
[9] Eugène Schkaff, *La question agraire en Russie* (Paris: Rousseau, 1922),
p. 118.

means of shackling the peasant to the land and, at the same time, of keeping his emigration down to a minimum. The peasant was forced to work on the landlord's latifundium not only because of the miserable existence he wrested from his miniscule plot of land but also because the landlord owned pastures, woods, mills, water, et cetera.

The coexistence of "community" and latifundium in Peru is, therefore, fully explained both by the characteristics of the colonial regime and by the experience of feudal Europe. But the "community," under this system, was tolerated rather than protected. It was subject to the despotic law of the latifundium, and the state could not possibly intervene. The "community" survived, but in a condition of servitude. Previously, it had been the very nucleus of the state, which assured it the energy necessary to the welfare of its members. Colonialism petrified it within the great property that supported a new state, alien to its destiny.

The liberalism of the laws of the republic, powerless to destroy feudalism and create capitalism, later denied the "community" the formal protection that it had been granted by the absolutism of colonial laws.

The War of Independence and Agrarian Property

We shall now examine the problem of land under the republic. In order to define my points of view about this period as regards the agrarian question, I must emphasize an opinion that I already have expressed about the character of the War of Independence in Peru. Independence found Peru to be backward in the formation of its bourgeoisie. The elements of a capitalist economy were less developed in our country than in other countries of America, where the struggle for independence could count on an emerging bourgeoisie.

If the War of Independence had been a movement of the indigenous masses or had championed their cause, it would necessarily have had an agrarian cast. It is already clearly demonstrated that the French Revolution especially benefited the rural class and depended on it to prevent the return of the old regime. This phenomenon, furthermore, seems in general to be true of bourgeois as well as Socialist revolution judging by the more precise and enduring results of the overthrow of feudalism in Central Europe and czarist Russia. Although mainly the urban bourgeoisie and proletariat have directed and carried out both kinds of revolution, the peasant has been the immediate beneficiary. Particularly in Russia, the rural class has gathered the first fruits of the Bolshevik revolution, because there was no bourgeois revolution to destroy feudalism and absolutism and to initiate a liberal democratic regime.

But achievement of these objectives by a liberal democratic revolution presupposes two conditions: the existence of a bourgeoisie that knows where it is going and why; and the existence of a revolutionary spirit in the peasant class and, above all, of a declaration of the peasants' right to land, in defiance of the power of the landowning aristocracy. In Peru these conditions existed even less than in other countries at the time of the War of Independence. The revolution had triumphed because the peoples of the continent had been obliged to join together against Spanish rule and because world political and economic circumstances were in its favor. The continental nationalism of the Spanish American revolutionaries and the enforced association of their destinies combined to bring the most backward abreast of the most advanced peoples in their march toward capitalism.

In his study of the Argentine and, therefore, of the American revolution, Echevarría classifies society in the following manner:

American society was divided into three classes with conflicting interests and without any moral or political bond. The first class was comprised of the lawyers, clergy, and authorities; the second class was made up of those who became rich through monopolies or good luck; the third class contained the workers, known as *gauchos* and *compadritos* in the Río de la Plata, *cholos* in Peru, *rotos* in Chile, and *léperos* in Mexico. The Indian and African castes were slaves who lived outside of society. The first class, with the power and privileges of the hidalgo, produced nothing and enjoyed a life of ease; it was an aristocracy largely composed of Peninsular Spaniards and included very few criollos. The second class also lived in comfort, peacefully engaged in industry or commerce; it was the middle class that sat on the municipal council. The third class was the only one that contributed manual labor to production and it was made up of artisans and every kind of proletariat. American descendants of the first two classes who had received some education in America or in Spain were the ones to raise the banner of the revolution.[10]

The struggle for independence in many cases united the landholding nobility and the bourgeois merchants, either because the former had been indoctrinated with liberal ideas or because it regarded the revolution as only a liberation movement from the Spanish crown. The peasant population, which in Peru was Indian, did not participate directly or actively in the war, and the revolutionary program did not represent its claims.

But this program was inspired by liberal ideology. The revolution could not exclude principles that supported agrarian reform founded on the practical necessity and theoretical justice of freeing the land from its feudal shackles. The republic introduced these principles into its statutes. Peru did not have a bourgeoisie to apply them in accordance with its economic interests and its political and legal doctrine. Although the republic—following the course and dictates of history—was established on liberal and bourgeois principles, the practical effects of independence on agricultural property could not help but be limited by the interests of the large landowners.

Therefore, the disentailment of agricultural property required by the basic policies of the republic did not attack the latifun-

[10] Esteban Echevarría, *Antecedentes y primeros pasos de la revolución de mayo.*

dium. And if, on the one hand, the new laws in compensation ordered the distribution of land to the Indian, on the other hand they attacked the "community" in the name of liberal precepts.

Thus was inaugurated a regime that, whatever its principles, made the condition of the Indian to some extent worse instead of better. And this was not the fault of the ideology that inspired the new policy, which, rightly applied, would have ended feudal control of land and converted the Indian into a small landowner.

The new policy formally abolished the *mita*, the *encomienda*, et cetera. It included a series of measures that signified the end of the Indian's serfdom. But since it nevertheless left the power and force of feudal property intact, it invalidated its own measures for protecting the small landowner and farmer.

Although the landholding aristocracy in principle forfeited its privileges, in fact it maintained its position. It continued to be the dominant class in Peru. The revolution had not really raised a new class to power. The professional and business bourgeoisie was too weak to govern. The abolition of forced labor, therefore, never became more than a theoretical declaration because it did not touch the latifundium, and servitude is only one of the aspects of feudalism, not feudalism itself.

The Agrarian Policy of the Republic

During the period of military caudillos that followed the War of Independence, a liberal policy on agricultural property obviously could not be developed or even be formulated. The military caudillo was the natural product of a revolutionary period that had not been able to create a new governing class. In this situation, power was taken over by the military leaders of the revolution, who, on the one hand, enjoyed the prestige of their wartime achievements and, on the other, were in a position to keep themselves in the government by means of armed force. Of course, the caudillo could not remain aloof from the influence of class interests or of opposing historical currents. He was supported by the spineless liberalism and rhetoric of the urban demos and by the colonial conservatism of the landowning class. He was sanctioned by the city's lawmakers and jurists and by the writers and orators of the latifundium aristocracy. In the contest between liberal and conservative interests, there was no direct and active campaign to vindicate the peasant, which would have compelled the liberals to include the redistribution of agricultural property in their program.

A true statesman, not one of our military bosses of this period, would have heeded and dealt with this basic problem.

The military caudillo, furthermore, seems organically incapable of so sweeping a reform, which first and foremost requires an informed legal and economic mind. His tyranny creates an atmosphere that is hostile to new legal and economic principles. Vasconcelos makes this observation:

On an economic level, the caudillo is always the main support of the latifundium. Although he sometimes declares himself to be an enemy of property, there is almost no caudillo who does not end up as an *hacendado*. The fact is that military power inevitably leads to land appropriation, whether by soldier, caudillo, king, or emperor; despotism and the latifundium go together. This is natural. Economic, like political, rights can only be preserved and defended within a regime of liberty. Absolutism always means poverty for the many and opulence and abusive power for the few. Only democracy, with all its defects, has been able to take us closer to the best achievements of social justice—at least, democracy as it is before it degenerates into the imperialism of republics that are too wealthy and that are surrounded by decadent peoples. In any event, among us the caudillo and military government have cooperated in the development of the latifundium. Just a glance at the property titles of our great landowners would reveal that almost all owe their wealth first to the Spanish crown and later to concessions and illegal favors granted to the influential generals of our false republics. Benefits and concessions have been granted over and over again without any regard for the rights of entire Indian or mestizo populations, who were helpless to assert their ownership.[11]

A new legal and economic order must be, in any case, the work of a class and not of a caudillo. When the class exists, the caudillo acts as its interpreter and trustee. His policy is no longer determined by his personal judgment but by a group of collective interests and requirements. Peru lacked a middle class capable of organizing a strong and efficient state. Militarism represented an elementary and provisional order that, as soon as it could be dispensed with, needed to be replaced by a more advanced and integrated order. It could not understand or even consider the agrarian problem. Elementary and immediate problems absorbed its limited action. Castilla was the military caudillo at his best. His shrewd opportunism, slyness, crudeness, and absolute empiricism prevented him from adopting a liberal policy until the very end. Castilla realized that the liberals of his time were a literary group, a coterie, not a class. Therefore, he cautiously avoided any act that would seriously oppose the interests and principles of the conservative class. But the merits of his policy lie in his reformist and progressive leanings. His acts of greatest historic significance—the abolition of Negro slavery and of forced tribute from the Indians—expressed his liberal attitude.

Since the enactment of the Civil Code, Peru has entered a period of gradual organization. It is hardly necessary to point out that the Code signified, among other things, the decline of militarism. Inspired by the same principles as the republic's early decrees on land, it reinforced and continued the policy of disentailment and redistribution of agricultural property. Ugarte,

---

[11] Vasconcelos, "Nacionalismo en la América Latina," in *Amauta*, No. 4. This opinion, which is true as regards relations between the military caudillo and agricultural property in America, is not as valid for all periods and historical situations. It cannot be subscribed to without making this specific qualification.

taking note of the progress made by national legislation on land, remarks that the Code "confirmed the legal abolition of the Indian communities and of the entailments; it introduced new legislation establishing occupation as one of the means of acquiring ownerless land; in its rules on inheritance, it tried to favor small property."[12]

Francisco García Calderón attributed to the Civil Code effects that it actually did not have or, at least, that were not as drastic and absolute as he believed. "The constitution had destroyed privileges and the civil law dividing up properties ended the unequal division of inheritances. This provision resulted, politically, in the death of the oligarchy, the aristocracy, the latifundium; socially, in the rise of the bourgeoisie and the mestizo; economically—by dividing inheritances equally—in the formation of small properties, previously blocked by the great estates of the nobility."[13]

This was undoubtedly the intention of the codifiers of rights in Peru. However, the Civil Code is merely one of the instruments of liberal policy and capitalist practice. As Ugarte recognizes, the Peruvian legislation "proposes to encourage the democratization of rural property, but by the purely negative means of removing obstacles rather than by giving the farmers positive protection."[14] Nowhere has the division, that is, redistribution, of agricultural property been possible without special expropriation laws that have transferred ownership of the land to the class that works on it.

Notwithstanding the Code, small property has not flourished in Peru. To the contrary, the latifundium has been consolidated and extended. And only the property of the Indian "community" has suffered the consequences of this twisted liberalism.

[12] Ugarte, *Historia económica del Peru*, p. 57.
[13] Francisco García Calderón, *Le Pérou contemporain*, pp. 98, 199.
[14] Ugarte, *Historia económica del Perú*, p. 58.

Large Property and Political Power

The two factors that kept the independence movement from taking up the agrarian problem in Peru—the extremely rudimentary state of the urban bourgeoisie and the extra-social situation, as Echevarría defines it, of the Indian—later prevented the governments of the republic from developing a policy aimed in some way at a more equitable distribution of land.

During the period of the military caudillo, it was the latifundia and not the urban demos that grew stronger. With business and finance in the hands of foreigners, the emergence of a vigorous urban bourgeoisie was not economically possible. Spanish education was absolutely incompatible with the ends and needs of industrialism and capitalism; instead of technicians, it trained lawyers, writers, priests, et cetera. Unless the latter felt a special vocation for Jacobinism or demagoguery, they joined the clientele of the landowning class. In turn, business capital, almost exclusively foreign, had no choice but to deal and associate with this aristocracy, which, moreover, tacitly or explicitly continued to dominate political life. In this way, the landholding aristocracy and its adherents became the beneficiaries of the fiscal policy and the exploitation of guano and nitrate. In this way, this group was compelled by its economic role to assume the function of the bourgeoisie in Peru, although it did not lose its colonial and aristocratic vices and prejudices. And in this way, the urban bourgeoisie—professionals and businessmen—were finally absorbed by *civilismo*.

The power of this class—*civilistas* or *neogodos*—was to a large measure derived from ownership of land. In the early years of independence, it was not exactly a class of capitalists, but a class of landowners. As a landowning rather than an educated class, it was able to merge its interests with those of foreign businessmen and creditors and by this token to negotiate with the state and to traffic in the country's natural resources. Thanks to the properties it had received under the viceroyalty, it possessed business capital under the republic. The privileges of the colony engendered the privileges of the republic.

Therefore, this class naturally and instinctively held the most conservative views on land ownership. The continued extra-social condition of the Indians, on the other hand, meant that there were no peasant masses ready to fight for their rights.

These have been the principal factors in the preservation and development of the latifundium. The liberalism of republican legislation was passive in its attitude toward feudal property and only took action against communal property. Although it could do nothing to the latifundium, it could do a great deal of damage to the "community." When a people are traditionally communist, dissolving the "community" does not help to create small properties. A society cannot be transformed artificially, still less a peasant society deeply atttached to its traditions and its legal institutions. Individualism has not originated in any country's constitution or civil code. It must be formed through a more complicated and spontaneous process. Destroying the "communities" did not convert the Indians into small landowners or even into free salaried workers; it delivered their lands to the *gamonales* and their clientele and made it easier for the *latifundista* to chain the Indian to the latifundium.

It is claimed that the key to the accumulation of agricultural property on the coast has been the need for an adequate water supply. According to this argument, irrigated agriculture in valleys formed by shallow rivers has caused large property to flourish and medium and small property to wither away. But this is a specious argument, with only a grain of truth. The overrated technical or material reasons on which it is based have affected the accumulation of property only since the establishment and development of large-scale commercial agriculture on the coast. Before coastal agriculture acquired a capitalist organization, the factor of irrigation was not important enough to determine the accumulation of property. It is true that the scarcity of irrigation water, because of the difficulties of its widespread distribution, favors the large landowner. But this is not what has kept property from being subdivided. The origins of the coastal latifundium go back to the colonial regime. The depopulation of the coast owing to colonial practices was at the same time one of the consequences of and one of the reasons for large property. The labor problem, which has been the only problem of the coastal landowner, is rooted in the latifundium. Landowners sought to solve it with the Negro slave in the colonial period and with the Chinese coolie in the time of the republic. A vain effort. The earth cannot be populated and, above all, made fruitful with slaves. Thanks to their policy, the great landholders own all the land possible, but they do not have enough men to till it and bring it to life. This is the defense of the large property; but it is also its misfortune and its weakness.

The agrarian situation in the sierra, on the other hand, shows the fallacy of the above argument. The sierra has no water problem. Abundant rainfall allows the latifundium owner and the communal farmer to grow the same crops. Nevertheless, property is also accumulated in the sierra. This circumstance proves that the question is essentially a socio-political one.

The development of commercial crops for an export agriculture in the coastal plantations appears to be wholly dependent on the economic colonization of the Latin American countries by Western capitalism. British businessmen and bankers became interested in these lands when they saw the possibility of using them profitably for the production of sugar, first, and cotton, later. From a very early date, a large part of agricultural property was mortgaged to foreign firms. *Hacendados* in debt to foreign businessmen and lenders served as intermediaries, almost as sharecroppers, for Anglo-Saxon capitalism in order to guarantee that their fields would be cultivated at minimum cost by wretched laborers bent double under the whip of colonial slave drivers.

But on the coast, the latifundium has reached a fairly advanced level of capitalist technique, although its exploitation still rests on feudal practices and principles. The yields of cotton and sugar cane are those of the capitalist system. Enterprises are heavily financed and land is worked with modern machines and methods. Powerful industrial plants operate to process these products. Meanwhile, in the sierra, yields are usually not higher for latifundium lands than for communal lands. And if we use an objective economic standard and judge a production system by its results, this fact alone hopelessly condemns the land tenure system in the sierra.

The "Community" under the Republic

We have already seen how the formal liberalism of republican legislation only acted against the Indian "community." The concept of individual property has had almost an antisocial function in the republic, because of its conflict with the existence of the "community." If the latter had been dissolved and expropriated by a capitalism in vigorous and independent growth, it would have been considered a casualty of economic progress. The Indian would have passed from a mixed system of communism and servitude to a system of free wages. Although this change would have denaturalized him somewhat, it would have placed him in a position to organize and emancipate himself as a class, like the other proletariats of the world. However, the gradual expropriation and absorption of the "community" by the latifundium not only plunged him deeper into servitude, but also destroyed the economic and legal institution that helped safeguard the spirit and substance of his ancient civilization.[15]

[15] Because of the length of this note, it has been placed at the end of the chapter. *Ed.*

During the republican period, national writers and legislators have shown a fairly uniform tendency to condemn the "community" as the residue of a primitive society or the survival of colonial organization. This attitude sometimes has been due to the pressures of *gamonalismo* and sometimes to the individualist and liberal thought that automatically dominated an overly literary and emotional culture.

Dr. M. V. Villarán, an able and effective representative of this school of thought, has written a study that indicates the need to carefully revise its conclusions concerning the Indian "community." Dr. Villarán theoretically maintains his liberal position by advocating the principle of individual property, but he accepts in practice the defense of the "communities" against the latifundium by recognizing that they have a function that the state should protect.

But Hildebrando Castro Pozo's book *Nuestra comunidad indígena* demonstrates that the first integrated and documented defense of the Indian "community" had to be inspired in socialist thought and be based on a concrete study of its nature carried out according to the research methods of modern sociology and economics. In this interesting study, Castro Pozo approaches the problem of the "community" with a mind free of liberal prejudices and prepared to evaluate and understand it. He reveals that, despite the attacks of a liberal formalism serving the interests of a feudal regime, the Indian "community" is still a living organism and that, within the hostile environment that suffocates and deforms it, it spontaneously shows unmistakable potentialities for evolution and development.

Castro Pozo maintains that "the *ayllu* or community has conserved its natural peculiarity, its character as an almost family institution that continued to harbor, after the conquest, its main constituents."[16]

---

[16] Hildebrando Castro Pozo, *Nuestra comunidad indígena.*

In this he agrees with Valcárcel, whose statements about the *ayllu* appear to some to be too colored by his ideal of an Indian renaissance.

What are the "communities" and how do they operate at present? Castro Pozo classifies them in the following way:

First—agricultural communities. Second—agricultural and livestock communities. Third—communities of pasture lands and watering places. Fourth—communities that have the use of the land. It should be borne in mind that in a country like ours, where a single institution acquires different characteristics according to the environment in which it has developed, no one type is actually so distinct and different from the others that it can be held up as a model. On the contrary, all the types have some characteristics in common. But since circumstances combine to impose a given kind of life in customs, work systems, properties, and industries, each group has predominant characteristics that make it agricultural, livestock, livestock with communal pastures and water, or usufructuary of the land which unquestionably belonged to the *ayllu*.[17]

These differences have developed, not through the natural evolution or degeneration of the ancient "community," but as a result of legislation aimed at the individualization of property and, especially, as a result of the expropriation of communal lands for the latifundium. They demonstrate, therefore, the vitality of the Indian "community," which invariably reacts by modifying its forms of cooperation and association. The Indian, in spite of one hundred years of republican legislation, has not become an individualist. And this is not because he resists progress, as is claimed by his detractors. Rather, it is because individualism under a feudal system does not find the necessary conditions to gain strength and develop. On the other hand, communism has continued to be the Indian's only defense. Individualism cannot flourish or even exist effectively outside a

[17] Ibid., pp. 16–17.

system of free competition. And the Indian has never felt less free than when he has felt alone.

Therefore, in Indian villages where families are grouped together that have lost the bonds of their ancestral heritage and community work, hardy and stubborn habits of cooperation and solidarity still survive that are the empirical expression of a communist spirit. The "community" is the instrument of this spirit. When expropriation and redistribution seem about to liquidate the "community," indigenous socialism always finds a way to reject, resist, or evade this incursion. Communal work and property are replaced by the cooperation of individuals. As Castro Pozo writes: "Customs have been reduced to *mingas* or gatherings of all the *ayllu* to help some member of the community with his walls, irrigation ditches, or house. Work proceeds to the music of harps and violins and the consumption of several quarts of sugar-cane *aguardiente*, packages of cigarettes, and wads of coca." These customs have led the Indians to the practice—incipient and rudimentary, to be sure—of the collective contract. Instead of individuals separately offering their services to landowners or contractors, all the able-bodied men of the cooperative jointly contract to do the work.

The "Community" and the Latifundium

The defense of the "community" does not rest on abstract principles of justice or sentimental traditionalist considerations, but on concrete and practical reasons of a social and economic order. In Peru, communal property does not represent a primitive economy that has gradually been replaced by a progressive economy founded on individual property. No; the "communities" have been despoiled of their land for the benefit of the feudal or semi-feudal latifundium, which is constitutionally incapable of technical progress.[18]

[18] After writing this essay, I find ideas in Haya de la Torre's book *Por la emancipación de la América Latina* that fully coincide with mine on the

On the coast, the latifundium has evolved in its crop cultivation from feudal routine to capitalist technique, while the communist farming of the Indian "community" has disappeared. But in the sierra the latifundium has preserved its feudal character intact and has put up a much stronger resistance than the "community" to the development of a capitalist economy. In fact, when a "community" is connected by railway to commerce and central transportation, it spontaneously changes into a cooperative. Castro Pozo, who, as head of the Section of Indian Affairs of the Ministry of Development, collected a great deal of information on the life of "communities," points to the interesting case of the Muquiyauyo "community," which, he says, combines the characteristics of producer, consumer, and credit cooperative. "As the owner of a magnificent electric plant on the banks of the Mantaro River, which furnishes light and power to the small industries of the districts of Jauja, Concepción, Mito, Muqui, Sincos, Huaripampa, and Muquiyauyo, it has become a communal institution par excellence. Instead of neglecting its indigenous customs, it has utilized them to carry out the work of the enterprise. It has purchased heavy machinery with the money saved on labor done by the cooperative, which even used women and children to help cart building materials, just as in the *mingas* that worked on communal construction."[19]

The latifundium compares unfavorably with the "community" as an enterprise for agricultural production. Within the capitalist system, large property replaces and banishes small agricultural property by its ability to intensify production through the employment of modern farm methods. Industrialization of agriculture is accompanied by accumulation of agrarian property. Large property seems to be justified by the interests

---

agrarian question in general and the Indian community in particular. Since we share the same points of view, we necessarily reach the same conclusions.

[19] Castro Pozo, *Nuestra comunidad indígena*, pp. 66–67.

of production, which are identified, at least in theory, with the interests of society. But this is not the case of the latifundium and, therefore, it does not meet an economic need. Except for sugar-cane plantations—which produce *aguardiente* to intoxicate and stupefy the Indian peasant—the latifundium of the sierra generally grows the same crops as the "community," and it produces no more. Lack of agricultural statistics does not permit an exact estimate of partial differences; but all available data indicate that crop yields of "communities" are not on the average less than those of latifundia. The only production statistics for the sierra are in wheat and they support this conclusion. Castro Pozo, summarizing the data for 1917–1918, writes:

Communal and individual properties harvested an average of 450 and 580 kilos per hectare, respectively. If it is taken into account that most fertile lands are in the hands of the large landowners, since the struggle for land in the south has reached the point where the Indian owner is gotten rid of by force or by murder, and that the ignorance of the communal farmer induces him to lie about the amount of his harvest in fear of new taxes or assessments by minor political authorities or their agents, it can readily be inferred that the higher production figure for individual property is not accurate and that the difference is negligible. Therefore, the two types of properties are identical in means of production and cultivation.[20]

In feudal Russia of the last century, the latifundium showed higher yields than small property. The figures in hectoliters per hectare were as follows: for rye, 11.5 against 9.4.; for wheat, 11 against 9.1; for oats, 15.4 against 12.7; for barley, 11.5 against 10.5; and for potatoes, 92.3 against 72.[21]

As a factor of production, the latifundium of the Peruvian sierra turns out to be inferior to the execrated latifundium of czarist Russia.

[20] Ibid., p. 434.
[21] Schkaff, *La question agraire en Russie*, p. 188.

The "community," on the one hand, is a system of production that keeps alive in the Indian the moral incentives that stimulate him to do his best work. Castro Pozo very correctly observes that "the Indian community preserves two great economic and social principles that up to now neither the science of sociology nor the empiricism of great industrialists has been able to solve satisfactorily: to contract workers collectively and to have the work performed in a relaxed and pleasant atmosphere of friendly competition."[22]

By dissolving or abandoning the "community," the system of the feudal latifundium has attacked not only an economic institution but also, and more important, a social institution, one that defends the indigenous tradition, maintains the function of the rural family, and reflects the popular legal philosophy so prized by Proudhon and Sorel.[23]

[22] Castro Pozo, *Nuestra comunidad indígena*, p. 47. The author has some very interesting comments to make about the spiritual elements of the community economy. "The vigor, industry and enthusiasm with which the communal farmer reaps and sheaves wheat or rye, *quipicha* (*quipichar*: to carry on one's shoulders. A widespread indigenous custom. The porters and stevedores of the coast shoulder their loads), and rapidly proceeds to the threshing floor, joking with his companion or with the man tugging on his shirt from behind, present a profound and decisive contrast to the indolence, indifference, apathy, and apparent fatigue with which the *yanacones* do the same or similar work. The former mental and physical state is so evidently more desirable than the latter that it raises the question of how the work process is affected by its results and concrete purpose."

[23] Sorel, who has examined carefully the ideas of Proudhon and Le Play on the role of the family in the structure and spirit of society, has made a penetrating study of "the spiritual part of the economic environment." If anything has been missing in Marx it has been an adequate legal spirit, although this aspect of production did not escape the dialectician of Trèves. "It is known," he writes in his *Introduction à l'économie moderne*, "that the family customs of the Saxon plain made a deep impression on Le Play when he started his travels and that they decisively influenced his thought. I have wondered if Marx was not thinking of these ancient customs when he accused capitalism of turning the proletarian into a man without a family." Returning to the comments of Castro Pozo, I want to recall another of Sorel's ideas. "Work depends to a very large measure on the feelings that the workers have about their task."

The Work System—Serf and Wage Earner

In agriculture, the work system is chiefly determined by the property system. It is not surprising, therefore, that to the same extent that the feudal latifundium survives in Peru, servitude survives in various forms and under various names. Agriculture on the coast appears to differ from agriculture in the sierra less in its work system than in its technique. Coastal agriculture has evolved rather rapidly toward a capitalist procedure in farming and in the processing and sale of crops. But it has made little progress in its attitude and conduct as regards labor. Unless forced to by circumstances, the colonial latifundium has not renounced its feudal treatment of the worker.

This phenomenon is not altogether explained by the fact that the old feudal lords have kept their properties and, acting as intermediaries for foreign capital, have adopted the practice but not the spirit of modern capitalism. It is also due to the colonial mentality of a landholding class accustomed to regard labor with the criteria of slave owners and slave traders. In Europe, the feudal lord to some extent represented the primitive patriarchal tradition, so that he naturally felt superior to his serfs but not ethnically or nationally different from them. The aristocratic landowner of Europe has found it possible to accept a new concept and a new practice in his relations with the agricultural worker. In colonial America, however, the white man's arrogant and deeply rooted belief in the colored man's inferiority has stood in the way of this transition.

When not Indian, the agricultural worker of the Peruvian coast has been the Negro slave and the Chinese coolie, who are, if possible, held in even greater contempt. The racial prejudices of the medieval aristocrat and the white colonizer have combined in the coastal *latifundista*.

Yanaconazgo and indenture are not the only expressions of feudal methods that still persist in coastal agriculture. The hacienda is run like a baronial fief. The laws of the state are not applied in the latifundium without the tacit or formal consent of the large landowners. The authority of political or administrative officials is in fact subject to the authority of the landowner in his domain. The latter considers his latifundium to be outside the jurisdiction of the state and he disregards completely the civil rights of the people who live within his property. He collects excise taxes, grants monopolies, and imposes sanctions restricting the liberty of the laborers and their families. Within the hacienda, transportation, business, and even customs are controlled by the landlord. And frequently the huts that he rents to the laborers do not differ greatly from the sheds that formerly served as slave quarters.

The great coastal landowners are not legally entitled to their feudal or semi-feudal rights; but their position of dominance and their vast estates in a territory without industries and without transportation give them almost unrestricted power. Through indenture and *yanaconazgo*, the large proprietors block the appearance of free-wage contracting, a functional necessity to a liberal and capitalist economy. Indenture, which prevents the laborer from disposing of his person and his labor until he satisfies the obligations he has contracted with the landlord, is unmistakably descended from the semi-slave traffic in coolies; *yanaconazgo* is a kind of servitude in politically and economically backward villages that has prolonged feudalism into our capitalist age. The Peruvian system of *yanaconazgo* is identified, for example, with the Russian system of *polovnischestvo*, under which crops sometimes were divided equally between landlord and peasant and sometimes only a third was given to the latter.[24]

The coast is so thinly populated that agricultural enterprises constantly face a labor shortage. *Yanaconazgo*, by giving the scanty native population a minimal guarantee of the use of the

[24] Schkaff, *La question agraire en Russie*, p. 135.

land, discourages emigration. Indenture attracts the laborers of the sierra to coastal agriculture by offering them better pay.

This indicates that, in spite of everything and although perhaps only superficially or partially,[25] the situation of the laborer on the haciendas of the coast is better than on the haciendas of the sierra, where feudalism has remained all-powerful. Coastal landowners are compelled to accept, albeit in a restricted and attenuated form, the system of free labor and wages. The laborer keeps his freedom to emigrate as well as to refuse his services to the employer who mistreats him. The proximity of ports and cities and the accessibility of modern transportation and commerce, furthermore, offer the laborer the possibility of escaping his rural destiny and of trying to support himself in another way.

If the agriculture of the coast had been more progressive and capitalist, it would have sought a logical solution to the labor problem. The more enlightened landowners would have realized that the latifundium as it now operates leads to depopulation and that, therefore, the labor problem is one of its most obvious and inevitable consequences.[26]

As capitalist technique advances in coastal agriculture, the wage earner replaces the *yanacón*. Scientific farming—the use of machinery, fertilizer, et cetera—is incompatible with routine and primitive agriculture. But the demographic factor—"the labor problem"—is a serious obstacle to this process of capitalist development. In the valleys, *yanaconazgo* and its variations

[25] It must not be forgotten that the laborers of the sierra suffer in the hot and unhealthy coastal climate; they soon contract malaria, which weakens them and predisposes them to tuberculosis. Nor should it be forgotten that the Indian is deeply attached to his home and his mountains. On the coast he feels an exile, a *mitimae*.

[26] This topic makes clear how closely our agrarian problem is related to our demographic problem. The concentration of land in the hands of the *gamonales* is a cancer in national demography. Only when it has been extirpated can Peru progress and really adopt the South American principle: "To govern is to populate."

guarantee the enterprises a minimum of permanent workers. Furthermore, the family of the native resident laborer or *yanacón* represents a source of future workers for the *hacendado*.

The large landholders themselves have recognized the advisability of establishing—very gradually and cautiously—colonies of small property owners. Part of the irrigated land in the Imperial Valley has been set aside for small farms. The same principle will be applied to other irrigated zones. An intelligent and experienced landowner recently told me that it was essential for the large estate to have small farms nearby from which to draw labor, in order not to have to depend on migrant workers or indenture. The program of the Agrarian Subdivision Company is part of the official policy to gradually establish small properties.[27]

But since this policy systematically avoids expropriation or, more precisely, large-scale expropriation by the state, for reasons of public interest or distributive justice, and since its possibilities of development are for the moment restricted to a few valleys, it is not likely that small property will promptly and extensively replace *yanaconazgo* in its demographic function. In valleys where plantation owners cannot contract a supply of labor from the sierra on favorable terms, *yanaconazgo* in its various forms will coexist with the wage earner for some time.

The forms of sharecropping and tenant farming vary on the

[27] The government's project to create small agricultural property is based on liberal economic and capitalist theory. Its application on the coast, subject to the expropriation of estates and the irrigation of uncultivated land, can offer fairly broad possibilities of settlement. In the sierra, its effects would be much more limited and doubtful. Like all attempts to distribute land in the history of our republic, it disregards the social value of the "community" and is overly solicitous of the latifundista, who jealously protects his own interests. In regions where there is still no monetary economy, lots should not have to be paid for in cash or in twenty annual installments. In these cases, payment should be specified in kind instead of money. The state's system of acquiring estates to be distributed among the Indians shows its extreme concern for the latifundista, who is given the opportunity to sell unproductive or rundown estates for a profit.

coast and in the sierra according to regions, practice, or crops.
They also have different names. But within their diversity, they
can generally be identified with precapitalist methods of farming observed in other countries of semi-feudal agriculture, for
example, czarist Russia. The system of the Russian *otrabotki*
presented all the ways that exist in Peru of paying rent—by
work, money, or crops. This can be confirmed simply by reading what Schkaff has to say about this system in his documented book on the agrarian question in Russia:

Between servitude based largely on violence and coercion and free
labor based on purely economic necessity there extends a whole
transitional system of extremely varied forms that combine the features of the *barchtchina* and the wage earner. It is the *otrabototsch-
nai* system. Wages are paid either in money, where services are contracted, or in produce or in land. In the last case (*otrabotki* in the
strict sense of the word), the landlord lets the peasant use his land
in return for the latter's work on his estate. . . . Payment for work
in the *otrabotki* system is always less than the wages of capitalist
free contracting. Payment in produce makes landlords more independent of price fluctuations in the wheat and labor markets. Since
nearby peasants supply them with cheaper labor, they enjoy a real
local monopoly. . . . Rent paid by the peasant takes several forms:
in addition to his labor, the peasant is obliged to give money and
produce. If he receives a *deciatina* of land, he agrees to work a *deciatina* and a half of the landlord's estate, to give ten eggs and one hen.
He will also deliver his cattle's manure; for everything, including
manure, is used for payment. Frequently, the peasant is even required "to do all that the landlord demands of him," to transport
crops, cut firewood, and carry loads.[28]

In the agriculture of the sierra exactly those features of feudal
property and work are found. The free labor system has not
developed there. The planation owner does not care about the

---

[28] Schkaff, *La question agraire en Russie*, pp. 133, 134, 135.

productivity of his land, only about the income he receives from it. He reduces the factors of production to just two: land and the Indian. Ownership of land permits him to exploit limitlessly the labor of the Indian. The usury practiced on this labor— translated into the Indian's misery—is added to the rent charged for the land, calculated at the usual rate. The *hacendado* reserves the best land for himself and distributes the least fertile among his Indian laborers, who are obliged to work the former without pay and to live off the produce of the latter. The Indian pays his rent in work or crops, very rarely in money (since the Indian's labor is worth more to the landlord), and most often in mixed forms. I have before me a study made by Dr. Ponce de León of the University of Cuzco that gives first-hand documentation of all the varieties of tenant farming and sharecropping existing in that huge department. It presents a quite objective picture—in spite of the author's conclusions about the privileges of the landlords—of feudal exploitation. Here are some of his statements:

In the province of Paucartambo, the landlord grants the use of his land to a group of Indians on the condition that during the entire year they do all the farming needed on the hacienda lands reserved to the owner. The tenants or *yanacones*, as they are called in this province, are obliged to transport the plantation crops to this city on their own animals and do domestic service in the hacienda itself or more usually in Cuzco, where the landlords prefer to reside. . . . In Chumbivilcas, there is a similar arrangement. Tenants farm as much land as they can and in exchange must work for the owner as often as he requires. . . . In the province of Anta, the landlord grants the use of his land on the following conditions: the tenant furnishes the capital (seeds and fertilizer) and all the labor needed to bring the crop to harvest, when he divides it equally with the landlord. That is, each one collects fifty percent of the produce, although the landlord has contributed nothing but the use of his land, without even fertilizing it. But this is not all. The tenant farmer is required to attend personally to the work of the landlord, receiving the customary wages of twenty-five *centavos* a day.[29]

A comparison of the foregoing with Schkaff's report on Russia demonstrates that none of the dark aspects of precapitalist property and work is lacking in the feudal sierra.

The "Colonialism" of Our Coastal Agriculture

The industrialization of agriculture in the coastal valleys under a capitalist system and technique has reached its present level of development thanks mainly to British and American investment in our production of sugar and cotton. Landlords have contributed little in industrial ability and capital to the expansion of these crops. Financed by powerful export firms, they grow cotton and sugar cane on their lands.

The best lands of the coastal valleys are planted with cotton and sugar cane, not exactly because they are suited to these crops, but because only these crops are important at present to English and American businessmen. Agricultural credit—absolutely dependent on the interests of these firms until a national agricultural bank is established—does not promote any other crop. Food crops intended for the domestic market generally are grown by small landowners and tenant farmers. Only in the valleys of Lima, because of the proximity of sizable urban markets, do large estates grow food crops. Often cotton and sugar-cane haciendas do not raise enough food to supply their own rural populations.

Even the small landowner or tenant farmer may be driven to plant cotton by these interests that do not take into account the special needs of the national economy. One of the most evident causes of the rise in food prices in coastal towns is the displacement of traditional food crops by cotton on the farmland of the coast.

[29] Francisco Ponce de León, *Sistema de arrendamiento de terrenos de cultivo en el departamento del Cuzco y el problema de la tierra.*

Commercial aid is given to the farmer almost exclusively for raising cotton. Loans are reserved, at all levels, for the cotton farmer. The production of cotton is not governed by any consideration of the national economy. It is produced for the world market, with no control to safeguard this economy against possible drops in prices due to periods of industrial crisis or of overproduction of cotton.

A cattle rancher recently told me that whereas a loan extended on a cotton crop is limited only by price fluctuations, a loan on a herd or ranch is entirely ad hoc and uncertain. A cattle rancher on the coast cannot obtain a substantial bank loan for expanding his business, and unless a farmer can put up as security either a cotton or sugar-cane crop, he is no better off.

If domestic consumption were met by the country's agricultural output, this would not be such an artificial situation. But the country still does not produce all the food that the population needs. Our heaviest imports are in "foodstuffs": *Lp.* [*libras peruanas*] 3,620,235 in 1924. This figure, within total imports of eighteen million pounds, reveals one of the problems of our economy. Although we cannot stop importing foodstuffs, we can eliminate its leading items, for example, wheat and flour, which reached more than twelve million *soles* in 1924.

For some time, the Peruvian economy has clearly and urgently called for the country to grow enough wheat for the bread of its people. If this had been accomplished, Peru would no longer have to pay twelve or more million *soles* a year to foreign countries for the wheat consumed in its coastal cities.

Why has this problem of our economy not been solved? It is not just because the state has failed to work out a policy on foodstuffs. Nor, I repeat, is it because sugar cane and cotton are the best crops for the soil and climate of the coast. A single valley, a single Andean tableland, if opened up with a few kilometers of railway or roads, can supply the entire Peruvian population with more than enough wheat, barley, et cetera. In the early colonial years, the Spaniards raised wheat on that same coast until the cataclysm that changed the climatic conditions of the littoral. Subsequently, no scientific and integrated study was made of the possibility of reestablishing its cultivation. The diseases that attack wheat grown on the coast went unchecked by the indolent criollo until recently, when experiments carried out in the north on the lands of the "Salamanca" demonstrated that there are varieties of wheat resistant to disease.[30]

The obstacle to a solution is in the very structure of the Peruvian economy, which can only move or develop in response to the interests and needs of markets in London and New York. These markets regard Peru as a storehouse of raw materials and a customer for their manufactured goods. Peruvian agriculture, therefore, obtains credit and transport solely for the products that benefit the great markets. Foreign capital is one day interested in rubber, another in cotton, another in sugar. When London can obtain a commodity more cheaply and in sufficient quantity from India or Egypt, it immediately abandons its suppliers in Peru. Our *latifundistas*, our landholders, may think that they are independent, but they are actually only intermediaries or agents of foreign capital.

Final Propositions

To the basic propositions already stated in this story on the agrarian question in Peru, I should add the following:

1. The nature of agricultural property in Peru is one of the greatest obstacles to the development of a national capitalism. Large or medium tenant farmers work a very high percentage of land, which is owned by landlords who have never managed their own estates. These landlords, completely ignorant of and

---

[30] The Commission for the Promotion of Wheat Farming has announced the success of its experiments in different parts of the coast. It has obtained substantial yields from the rust-immune "Kappli Emmer" variety, even in semi-arid areas.

remote from agriculture and its problems, live from their property income without contributing any work or intelligence to the economic activity of the country. They belong to the category of aristocrats or *rentiers* who are unproductive consumers. Through their inherited property rights they receive an income that may be considered a feudal privilege. The tenant farmer, on the other hand, is more like the head of a capitalist enterprise. Under a true capitalist system, this industrialist and the capital financing him would benefit from his efforts to increase the value of his business. Control of the land by a class of *rentiers* imposes on production the heavy burden of maintaining an income that is not subject to the vicissitudes of agriculture. The tenant farmer generally is not encouraged by this system to improve the land and its crops and installations. Fear of a higher rent when his contract expires keeps his investments to a minimum. The tenant farmer's ambition is, of course, to become a property owner; but by his own industry he makes the property worth more to the landlord. The lack of agricultural credit in Peru prevents a more intensive capitalist expropriation of land for this class of industrialists. Capitalist exploitation and industrialization of land cannot develop fully and freely unless all feudal privileges are abolished; therefore it has made very little progress in our country. This problem is just as apparent to a capitalist as to a socialist critic. Edouard Herriot states a principle that is embodied in the agrarian program of the French liberal middle class when he says that "land requires the actual presence."[31] In this respect, the West is certainly less advanced than the East, since Moslem law establishes, as Charles Gide observes, that "the land belongs to the one who makes it fertile and productive."

2. The latifundium system in Peru is also the most serious barrier to white immigration. For obvious reasons, we hope for

[31] Edouard Herriot, *Créer* (Paris: Payot, 1919).

the immigration of peasants from Italy, Central Europe, and the Balkans. The urban population of the West emigrates to a lesser degree and industrial workers know, moreover, that there is little for them to do in Latin America. The European peasant does not come to America to work as a laborer except where high wages would permit him to save a great deal of money; and this is not the case in Peru. Not even the most wretched farmer in Poland or Rumania would accept the living conditions of our day laborers on the sugar-cane and cotton haciendas. His ambition is to become a small landowner. To attract such immigrants, we must offer them land complete with living quarters, animals, and tools and connected with railroads and markets. A Fascist official or propagandist who visited Peru about three years ago declared to local newspapers that our system of large properties was incompatible with a colonization and immigration program that would attract the Italian peasant.

3. The subjugation of coastal agriculture to the interests of British and American capital not only keeps it from organizing and developing according to the specific needs of the national economy—that is, first of all to feed the population—but also from trying out and adopting new crops. The largest undertaking of this kind in recent years, the tobacco plantations in Tumbes, was made possible only by state aid. This is the best proof that the liberal laissez-faire policy which has been so sterile in Peru should be replaced by a social policy of nationalizing our great natural resources.

4. Agricultural property on the coast, despite the prosperity it has enjoyed, so far has been incapable of attending to the problems of rural health. *Hacendados* still have not complied with the modest requirements of the Office of Public Health concerning malaria. There has been no general improvement in farm settlements. The rural population of the coast has the highest rates of mortality and disease in the country (except, of course, for the extremely unhealthy regions of the jungle).

Demographic statistics for the rural district of Pativilca three years ago showed a higher death rate than birth rate. Sutton, the engineer in charge of the Olmos project, believes that irrigation works may offer the most radical solution to the problem of marshes and swamps. But outside of the project in Huacho to use the overflow of the Chancay River (it is directed by Antonio Graña, who is also responsible for an interesting colonization scheme), the project in "Chiclín" to use ground water, and a few other undertakings in the north, private capital has done very little to irrigate the Peruvian coast in recent years.

5. In the sierra, agrarian feudalism is unable to create wealth or progress. With the exception of livestock ranches that export wool and other products, the latifundia in the valleys and table-lands of the sierra produce almost nothing. Crop yields are negligible and farming methods are primitive. A local publication once said that in the Peruvian sierra the *gamonal* appears to be relatively as poor as the Indian. This argument—which is absolutely invalid in terms of relativity—far from justifying the *gamonal*, damns him. In modern economics, understood as an objective and concrete science, the only justification for capitalism with its captains of industry and finance is its function as a creator of wealth. On an economic plane, the feudal lord or *gamonal* is the first one responsible for the worthlessness of his land. We have already seen that, in spite of owning the best lands, his productivity is no higher than the Indian's with his primitive farming tools and arid communal lands. The *gamonal* as an economic factor is, therefore, completely disqualified.

6. To explain this situation it is said that the agricultural economy of the sierra depends entirely on roads and transportation. Those who believe this undoubtedly do not understand the organic, fundamental difference existing between a feudal or semi-feudal economy and a capitalist economy. They do not understand that the medieval, patriarchal, feudal landowner is

substantially different from the head of a modern enterprise. Furthermore, *gamonalismo* and *latifundismo* also appear to stand in the way of the execution of the state's present road program. The abuses and interests of the *gamonales* are altogether opposed to a strict application of the law conscripting road workers. The Indian instinctively regards it as a weapon of *gamonalismo*. Under the Inca regime, duly established work on road construction was a compulsory public service, entirely compatible with the principles of modern socialism; under the colonial regime of latifundium and servitude, the same service turned into the hated *mita*.

NOTE 15

If the historical evidence of Inca communism is not sufficiently convincing, the "community"—the specific organ of that communism—should dispel any doubt. The "despotism" of the Incas, however, has offended the scruples of some of our present-day liberals. I want to restate here the defense that I made of Inca communism and refute the most recent liberal thesis, presented by Augusto Aguirre Morales in his novel *El pueblo del sol*.

Modern communism is different from Inca communism. This is the first thing that must be learned and understood by the scholar who delves into Tawantinsuyo. The two communisms are products of different human experiences. They belong to different historical epochs. They were evolved by dissimilar civilizations. The Inca civilization was agrarian; the civilization of Marx and Sorel is industrial. In the former, man submitted to nature; in the latter, nature sometimes submits to man. It is therefore absurd to compare the forms and institutions of the two communisms. All that can be compared is their essential and material likeness, within the essential and material difference of time and space. And this comparison requires a certain degree of historical relativism. Otherwise, one is sure to commit the error made by Víctor Andrés Belaúnde when he attempted a comparison of this kind.

The chroniclers of the conquest and of the colonial period viewed the indigenous panorama with medieval eyes. Their testimony cannot be accepted at face value.

Their judgments were strictly in keeping with their Spanish and Catholic points of view. But Aguirre Morales is also the victim of fallacious reasoning. His position in the study of the Inca empire is not a relativist one. Aguirre considers and examines the empire with liberal and individualist prejudices. And he believes that under the Incas, the people were enslaved and miserable because they lacked liberty.

Individual liberty is an aspect of the complex liberal philosophy. A realistic critic would define it as the legal basis of capitalist civilization. (Without free will, there would be no free trade, free competition, or free enterprise.) An idealistic critic would define it as a gain made by the human spirit in modern times. In no case did this liberty fit into Inca life. The man of Tawantinsuyo felt absolutely no need of individual liberty—any more than he felt the need of a free press. A free press may be important to Aguirre Morales and to me, but the Indian could be happy without it. The Indian's life and spirit were not tormented by intellectual anxieties or creative pursuits. Nor were they concerned with the need to do business, make contracts, or engage in trade. Therefore what use would this liberty invented by our civilization be to the Indian? If the spirit of liberty was revealed to the Quechua, it was undoubtedly in a formula or rather in an emotion unlike the liberal, Jacobin, and individualist formula of liberty. The revelation of liberty, like the revelation of God, varies with age, country, and climate. To believe that the abstract idea of liberty is of the same substance as the concrete image of a liberty with a Phrygian cap—daughter of Protestantism and the French Revolution—is to be trapped by an illusion that may be due to a mere, but not disinterested, philosophical astigmatism of the bourgeoisie and of democracy.

Aguirre's denial of the communist nature of the Inca society rests altogether on a mistaken belief. Aguirre assumes that autocracy and communism are irreconcilable. The Inca system, he says, was despotic and theocratic and, therefore, not communist. Although autocracy and communism are now incompatible, they were not so in primitive societies. Today, a new order cannot abjure any of the moral gains of modern society. Contemporary socialism —other historical periods have had other kinds of socialism under different names—is the antithesis of liberalism; but it is born from its womb and is nourished on its experiences. It does not disdain the intellectual achievements of liberalism, only its limitations. It appreciates and understands everything that is positive in the liberal ideal; it condemns and attacks what is negative and selfish in it.

The Inca regime was unquestionably theocratic and despotic. But these are traits common to all regimes of antiquity. Every monarchy in history has been supported by the religious faith of its people. Temporal and spiritual power have been but recently divorced; and it is more a separation of bodies than a divorce. Up to William of Hohenzollern, monarchs have invoked their divine right.

It is not possible to speak abstractly of tyranny. Tyranny is a concrete fact. It is real to the extent that it represses the will of the people and oppresses and stifles their life force. Often in ancient times an absolutist and theocratic regime has embodied and represented that will and force. This appears to have been the case in the Inca empire. I do not believe in the supernatural powers of the Incas. But their political ability is as self-evident as is their construction of an empire with human materials and moral elements amassed over the centuries. The *ayllu*—the community—was the nucleus of the empire. The Incas unified and created the empire, but they did not create its nucleus. The legal state organized by the Incas undoubtedly reproduced the natural pre-existing state. The Incas did not disrupt anything. Their work should be praised, not scorned and disparaged, as the expression and consequence of thousands of years and myriad elements.

The work of the people must not be depreciated, much less denied. Aguirre, an individualistic writer, does not care about the history of the masses. His romantic gaze looks only for a hero. The remains of Inca civilization unanimously refute the charges of Aguirre Morales. The author of *El pueblo del sol* cites as evidence the thousands of *huacos* he has seen. Those *huacos* testify that Inca art was a popular art; and the best document left by the Inca civilization is surely its art. The stylized, synthesized ceramics of the Indians cannot have been produced by a crude or savage people.

James George Frazer—very remote spiritually and physically from the chroniclers of the colony—writes: "Nor, to remount the stream of history to its sources, is it an accident that all the first great strides towards civilisation have been made under despotic and theocratic governments, like those of Egypt, Babylon, and Peru, where the supreme ruler claimed and received the servile allegiance of his subjects in the double character of King and a god. It is hardly too much to say that at this early epoch despotism is the best friend of humanity and, paradoxical as it may sound, of liberty. For after all there is more liberty in the best sense—liberty to think our own thoughts and to fashion our own destinies—under the most absolute despotism, the most grinding tyranny, than under the apparent freedom of savage life, where the individual's lot is cast from the cradle to the grave in the iron mould of hereditary custom." *The Golden Bough*, abridged edition (London: Macmillan & Co., 1954), p. 48.

Aguirre Morales says that there was no theft in Inca society simply because of lack of imagination for wrongdoing. But this clever literary comment does not destroy a social reality that proves precisely what Aguirre insists on denying: Inca communism. The French economist Charles Gide states that Proudhon's famous phrase is less exact than the following one: "Theft is property." In Inca society there was no theft because there was no property or, if you like, because there was a socialist organization of property.

We dispute and, if necessary, reject the testimony of colonial chroniclers. But Aguirre seeks support for his theory precisely in their medieval interpretation of the form and distribution of the land and its products.

The fruits of the earth cannot be hoarded. It is not credible, therefore, that two-thirds of the crops were taken over for the consumption of the officials and priests of the empire. It is much more likely that the crops supposedly reserved for the nobility were actually put into a state storehouse for social welfare, a typically and singularly socialist provision.

Public Education

*The Colonial Heritage and French
and North American Influence*

Education in peru has been subject to three successive influences: the Spanish influence or, more precisely, legacy;
the French; and the North American. However, the initial Spanish influence has dominated. The other two have barely penetrated the Spanish framework and have not altered it basically.

The history of public education in Peru is divided into three
periods according to these influences.[1] The periods are not precisely defined. This is a common defect in Peru, where even
men are seldom clearly and unmistakably outlined and everything is a little blurred and confused.

A combination of foreign elements, unadapted to local conditions, is superimposed on public education, as on other aspects

[1] The participation of Belgian, German, French, Italian, English, and
other foreign educators in the development of our public education has been
episodic and contingent, and does not imply an orientation of our educational
policy.

of national life. Peru, fruit of the conquest, is not a country that assimilates the ideas of men of other nations and imbues them with its sentiments and customs, thereby enriching without deforming its national spirit. It is a country in which Indians and foreign conquerors live side by side but do not mingle with or even understand one another. The republic feels and declares its loyalty to the viceroyalty and, like the viceroyalty, it belongs more to the colonizers than to the rulers. The feelings and interests of four-fifths of the population play almost no role in the formation of the national identity and institutions.

Peruvian education, therefore, has a colonial rather than a national character. When the state refers to the Indians in its educational programs, it treats them as an inferior race; in this respect, the republic is no different from the viceroyalty.

Spain willed us, on the other hand, an aristocratic attitude and an ecclesiastical and literary concept of education, which closed the university to mestizos and made culture a class privilege. The purpose of teaching was to prepare priests and scholars, and the common people had no right to instruction.

The independence movement, nourished on Jacobin ideology, temporarily brought about the adoption of egalitarian principles. However, this verbal equality, meant only for the criollo, ignored the Indian. The republic, moreover, was born in poverty and could not afford the luxury of a broad educational system.

Condorcet's lofty concept did not figure among the ideals borrowed from the Revolution by our liberal leaders. In practice, independence perpetuated the colonial mentality in education as in everything else. After the fervor of liberal oratory and sentiment had died down, class privilege reasserted itself. The government of 1831 declared that education was to be free, a measure that was never carried out. The government was actually concerned not with the need to educate the people but, in its own words, with "the notorious depletion of private fortunes that had reduced countless fathers to the bitter situation of not being able to give their sons a good education, thereby ruining the future of many talented youths."[2]

The literary and rhetorical orientation was just as marked. Felipe Barreda y Laos cites as typical academic centers during the early days of the republic: Trinity College of Huancayo; the School of Philosophy and Latin Studies of Huamachuco; and the Schools of Philosophy, Theology, and Jurisprudence of the College of Moquegua.[3]

The liberals, the old landholding aristocracy, and the new urban middle class all studied together in the humanities. They liked to think of universities and colleges as factories producing writers and lawyers. The liberals enjoyed rhetoric as much as the conservatives. No one was interested in a practical orientation encouraging work in commerce or industry, still less in a democratic orientation making culture accessible to all.

The Spanish heritage was not only psychological and intellectual but above all economic and social. Education continued to be a privilege because the privileges of wealth and class continued. The aristocratic and literary concept of education was typical of a feudal system and economy. Not having abolished feudalism in Peru, independence would not abolish its ideas about education.[4]

Dr. Manuel Vicente Villarán, who stands for democratic-bourgeois beliefs in the Peruvian educational system, deplores this legacy. Twenty-five years ago he stated in a speech on the liberal professions:

There are a thousand economic and social reasons why Peru should be like the United States, a country of farmers, settlers, miners, tradesmen, and laborers. But the vagaries of history and the will of

[2] Circular by the Minister Matías León, dated 19 April 1831.
[3] "Las reformas de la instrucción pública," a speech delivered at the beginning of the academic year 1919 and published in the *Revista Universitaria*, 1919.
[4] See the essays on the national economy and the land problem in this book.

man have converted this country into a literary center, homeland of
intellectuals and breeder of bureaucrats. Let us look at society and
examine any family: with luck, we might find one of its members
in agriculture, business, industry, or shipping; but we shall certainly find a lawyer or physician, a military officer or government em-
ployee, a judge or a politician, a professor or a scholar, a journalist
or a poet. We are infected with the sickness of the old, decadent
countries, with their preoccupation with speaking and writing instead of acting, with "moving words instead of things," an illness
that is a sign of indolence and weakness. Almost all of us look with
horror on the active professions that require energy and the will to
succeed, because we do not want to fight, suffer, take risks, and
make our own way to prosperity and independence. How few of us
decide to bury ourselves on a mountain, live in the *puna*, sail the
seas, explore the rivers, irrigate the fields, work the mines. We are
even frightened of the risks and responsibilities connected with
manufacturing and commerce, while at the same time we are encouraged by society to join the swelling multitude of people who
want at any price the tranquility, security, the semi-idleness of public employment and the literary professions. Every father hopes that
his son will be a lawyer, scholar, office employee, writer, or teacher.
Knowledge is triumphant, the spoken and written word is in its
glory, and if this evil is not corrected, Peru will become like China,
the promised land of bureaucrats and scholars.[5]

A study of the history of capitalist civilization makes clear the
causes of the social situation in Peru as described by Dr. Villarán in the above paragraph.

Spain is a country that has never emerged from the Middle
Ages and joined the march of capitalism. Whereas in Central
and Eastern Europe the last bastions of feudalism were demolished by the World War, in Spain they have been maintained
by the monarchy. Spanish history reveals that this country has
never had a liberal-bourgeois revolution with a victorious third
estate. Capitalism more and more appears to be closely related

[5] Manuel Vicente Villarán, *Estudios sobre educación nacional*, pp. 8–9

to liberalism and Protestantism. This is an empirical observation based on experience, rather than a principle or theory. The countries that have most highly developed capitalism—industrialism and mechanization—are the Anglo-Saxons.[6] Of all the Latin countries, Spain is the one that has been least able to adapt to capitalism and liberalism. The famous Spanish decadence, which has been romantically attributed to the most varied and exotic origins, consists simply of this inability to adapt, to Europeanize, to assimilate into a democratic, bourgeois, and capitalist society. The colonies founded by Spain in America were bound to suffer from the same weakness. It is perfectly clear that the colonies of England, a nation destined to be supreme in the capitalist age, received the spiritual and material energies of a society at its zenith, whereas the colonies of Spain, a nation chained to the aristocratic age, received the sickness of a decadent society.

The medieval Spaniard came to America as a conquistador, not a colonizer. When Spain stopped sending conquistadors, it began sending viceroys, priests, and lawyers.

It is now believed that Spain experienced its bourgeois revolution in America. Its liberal bourgeois class, suppressed at home, organized itself in the colonies. The countries most benefited by the historical process launched by this revolution were those which had the strongest elements of a liberal, bourgeois society and economy. In Peru, the viceroyalty had constructed on the scattered remains of the Inca economy and society an aristocratic and feudal regime that reproduced the regime of the decaying metropolitan country with all its evils and without its roots.

The responsibility for the social situation denounced in 1900 by Dr. Villarán belongs to the Spanish heritage. Dr. Villarán admitted as much in his speech, although he could not show

[6] It is interesting and significant that French reactionaries call France a bourgeois rather than a capitalist nation.

much intellectual independence because of his affiliation with *civilismo*, the class represented by his party and heir to all the privileges of the viceroyalty:

America was not a colony to be settled and developed but to be exploited. The Spaniards came in search of easy wealth, ready and waiting, the kind of wealth that attracts the adventurer, the nobleman, the soldier, and the sovereign. In any event, the Indians were there to do the work. They were numerous, docile, industrious, and used to the land and the climate. The servile Indian produced the idle and wasteful rich. Still worse, labor was associated with servitude, because the worker was nothing but a servant. All labor came to be instinctively regarded as dishonorable. This instinct has been handed down to us by our grandparents as part of ourselves. By race and by birth we despise work and we yearn for wealth without effort, for a life of indolence, parties, and luxury.[7]

The United States was created by the pioneer, the puritan, the Jew, all men of strong will who directed their energies toward utilitarian and practical ends. Peru received a race that in its homeland could only be indolent, feckless, dreamy, and completely unfit for industrial and capitalist enterprises. The descendants of this race have inherited its defects.

The argument that the Spanish race could not liberate itself from the Middle Ages and adapt to a liberal and capitalist century is corroborated by a scientific interpretation of history.[8] We, who have always tended to an undiscriminating idealism in our approach to history, now have a realistic critic, César A. Ugarte. In his *Bosquejo de la historia económica del Perú* he states:

What forces did the new race bring to Peru? The Spaniard of the sixteenth century was not psychologically equipped to undertake the economic development of a hostile, harsh, unexplored land. A

---

[7] Villarán, *Estudios sobre educación nacional*, p. 27.

[8] Spain is the country of the Counter Reformation and therefore the antiliberal and antimodern state *par excellence*.

warrior who had recently emerged from eight centuries of the reconquest of Spain into the political unification of his country, he
lacked the virtues of diligence and thrift. His noble prejudices and
bureaucratic predilections turned him against agriculture and industry, which he considered to be occupations of slaves and com-
moners. Most of the conquistadors and explorers of the sixteenth
century were destitute, but they were not interested in finding a
free and bountiful land out of which they could carve a prosperous
future; they were driven only by greed for easy and fabulous wealth
and the possibility of attaining power and glory. The few cultured
and worthwhile men who accompanied this mass of ignorant adventurers were inspired by religious faith and proselytizing zeal.[9]

In my opinion, a religious spirit was not an obstacle to the
economic organization of the colonies. The devout puritans of
New England applied precisely this spiritual drive to their economic enterprises. Spanish colonization did not suffer from an
excess of religion.[10]

The republic, which inherited the institutions and methods
of its public education from the feudal and aristocratic viceroyalty, used France as a model as soon as its budding capitalist
economy and class induced the government to become interested
in reforming its educational system.

The French influence only added its defects to the original
ones of the Spanish heritage. Instead of correcting the literary
and rhetorical concepts of education handed down to the republic by the viceroyalty, it simply intensified and complicated
them.

Capitalist civilization did not develop as fully in France as it
did in England, Germany, and the United States, partly because
of the failings of the French educational system. That nation,
from which we have anachronistically copied so much, still has

[9] César Antonio Ugarte, *Bosquejo de la historia económica del Perú.*
[10] See the essay on the religious factor in this book.

not solved such basic problems as a uniform primary-school system and technical training.

Carefully studying this question in *Créer*, Herriot makes the following statements. "Consciously or not, we have remained faithful to that taste for universal culture which our fathers thought was the best way to refine the spirit. The Frenchman loves the general idea without always knowing what it stands for. Our press and our speeches are nourished on generalities."[11] "In the middle of the twentieth century, we still do not have a national program for education. Every political regime inflicted on us has imposed its theories on education. Looked at in perspective, their efforts have been disastrous."[12]

Further on, after recalling that Renan blamed part of the misfortunes of 1870 on a public education closed to all progress and thereby stifling the spirit of France, Herriot adds: "The men of 1848 had planned for our country a program of instruction that has never been carried out or even understood. Our teacher, Constantin Pecqueur, deplored the fact that public education was still not organized socially and that the privileges of birth should be extended into the education of children."[13]

Herriot, whose democratic principles cannot be questioned, supports his thesis with declarations of the Compagnons de l'Université Nouvelle and other advocates of a radical reform in education. According to his outline of the history of public education in France, the Revolution had broad and modern theories on education. "With remarkable decisiveness, Condorcet demanded for all citizens all the possibilities of instruction, free at all levels, the triple development of body, mind, and morals." But after Condorcet came Napoleon.

The work of 1808 [Herriot writes] is the antithesis of the efforts of 1792. From then on, the two opposing principles were in constant

[11] Edouard Herriot, *Créer* (Paris: Payot, 1919), p. 95.
[12] Ibid., p. 125.
[13] Ibid., p. 127.

conflict. We find them both underlying our institutions, which to this day are badly coordinated. Napoleon's primary interest in secondary education was to train his bureaucrats and government officials. We believe that he was largely responsible for the prolonged ignorance of our people during the nineteenth century. The men of 1793 had other hopes. Even in the colleges and lycées, there was nothing to awaken intellectual freedom; even in the university, there was no place for the independent study of science or letters. The Third Republic has been able to free the universities from this bondage and return to the sectarian aims of the Normal School, the Conservatory of Arts and Trades, and the Institute. But it has not been able to break away completely from the narrow concept tending to isolate the university from the rest of the nation. It has perpetuated the exaggerated concern for academic degrees and respect for procedures that made Jesuit education so strong and, at the same time, so dangerous a force.[14]

This, according to a democratic and liberal statesman of the French middle class, is the situation of education in the nation from which for so many years we have misguidedly imported methods and texts. Our mistake derives from the viceroyal aristocracy which, disguised as the republican bourgeoisie, has maintained in the republic the privileges and principles of a colonial society. This class wanted its children to have, if not the severely dogmatic education of the mother country, at least the elegantly conservative education of the Jesuit colleges that existed in France during the Restoration.

Dr. Villarán, proponent of a North American orientation, writing in 1908 on foreign influences in education, pointed out the error of using France as a model. "With all its admirable intellectual qualities," he said, "that country still has not been able to become sufficiently modern, democratic, and united in its system and methods of education. Leading French writers are the first to recognize this."[15] Dr. Villarán cited the opinion of

[14] Ibid., pp. 120, 123–124.
[15] Villarán, *Estudios sobre educación nacional*, p. 74.

Taine as an indisputable authority for the intellectual *civilistas* whom he was addressing.

French influence has not yet disappeared. There are still too many traces of it in the programs and, above all, in the spirit of secondary and university education. But with the recent reforms based on North American models, its period has ended. Therefore, an accounting can be made of this influence, which we already know represents an enormous liability. It is responsible for the predominance of the liberal professions. Unable to prepare a competent ruling class, education in Peru, from a strictly historical point of view, suffers from its failure to meet the needs of the developing national economy and from its indifference to the indigenous element. This is the same defect that we find throughout almost the entire political process of the republic.

When in 1895 the Piérola administration began to reorganize the economy of the country along the lines of *civilismo*, it also revised the system and methods of education. The creation of a capitalist economy had been interrupted by the War of '79 and its aftermath; now public education had to be adapted to the needs of this developing economy.

Primary education, which had been turned over to the municipalities by an impoverished government, again became the responsibility of the state. With the foundation of a Teachers' Normal School, it was taken out of the hands of criollo dilettantes and made truly public, that is, for the people. Technical education was assured by the reestablishment of the School of Arts and Trades.

This period of public education was characterized by its progressive orientation toward the Anglo-Saxon model. Although the 1902 reform of secondary education was a first step in this direction, it was a false step because it was limited to a single phase of education. The *civilismo* regime of Piérola neither knew how nor was able to conduct a sound educational policy. Its intellectuals, educated in garrulous and swollen verbosity or in lymphatic and academic erudition, had the mediocre mentality of law clerks. Its leaders or directors, when they rose above the mental level of traffickers in coolie labor or dealers in sugar cane, were hopelessly attached to their outdated aristocratic prejudices.

Since 1900 Dr. Villarán has been advocating a reform consistent with the burgeoning capitalist development of the country. His speech of that year on the liberal professions was the first effective protest against the literary and aristocratic approach to education that had been passed on to the republic by the viceroyalty. In the name of a frankly materialist or capitalist concept of progress, his speech condemned the vaporous and archaic foreign idealism that until then had prevailed in public education—limited to the education of "decent" young men. He concluded with the statement that it was "urgent to reorganize our educational system to produce fewer degree-holders and scholars and more men useful and productive to society." He added that "the great nations of Europe today are remodeling their educational programs, largely along North American lines, because they understand that this century requires men of enterprise rather than men of letters and also because they are all to some extent engaged in extending their trade, their culture, and their race throughout the world. Following the example of the great nations of Europe, we should also correct our mistakes and educate practical, industrious, and energetic men, the ones the country needs in order to become wealthy and by the same token powerful."[16]

The reform of 1920 marked the victory of the orientation ad-

16 Ibid., p. 33.

vocated by Dr. Villarán and, therefore, the predominance of North American influence. On the one hand, the Organic Law of Education, which took effect that year, originated in a proposal drawn up by a committee headed by Villarán. On the other hand, its final text was revised by Dr. Bard, chief of the North American mission contracted by the government to reorganize public education and for some time charged with applying the principles of this law.

The importation of North American methods cannot be attributed to weariness with Latin bombast, but rather to the spiritual drive that affirmed the development of a capitalist economy. Politically, the historical process meant the fall of a feudal oligarchy because of its inability to become capitalist. In the sphere of education, it meant an educational reform inspired by the example of the most prosperous and highly industrialized nation.

Therefore, the 1920 reform is consistent with the country's historical evolution. But, like the political movement which it paralleled and to which it was linked, the educational movement was sabotaged by the continued and widespread existence of a feudal regime. It is not possible to democratize the education of a country without democratizing its economy and its political superstructure.

A country cannot conscientiously fulfill its historical destiny unless it carries out its own educational reform, using foreign experts only as consultants. For this reason, the North American mission was a failure and the new Organic Law remained more a program of theory than of action.

There is a hopeless gap between the main provisions of the Organic Law and the practice of education. In a study that is not intended to be either negative or polemical, Dr. Bouroncle reviews the troubled history of this reform and notes several of its failures and amendments.

A superficial analysis [he writes] of the present legal situation of education reveals that many of its provisions and regulations have not had and never can have practical application. In the first place, the National Bureau of Education and the National Council of Education have been modified on the basis of legislative authorization; and the regional bureaus, which were the executive bodies with the highest technical and administrative competence, have been eliminated. The bureaus and offices have been changed and the study programs of primary and secondary education have had to be revised; examinations and degrees for teachers have had to be completely reformed. No work has been done on the division of schools into the different categories envisaged by the law or on the complicated classification of secondary schools that was proposed by the regulation on secondary education. The National Examining Board has been replaced by an Office of Examinations and Studies and the whole system has been modified. Higher education, which was dealt with in greatest detail, has only partially complied with the provisions of the law. The University of Technical Schools failed in its early stages and the Advanced Schools of Agriculture, Pedagogical Science, Industrial Arts, and Commerce have not been created. The study program for the University of San Marcos [also called the University of Lima] has not been fully implemented and the University Student Center, for which special personnel was contracted, has not even been founded. If we examine the present regulations for primary and secondary education, we shall likewise see an endless number of provisions that have been amended or that have not been applied. In Peru, few laws have been modified as rapidly and broadly as that of education, which today has more amendments and unapplied provisions than effective regulations.[17]

This is the thoughtful criticism of a sympathetic official. There is no lack of other statements, even one that declares the 1920 reform a failure because primary education still does not re-

---

[17] Dr. Bouroncle, "Cien años de política educacional," *La Prensa* (Lima), 9 December 1924.

ceive ten percent of the fiscal revenue as stipulated by law.[18] Furthermore, this statement is implicit in the revision of the Organic Law by the National Committee on Education.

Those of us whose ideology is revolutionary must declare that the failure of the 1920 reform was not due to overly ambitious or idealistic provisions. In many ways, the reform is limited in its objectives and conservative in its scope. It does nothing to diminish the privileges of rank and fortune. It does not open higher education to selected students from primary schools, because it does not provide for such a selection. It creates a dual school system according to whether or not the student will continue to secondary school, thereby restricting working-class children to a primary education in schools that do not prepare them to pursue a professional career. It perpetuates the private primary school, which from childhood rigidly separates the social classes. It establishes only free primary instruction, without even maintaining the principle that entrance into secondary school, which the government offered to a small percentage under its old system of scholarships, is expressly reserved for the best students. As regards scholarships, the terms of the Organic Law are very vague and in practice only students already in secondary schools are eligible for government support. Article 254 says: "By law, exemption from fees for tuition and residence may be awarded to needy youths who are outstanding in ability, morals, and dedication to study. These scholarships will be granted by the regional director on the recommendation of the faculty of the respective secondary school.[19]

In the light of its many limitations, the 1920 reform cannot be considered the democratic-bourgeois reform proposed by Dr. Villarán.

---

[18] In 1926 the budget expenditures were *Lp.* [*Libras peruanas*] 10,158,960 with *Lp.* 1,000,184 for education but only *Lp.* 859,807 for primary education.
[19] Ley Orgánica de 1920. Edición oficial, p. 84. [There is no footnote no. 20 in the original. *Ed.*]

University Reform
IDEOLOGY AND PROTEST

The student movement, which began in Córdoba with student demands for university reform, signals the birth of a new generation of Latin Americans. The documents on university reform in Latin America that were collected by Gabriel del Mazo at the request of the University Federation of Buenos Aires testify to the spiritual unity of this movement.[21] University unrest, whether in Argentina, Chile, or Peru, is caused by the same forces. Almost always sparked by a minor incident, it is spread and directed by a mood, a current of ideas called—not without risk of error—the "new spirit." Therefore, the desire for reform is found to have identical characteristics in all Latin American universities. Students throughout Latin America, although moved to protest by local problems, seem to speak the same language.

This movement is also closely connected with the postwar wave of messianic hopes, revolutionary sentiments, and mystic fervor which especially affected the university youth of Latin America. Convinced that the world had entered a new era, youth yearned to play a heroic role and to perform deeds that would go down in history. As is natural, the prevailing socio-economic system, with its evils and shortcomings, acted as a powerful stimulus to their desire for reform. The world crisis made it urgent for the Latin American people to examine and resolve their problems of organization and growth. Logically, the new generation felt these problems with an intensity and passion unknown to previous generations. Whereas the latter, in keeping with the tempo of the past, had been evolutionary— at times completely passive—the new generation was instinctively revolutionary.

[21] *La reforma universitaria*, 6 vols. (Buenos Aires: Publicaciones del Círculo Médico Argentino y Centro de Estudiantes de Medicina, 1926–1927).

At the beginning, the ideology of the student movement was neither homogeneous nor autonomous. It was overly influenced by the Wilsonian philosophy. The liberal and pacifist sentiments made popular by Wilson in 1918–1919 circulated as good revolutionary currency among Latin American youth. This is easily explained. In Europe, too, not only the bourgeois Left but the old Socialist reformers accepted as new the liberal ideas so eloquently expounded by the North American president.

Only through closer cooperation with labor unions, through battle with the conservative forces, and through criticism of the interests and principles of the established order could the university vanguard define its ideology. This is the belief of the spokesmen for the new student generation, after examining the origins and consequences of the reform movement.

Everyone agrees that the objectives of this movement, which hardly has a program, are not related exclusively to the university. Because of its increasing concern with improvement of the working classes and with reduction of the old economic privileges, it can only be understood as one of the aspects of a profound Latin American renovation. Palacios, taking into account all the recent consequences of the struggle, states that "as long as the present regime continues, the reform will not touch the hidden roots of the educational problem." He adds:

It will have achieved its purpose if it rids the universities of professors who think of themselves as bureaucrats; if it gives—as in other countries—to all who are competent the possibility of becoming professors, without being excluded because of their social, political, or philosophical beliefs; if it neutralizes, at least somewhat, chauvinism and encourages teachers to do research and accept responsibility. At best, the reform, correctly understood and applied, can help prevent the university from becoming, as is the rule in most countries, as it was even in Russia—whose intellectuals, although superior to those of any other country, betrayed the Revolution—a

stronghold of reaction. The reform can do this by making an effort
to attain the highest aspirations of the century.[22]

As might be expected, interpretations of the significance of
the movement do not exactly agree. But, with the exception of
the reactionaries, who are interested in limiting the reform to
the university and to education, all those who are sincerely
inspired by true ideals define it as the affirmation of the "new
spirit," understood as the revolutionary spirit.

As a philosopher, Ripa Alberdi considers that this affirmation
is a victory of the idealism of the first two decades of this century over the positivism of the nineteenth century. "The renaissance of the Argentine spirit," he said, "operates through the
younger generation, which, while crossing the fields of philosophy, has felt the wing of liberty brush its forehead." But Ripa
Alberdi himself realized that the purpose of the reform was to
enable the university to carry out "that social function which is
the very reason for its existence."[23]

Julio V. González, who has collected his writings on the university movement into two volumes, reaches more precise conclusions:

The university reform acknowledges the appearance of a new generation with no ties binding it to the preceding generation and with
its own feelings, ideals, and mission in life. This is not a simple, isolated fact: it is related in cause and effect to recent events in our
country which, in turn, are the consequence of world events. It
would be a mistake bordering on the ridiculous to think of university reform as a problem of lecture halls and, even then, to assume
that its importance lay in its effects in cultural circles alone. Such
a mistake would inevitably lead to a solution of the problem that
has nothing to do with actual circumstances. In other words: the

[22] Ibid., I, 55.
[23] Ibid., p. 44.

university reform is part of the material and moral development of our society since the war.[24]

González goes on to list the World War, the Russian Revolution, and the rise of the Radical party as decisive factors in the reform in Argentina.

José Luis Lanuza points to another factor: the evolution of the middle class. The majority of the students belong to some level of this class. However, one of the social and economic results of the war is the proletarization of the middle class. Lanuza argues that

a collective student movement of such broad social implications as the university reform would not have been possible before the World War. It became evident that methods of study would have to be modernized and that the university had not kept up with the development of universal thought since the time of Alberdi, when our country began to industrialize. But at that time, the university middle class was content to be a select group. To its misfortune, its privileges diminished with the growth of industry, class distinctions became more marked, and the proletarization of the intellectual followed. Teachers, journalists, and tradesmen organized into unions. Students could not escape the general movement.[25]

Mariano Hurtado de Mendoza agrees substantially with the observation by Lanuza:

The university reform is first and foremost a social phenomenon that results from another, more general, and far-reaching social phenomenon related to our country's level of economic development. It would therefore be a mistake to study the reform, in terms of the university, as a problem of modernizing its administration; or, in terms of education, as an attempt to apply new research methods in the pursuit of culture. We would also be wrong to think of it only as a current of new ideas produced by the World War and the Russian Revolution, or as the work of the new generation that ap-

24 Ibid., pp. 58, 86.
25 Ibid., p. 125.

pears "with no ties binding it to the preceding generation and with its own feelings, ideals, and mission in life.

And later on he adds:

The university reform is no more than a consequence of the proletarization of the middle class which inevitably occurs when a capitalist society reaches a certain stage of economic development. This means that in our society the proletarization of the middle class is taking place and that the university, which is composed almost entirely of this class, has been the first to be affected because it was the prototype of the capitalist institution.[26]

In any case, the reform generally has inspired the formation of groups of students who demonstrate their sympathy with the proletariat by spreading progressive social ideas and studying Marxist theories. Popular universities, very different in concept from earlier timid attempts at university extension courses, have sprung up all over Latin America as a visible adjunct to the student movement. Throughout Latin America the university has produced students of economics and sociology who have used their knowledge to help the working class, giving the latter, in some countries, an intellectual guidance that it formerly lacked. Finally, the most enthusiastic propagandists and supporters of the political union of Latin America are for the most part former leaders of the university reform who thereby conserve their continentalism, another badge of the "new generation."

A comparison of this movement with that of the universities of China and Japan proves that it has historical justification. In Japan, the university has been the principal classroom of socialism. In China, for obvious reasons, it has been even more active in the creation of a national conscience. Chinese students are in the vanguard of a revolutionary nationalism which has given that immense Asiatic nation a new soul and organization and

[26] Ibid., p. 130.

assigned to it a role of influence in world affairs. The most authoritative Western observers agree on this point.

But I shall not enter into a study of all the consequences of
the university reform and of its relationship with the great problems of the political evolution of Latin America. Having established the solidarity of the student movement with the general
historical movement of these peoples, we shall try to define its
characteristics.

What are the basic objectives or demands of the reform?

In 1921, the International Congress of Students held in Mexico proposed: (1) student participation in university government; (2) open courses and optional attendance. Chilean students supported the following principles: (1) autonomy of the
university, understood to be an institution composed of students,
professors, and graduates; (2) reform of the teaching system by
means of open courses and optional attendance, so that when
two professors teach the same subject, student attendance will
testify to the better teacher; (3) revision of study methods and
content; and (4) university extension courses to effectively link
the university and society. In 1923, students of Cuba expressed
their demands as follows: (1) a really democratic university;
(2) a real pedagogical and scientific modernization; (3) an educational system really for the people. In their 1924 program, the
students of Colombia advocated that the university be organized
to ensure its independence, the participation of students in its
government, and the adoption of new study methods. "Not only
lectures," this program says, "but also seminars and special
courses should be offered, and journals should be published. Professors should have assistants and the teaching profession should
offer security and be open to all who are qualified to occupy a
chair in the university." The vanguard students of the University of Lima, loyal to the principles proclaimed in 1919 and
1923, presented in 1926 the following platform: defense of university autonomy; participation of students in the administra-

tion and in the orientation of their respective universities or special schools; the right of students to vote in the election of the university rector; modernization of teaching methods; student voice in the establishment of courses; incorporation into the university of values outside the university; social content in culture; popular universities. The principles upheld by the Argentine students probably are better known because of their extensive influence on the student movement of America since its first declaration at the University of Córdoba. Furthermore, they are largely the same principles that were announced by the other Latin American universities.

This rapid review makes it clear that the main proposals of university reform are, first, student participation in university government and, second, open courses alongside the regular courses and with identical standing, to be given by competent teachers.

The meaning and origin of these two demands help us to understand what the reform stands for.

UNIVERSITY POLICY AND TEACHING IN LATIN AMERICA

The economic and political system created by the colonial aristocracy—which in some Spanish American countries still exists, although it is steadily and irreversibly declining—has long kept the Latin American university under the tutelage of these oligarchies and their supporters. Because university education has turned into a privilege of wealth, if not of position, or at least of a social class absolutely bound to the interests of either wealth or position, the university has tended to become an academic bureaucracy. Even the temporary influence of some outstanding personality could not save it from this fate.

The purpose of the university was chiefly to provide lawyers and other professionals for the ruling class. The rudimentary development and limited scope of public instruction closed the doors of higher education to the poor. Even primary education did not reach, and still does not reach, more than a fraction of the people. The university, controlled intellectually and materially by a class that in general lacked any creative drive, could not aspire to the formation and selection of skills. Its bureaucratization inevitably led to spiritual and scientific impoverishment.

This was not a phenomenon peculiar to Peru. We have had it longer because of the survival of our semi-feudal economic structure. But even among countries like Argentina, which have led the way in industrialization and democracy, the university has been the last to join the march of progress and change. The history of the University of Buenos Aires before the reform is summarized by Dr. Florentino V. Sanguinetti as follows:

Early in Argentine history, it promoted culture on a modest scale and formed urban centers which gave the masses an awareness of political unity and institutional order. Although its technical level was low, it was adequate to the needs of the country and to apply the slowly acquired knowledge of the civilian sector. After our country became a nation, the aristocratic and conservative university created a new social type: the professional. These men were the patricians of the second republic, gradually replacing the rural caciques in the managing of businesses, but they were not intellectually qualified to participate actively in the educational system or to guide the energies bursting from the wealth of pampas and tropics. During the last fifty years, our farming and ranching nobility has been excluded first from the economic field by the technically more skilled and progressive immigrant and then from the political field by the emergence of the middle-class parties. In search of an area where they could still wield influence, they took over the university, which soon became the vehicle of class privilege—where a succession of lifetime directors held the most important posts and where teachers, recruited by hereditary levy, imposed a veritable academic servitude of narrow-mindedness and conservatism.[27]

---

[27] Ibid., pp. 140–141.

The reform movement had to attack, first of all, this conservative stratification of the university. The arbitrarily imposed courses, the incompetent professors, and the exclusion of independent and progressive minds from the faculty were simply consequences of the oligarchical system of education. These evils could be attacked only through student participation in the government of the university and through the establishment of open courses and optional attendance so that students could eliminate the bad professors by demonstrating their preference for the classes given by better qualified teachers.

Through the history of the reform, the conservative oligarchy invariably has followed two courses of action. First, it has been united in its support of the incompetent, unpopular professor, whenever the interest of a family of its group was involved. Second, it has been no less stubborn in its resistance to any new, non-university, or simply independent teaching values. The two basic demands of the reform are, therefore, unquestionably dialectical, because they do not grow out of purely doctrinaire concepts but out of specific student action.

The majority of the teachers were unbending in their opposition to the important principles of the university reform, the first of which had been declared at the Student Congress of Montevideo and, thanks to favorable political circumstances, was officially recognized in both Argentina and Peru. When these circumstances changed, the conservative elements in education began a counter-movement, which in Peru has already wiped out almost all the gains of the reform and which in Argentina has stirred up recent student demonstrations against reactionary trends.

But the ideals of the reform cannot be attained without honest acceptance of the two principles discussed here. The vote of the students, even if used only as a moral check on teaching policy, is the sole dynamic and progressive elements in a university which otherwise would be hopelessly dominated by re-

actionary forces. Without this premise, the second principle of
the reform, open courses, cannot be carried out. Moreover, the
"hereditary levy" so accurately described by Dr. Sanguinetti
becomes the method of recruiting new professors. And scientific
progress loses its main stimulus, because nothing lowers the
level of teaching and of science as much as an oligarchical bureaucracy.

THE UNIVERSITY OF LIMA

In Peru, for several reasons, the university has been the
stronghold of the colonial spirit. The first reason is that under
the republic the old colonial aristocracy continued in power.

But this fact has been brought to light only since the new generation, having freed itself of the colonialist mentality or *civilista*
historiography, has been able to judge Peruvian reality objectively. The breakdown of the old class was foretold in 1919 by
the "secessionist" character of the change in government.

When Dr. V. A. Belaúnde described the university as "the
link between republic and colony" and praised it as the unique
and essential organ of historical continuity, he seemed to think
that he had made a valuable discovery. Until then, the ruling
class had maintained the intellectual illusion of a republic different from and independent of the colony, although its real
feelings were betrayed by its instinctive nostalgia for the viceroyal period. The university, which according to a cliché was
the national alma mater, had always been officially defined as
the highest seat of the principles and ideals of the republic.

Except for a moment of liberalism under Gálvez y Lorente,
who reestablished and carried on the ideology of Rodríguez de
Mendoza, the university had remained faithful to its scholarly,
conservative, and Spanish tradition. The divorce between the
work of the university and national reality—which although
commented on sorrowfully by Belaúnde, did not prevent him

from praising the university as the unique and sacred embodiment of the country's historical continuity—is entirely due to the divorce, little recognized but nonetheless true, between the old ruling class and the Peruvian people. Belaúnde wrote: "An unhappy fate has decreed that our university should serve professional interests and a certain scientific snobbism; but it has not been an instrument of education nor has it created a national conscience. A rapid review of the history of the university from its founding to the present makes tragically clear that it is out of contact with our national reality, with the life of our society, with the needs and aspirations of our country."[28] Belaúnde could say no more. Bound by education and temperament to the feudal class, and a member of the party that was led by one of its most authentic representatives, he had to be content to disagree, without going into his reasons. He even had to offer as explanation an "unhappy fate."

The truth is that the colony survived in the university because it also survived—in spite of independence and a liberal government—in the social and economic structure of the country, thereby slowing down its historical evolution and weakening its vitality. The university did not play a progressive and creative role in Peruvian life. It was not only isolated from but also opposed to the country's requirements and expectations. The colonial landholders, who rose to power in the republic during the turbulent period of military caudillos, are the least nationalist, the least Peruvian, of the factors in the history of independent Peru. This alone has determined the "unhappy fate" of the university.

After Gálvez y Lorente and until the student movement of 1919, the university was heavily influenced by the spirit of the colony. In 1894, Dr. Javier Prado spoke on "the social condition

28 Víctor Andrés Belaúnde, *La vida universitaria*, p. 3.

of Peru under Spanish rule" and tried to give an objective and balanced criticism of colonialism. This speech could have initiated measures to bring the university closer to our history and people. But Dr. Prado was closely associated with interests and beliefs with which this movement inevitably would have conflicted. He therefore preferred to head a mediocre program of positivism which, in the name of Taine, attempted to justify *civilismo* by endowing it with a superficially modern political doctrine and which did not even succeed in orienting the university away from its literary preoccupations toward the scientific disciplines that it still lacks. In 1900, Dr. M. V. Villarán delivered a significant speech on the liberal professions in Peru in which he charged the colonialism of the university with being responsible for the aristocratic prejudices that nourished and perpetuated a surplus of lawyers and men of letters. But this rebuke, like all the other sporadic outbursts of *civilismo*, barely ruffled the waters of this placid intellectual pond.

The generation arbitrarily known as "futurist" should have been, chronologically, the one to begin a reform of the methods and spirit of the university. To this group belonged the students, later professors, who represented Peru in the Student Congress of Montevideo and who organized the University Center, in which they laid the foundations of a solidarity that would have made possible a definition of the procedures and objectives of the reform. But under the direction of Riva Agüero, who acted as spokesman for the colonialist spirit in his writings on Peruvian literature, that university generation was given a conservative and traditional orientation. Furthermore, because of its origins and ties, it appeared to be the generation designated to react against the literary movement of González Prado and to reestablish the intellectual hegemony of *civilismo*, which was threatened by the popularity of Radical literature, especially in the provinces.

The Peruvian student movement of 1919 received its ideological stimulus from the triumphant rebellion of the students of Córdoba and from the eloquent exhortations of Professor Alfredo L. Palacios. But it originated chiefly as a student uprising against certain obviously unqualified professors. A minority of the students extended and elevated the objectives of this unrest, transforming what had started out as only a repudiation of bad professors and an archaic system into a repudiation of the old spirit of the university. The movement was supported by students who conformed to *civilista* ideas but who followed the proponents of the reform as much because they thought they were participating in a relatively innocuous school rumpus as because they also objected to the obvious incompetence of the professors.

This shows that if the teaching oligarchy had shown any interest in maintaining its intellectual prestige and had promptly carried out a minimum of the scandalously overdue improvements and modernizations in the educational system, it would easily have kept its position intact for a few more years.

The crisis that it dealt with so ineptly was brought on by the protracted and flagrant discrepancy between the academic level of the professor and the general advance of our culture in more than one field. This lag was particularly striking in literature and the arts. The "futurist" generation had reacted against the romantic "radical" generation outside the university by trying to reinforce the spiritual power of the university and concentrate in its classrooms all the forces directing national culture. They did not, however, have the knowledge, the desire, or the power to replace the old, backward, and incompetent faculty of the most vulnerable department, which was the School of Literature.

The glaring contrast between the teaching of literature in this department and the country's heightened literary awareness and production could no longer be ignored once the new generation broke with the conservatism of our paradoxical "futurists" and launched a renaissance in national literature. Young people attending the literature courses had acquired outside the university an aesthetic discrimination that enabled them to judge how outdated and inept some of their professors were. Whereas these students, reading on their own, had left "modernism" behind, the university faculty was still in the grip of the criteria and precepts that prevailed in Spain in the early 1800's. Because of its historical and literary orientation, the group that headed the 1919 movement in San Marcos was more severe in its criticism and more categorical in its condemnation of the professors it accused of being backward and anachronistic.

The reform spread from the School of Literature to the other departments where vested interests and the oligarchical system maintained unqualified professors. But the first breach was made in the School of Literature; only some time later was the struggle directed against "bad methods" rather than "bad professors."

The students began their offensive by drawing up a list of criticisms which they carefully tried to keep impartial and dispassionate. At this time, the evaluation was made on the basis of academic competence, without any ideological judgments.

When the rector and the council declared their support of the professors under attack, the movement intensified. The student insurgents, realizing that the oligarchical character of teaching and the bureaucratization and stagnation of teaching were two aspects of the same problem, expanded their protests and made them more detailed.

The first national congress of students, which met in Cuzco in March 1920, revealed that the reform movement still lacked a well directed and defined program. The most important act of this congress was the creation of popular universities in order to link revolutionary students with the proletariat and to broaden the scope of student protest.

Later, in 1921, during the conflict between university and government, student behavior was profoundly disoriented. Furthermore, reactionary professors, who attempted to smuggle in colonialist superstitions and nostalgias under the guise of an opportunistic and democratic oratory, found an enthusiastic audience among university youth, most of whom persisted in revering their old masters.

It was, nonetheless, evident that the defeat suffered by traditional *civilismo* had contributed to the triumphs achieved in 1919 by student protest. In that year, the decree of September 20 established open courses and student representation on the university council, and by means of Laws 4002 and 4004 the government declared vacant the chairs occupied by the blacklisted professors.

Once the university reopened—after a recess which strengthened the bonds between teachers and part of the students—the gains of the reform largely vanished because of the new organization. On the other hand, the students were more deeply imbued with the "new spirit" and were less confused ideologically than before the closing.

The reopening of the university in 1922 under the rectorate of Dr. M. V. Villarán signified that the government and professors had reached an agreement to end the conflict which had forced the university to close the preceding year. The basis of this agreement was the Organic Law of Teaching promulgated in 1920 by the Executive under authorization from Congress in October 1919, when the latter passed Law 4004 sanctioning the principle of student participation in the government of the university. This law granted the university an autonomy that satisfied the teachers who, for obvious reasons, were more inclined than before to accept a compromise. The government, equally anxious to find a solution, managed to circumvent all difficulties and ratified the law in its entirety.

As is natural, the agreement endangered the gains of the students by solving, even if only temporarily, the situation that had sustained their struggle. In fact, soon there was a badly disguised attempt to gradually nullify the reforms of 1919. Some professors restored the attendance system. But now the students were alerted to such an attempt, and they were inspired first by the Student Congress of Mexico and then by the fervent message of the youth of the south delivered by Haya de la Torre.

On taking office, the new rector, in a spirit of moderation and fairness, had declared himself to be sympathetic to the reform and even critical of the law's provisions replacing the free association of students with the highly authoritarian and bureaucratic "university student center." In line with these declarations, he recognized the wisdom of working with a consensus of the students and of avoiding any arbitrary or reactionary action that could arouse student hostility.

With the recalcitrant conservative professors brought under control, Dr. Villarán's term of office marked a period of collaboration between faculty and students. The rector made himself popular by his support of Zulen's intelligent library reforms and by his frequent consultations with the students, whose opinions and ideas he respected. Dr. Gastañeta, dean of the School of Medicine, by following a similar policy, won the students' enthusiastic cooperation. And the work of some of the young professors helped improve relations between faculty and students.

This policy, however, prevented a renewal of the reform movement. On the one hand, the professors were careful to adhere to a progressive program or at least to avoid action that might be interpreted as reactionary. On the other hand, the students were in a mood to collaborate and many were convinced that this was the only way to guarantee the autonomy and even the survival of the university.

On May 23 the working class and the student vanguard demonstrated how closely they had become allied socially and ideologically. On that date, in exceptionally favorable circumstances, the new generation played a historical role when it advanced from student unrest to collective and social protest. This event sparked a revolutionary current that swept through the university halls, strengthening the left wing of the Student Federation, reorganized soon after, and, above all, reviving and invigorating student discussion.

But the reform, apart from abolishing compulsory attendance, actually gained for the student no more than a theoretical control of the orientation or, more precisely, the administration of education. The principle of student representation on the university council was formally recognized; but the students, who used the assembly to express their opinions on any problem, neglected to designate permanent delegates and preferred to influence the council through spontaneous action and student plebiscites.

Although student leaders were extremely aggressive and dynamic, they did not use the assembly, where there was more uproar than discussion, to demand and obtain new teaching methods. They may have been distracted by the struggle against reactionary forces within and outside the university or they may not have been sufficiently aware of the problems of education. In any event, they were satisfied to accept token efforts or vague promises that melted away once they relaxed their vigilance in the classrooms.

Therefore, the university reform made little progress as an educational reform, despite the new Organic Law and the more sympathetic attitude of some of the professors. The comments of Alfredo Palacios on a similar phase of the reform in Argentina can be applied to our university.

In its first stage, university reform consisted only of student participation in the university government and of optional attendance. It
had failed to achieve its most important objectives: modernized
teaching methods and intensified studies. These were very difficult
to accomplish in the School of Law, which was petrified in its old
procedures of pure theory and pure abstraction. There was no teaching by observation and experience. It was always believed that from
this school would emerge the social elite who would become the
governing class: the financier, the diplomat, the writer, the politician. What emerged, to the contrary, were youthful materialists,
knowing nothing about everything, but versed in all the tricks
needed to embrangle a litigation and employed to perpetrate the injustices of daily life. Students listened to lectures without showing
any curiosity or any interest in research; without laboratories to
spur their enthusiasm, to test their character, to discipline their
will, and to exercise their intellect.[29]

Because our university did not have directors like Dr. Palacios, capable of understanding the reform required in the educational system and of dedicating passion and optimism to the task
of realizing it, our reform movement never went beyond the
stage to which it was carried by student activity.

The years 1924–1927 were adverse to the movement to reform the university in Peru. The expulsion of twenty-six students from the University of Trujillo was a prelude to an
offensive by the reactionaries. Soon after, all the conservative
forces in the University of Lima were mobilized against the provisions laid down in 1919 and 1923. The repressive measures
taken by the government against the student leaders of San
Marcos freed the professors from the watchful presence of most
of those who had kept the reform spirit alive among the students.
With the deaths of the two young teachers Zulen and Borja y
García, almost no professors remained to champion reform. After

[29] Alfredo L. Palacios, *La nueva universidad.*

the departure of Dr. Villarán, his policy of cooperation with students was abandoned. Left vacant, the rectorate fell into the paralysis and sterility typical of an interim administration.

This combination of unfavorable circumstances inevitably produced a resurgence of the conservative and oligarchical spirit. As the forces of progress and reform weakened, teachers went back to the old system and representatives of the *civilista* mentality regained absolute control. The expedient of a provisional administration, constantly extended, temporarily masked the reestablishment of conservatism in positions from which it had been dislodged by the reform movement.

There was a noticeable concentration of left-wing students in the 1920 election of delegates. The platform presented by this group, which dominated the new federation, reaffirmed all the basic principles of the reform.[30] But once again repression came to the aid of conservative interests.

A characteristic of this period of reaction was the support given to the university's conservative elements by the same forces which, riding the historical wave that swept away traditional *civilismo*, had been decisive in the triumph of the reform in 1919.

These are not, however, the only factors in the crisis of the university movement. Youth is not exempt from responsibility. Their rebellious behavior usually has been the result of their susceptibility to superficial enthusiasms. This is actually a failing common to all Spanish America. In a recent article, Vasconcelos writes: "The principal weakness of our race is its instability. We are incapable of sustained effort and, for that same reason, we cannot develop a plan or execute a project." He goes on to say: "In general, one should beware of enthusiasts. 'Enthusiastic' is the most dangerous adjective in our vocabulary. With that noble epithet, we have learned to cover up our

[30] *Amauta*, no. 3 (November 1926).

national weakness: we start out well and promise much; we fail to finish or make good."[31]

Erratic and unstable though he is, the student does more damage to the movement because he is vague and imprecise about its program and character. The objectives of the reform are not sufficiently defined nor are they fully understood. Discussion and study proceed slowly. Reaction cannot conquer youth intellectually and spiritually; its victories are only conditional. The reform, on the other hand, continues to act on student spirit and, despite momentary lapses, keeps alive the ardor that fired youth in the days of 1919–1923.

If the reform movement is in a precarious situation in Lima, it nevertheless flourishes in the University of Cuzco, where the most distinguished faculty members accept and approve the principles maintained by the students. Proof of this is the project to reorganize the University of Cuzco, which was drawn up during its recess by a committee appointed by the government for this purpose.

This project, signed by Professors Fortunato L. Herrera, José Gabriel Cosío, Luis E. Valcárcel, J. Uriel García, Leandro Pareja, Alberto Araníbar P., and J. S. García Rodríguez, undoubtedly is the most important official document produced to date on university reform in Peru. It represents the first time university teachers have spoken on this problem at so high a level, as well as a break with tradition and with official routine. The plan envisages the transformation of Cuzco into a great cultural center capable of supervising and directing the social and economic development of the Andes region. Its statutes incorporate the cardinal principles of the university reform in Spanish America.

The committee includes among its "basic proposals": open courses to complement those taught by regular professors; elimination of the final examination as the deciding grade; full-time

[31] *Repertorio Americano*, vol. 15 (1927), p. 145.

professors; participation of students and alumni in the election of university authorities; student representation on the university council and on every faculty; democratization of teaching.[32]

The report also emphasizes the necessity of organizing the university in such a way as to give it a broad practical application and a complete scientific orientation. The University of Cuzco hopes to become a true center of scientific research, wholly dedicated to the betterment of society.

In order to understand the growing conflict between the principles of university reform, as they have been formulated and subscribed to by student assemblies in various Spanish American countries, and the situation of the University of Lima, these principles may be compared with the corresponding aspects of teaching and administration in the latter university.

Participation of students in the government of the university. Reactionary forces are determined to reestablish the old, rigid concept of discipline, understood as absolute deference to the judgment and authority of the teaching staff. The Council of Deans, or the rector on its behalf, frequently refuses to give students permission to hold meetings. For the first time, it is possible to deny the right of students to use the university for discussion. Student delegates who are not acceptable to the faculty are not recognized. The last committee of the Student Federation could not begin work or even make up its membership because it lacked approval of the council. The crisis of the federation thus depends on a factor beyond the students' control. Student opinion has lost not only its influence in the council but even the possibility of expressing itself freely and in an orderly fashion. In these conditions, student representation in the government of the university would be a farce.

Modernization of teaching methods. With the exception of

[32] *Revista Universitaria del Cuzco*, no. 55 (1927).

innovations introduced by one or two professors, the old methods reign supreme. A short time ago, a high official of the Department of Education, Dr. Luis E. Galván, demanded in an
article: "What does our university do for scientific research?"[33]
In spite of his feelings of loyalty to San Marcos, Dr. Galván was
obliged to give a totally negative answer. Changes in methods
and studies have been minimal and left to the initiative of a few
responsible professors. Courses continue to be given orally and
dogmatically. Reforms that were begun in the 1922–1924 period have been suspended or have been bungled, as in the case
of Zulen's projected reorganization of library methods.

Reform of the teaching system. Open courses still have not
been properly tried out and conditions do not favor their introduction. The oligarchy in control of education is opposed to
open courses. Academic chairs continue to be filled by means of
the "hereditary levy" denounced by Dr. Sanguinetti of the old
University of Buenos Aires.

All the formal gains of 1919 are therefore nullified. Despite
the mild purge brought about by the students at that time, the
percentage of incompetent teachers is certainly no lower now.
The School of Literature, where the reform was initiated, shows
almost no improvement in teaching methods and curricula.

The provisions of the reform, as established by the Organic
Law of 1920, are still largely unimplemented, and the University Council apparently has no intention of carrying out the
program outlined in that law.[34]

[33] *Amauta*, no. 7 (March 1927).

[34] After this book went to the printer, the government, with the express
authorization of the legislature, announced a new statute on university
teaching that goes into effect in the academic year 1928, which therefore will
begin late. This reform concerns almost exclusively the organization of university teaching, placed under the authority of a superior council presided
over by the Minister of Education. The character, the concept, of that teaching has not been altered: it could only be altered within an integral educational reform that made university teaching the highest level of professional
instruction, reserving it to the most capable and selecting them independ-

Nor has any progress been made in creating full-time teachers. The university professor is typically a dilettante for whom teaching is a very secondary activity. To a large extent, this is actually an economic problem. University teaching will remain in the hands of dilettantes until professors capable of dedicating themselves exclusively to research and study can be offered a decent salary. But even within its present economic resources, the university should begin to find a solution; for, as long as scientific research and specialization are not encouraged, this problem will not be solved automatically by a share of the university budget.

The crisis at San Marcos is reproduced on a smaller scale in the provincial universities. The reactionary assault began in the most inadequate and weakest of them all, the University of Trujillo. An institution that expels twenty-six of its students, when its enrollment is perilously low, reveals how deeply committed it is to the reactionary spirit. I am told that, in order not to appear deserted, this university sends out its staff every year to recruit students. Using local pride as an argument, the pro-

---

ently of economic privilege. The reform, which is above all administrative, tends in spirit to follow the principles of the 1920 law, although at some points it adopts different means. The speech by the president of the republic inaugurating the academic year assigned to the reform the mission of accommodating university teaching to the practical needs of the nation in this century of industrialism, and, by way of underlining this statement, explicitly condemned the orientation of those who favor an abstract, classical culture exempt from utilitarian preoccupations. But the rectorate, in the university's new era (which seems so much like the old one), has been conferred upon Dr. Deustua, who, if he is a concientious scholar and university man, is also the most conspicuous of those who support the very tendency on which the president's speech passes summary judgment. This contradiction could not be easily explained in any of the countries where ideological and doctrinal consistency is habitual. But Peru, we know, is not one of those countries. The statute—there is not room for a general discussion of it in this brief note—establishes the means for creating university careers, specialized teaching positions. In this sense it is a legal instrument for a technical transformation of teaching. The efficacy of this instrument depends on how it is used.

fessors try to persuade fathers not to send their sons to the University of Lima. If, in spite of its scarcity of students, the University of Trujillo was prepared to lose twenty-six, the extent of conservative intransigence can easily be imagined.

The University of Arequipa traditionally has been resistant to modernization. The conservative atmosphere of the city shields it from any outside influence that might disturb its repose. The reformist element, which in recent years has given hopeful signs of growth and activity, is still in the minority. Only the University of Cuzco is making serious efforts to transform itself. I have already referred to the reorganization scheme presented to the government by its leading professors; it is obviously the most advanced project for university reform in Peru.

The concept of reform, meanwhile, is daily gathering strength and substance. The problem of education is defined by the student leaders of La Plata in the following terms:

(1) Education is only one aspect of the social problem; for that reason, it cannot be solved separately. (2) The culture of all societies is the ideological expression of the interests of the class in power. The culture of society at present is therefore the ideological expression of the interests of the capitalist class. (3) The last imperialist war, by upsetting the bourgeois economy, has produced a crisis in the corresponding culture. (4) Only the advent of a socialist culture can put an end to this crisis.[35]

Whereas the new generation's message, which began as a confused announcement from Córdoba in 1918, reaches its clearest and most significant revolutionary expression in Argentina, the signs of reaction multiply on our university scene. The university reform is constantly threatened by the determination of the teaching oligarchy to regain full control.

[35] *Sagitaria* (La Plata), no. 2, 1925.

Conflicting Ideologies

In the stage of practical trials and theoretical digressions that slowly led to the importation of North American systems and methods, Dr. Deustua represented the reaction of the old aristocratic spirit, more or less dressed up in modern idealism. Dr. Villarán used the language of liberalism to present the program of bourgeois and, therefore, liberal *civilismo*. Dr. Deustua, in the modern guise of a university professor and philosopher, embodied the mentality of feudal *civilismo*, of the viceroyal landholder. (There had to be a reason why one sector of the party was called "historical *civilismo*").

The real meaning of the controversy between Deustua and Villarán escaped the reporters and public of that period. The so-called popular parties were incapable of taking a position in the debate. The Piérola party was reduced to railing against government taxes and loans—which by no means constituted all the economic policy of *civilismo*—and to proclaiming periodically that it stood for liberty, order, fatherland, citizenship, et cetera. The self-styled liberals were no different from the *piérolistas*, to whom they were linked in a sporadic, masonic anticlericalism and a vague, romantic, federalist vindication. (The ideological poverty and intellectual vulgarity of this opposition, clinging to the stale glory of its caudillo, permitted *civilismo* to monopolize discussion of one of the most weighty national problems.)

Only now is it historically possible to understand the meaning of that university debate, in which Francisco García Calderón, in his usual prudent and somewhat skeptical fashion, tried to play an eclectic and conciliatory role.

The ideological position of Dr. Deustua, in the discussion of public education, was decorated with all the rhetoric needed to impress our shallow intellectuals. In his metaphysical dissertations on education, Dr. Deustua represented himself as a defend-er of idealism against the positivism of his cautious and complaisant opponents. And the latter, instead of baring the antidemocratic and antisocial spirit behind his philosophical facade, preferred to declare their respect for his high ideals.

It would have been easy to demonstrate that the ideas of Dr. Deustua on education were based not on contemporary idealism but on the old aristocratic mentality of the great landholders. But no one undertook to reveal the true nature of Dr. Deustua's resistance to a reasonably democratic reform in education. University oratory was mystified by the abstruse doctrine of the reactionary *civilista* professor. The debate, furthermore, was conducted exclusively within the *civilismo* party, which was divided between feudalism and capitalism, with the latter spirit deformed and weakened by the former.

In order to identify the thought of Dr. Deustua and to perceive its medieval and aristocratic foundation, we need to study the prejudices and superstitions that sustain it. Dr. Deustua's ideas are contrary not only to the principles of modern education but to the essence of capitalism itself. His concept of work, for example, is in open conflict with the concept that for some time has governed human progress. In one of his philosophical studies of education, Dr. Deustua is just as disdainful of work as those who formerly considered that the only noble and worthwhile occupations were the military and the literary.

Values and work, virtue and self-interest [he wrote], are essential to the formation of character. But they play very different roles in that process, just as they play different roles in the process of education. Freedom is a value that educates; education consists in the realization of values. Work does not educate; it enriches and instructs; with practice it confers skill. But it is motivated by self-interest, which enslaves the soul. Even if work is inspired by a vocation, which brings to it happiness and joy, that motive is as egoistic as the others. Freedom does not spring from self-interest, but from moral and aesthetic values. Even in science, which in a way educates by disciplining the mind either through the orderly exercise of deduction or through the intuitive action of induction, the so-called value of logic does not bring to work the freedom that is the essence of the human personality. Work can contribute to spiritual expansion through the material wealth it produces. But that expansion may be and usually is a sign of blind egoism. And so it does not signify real freedom, freedom within, moral and aesthetic freedom, the freedom that is the goal and content of education.[36]

This concept of work, although advanced by Dr. Deustua only a little over a decade ago, is absolutely medieval and aristocratic. Western civilization is based entirely on work. Society strives to organize itself as a society of workers and producers. Therefore, work cannot be thought of as servitude; it must be given stature and dignity.

The dignity of work should not be interpreted as an egoistic sentiment peculiar to Western civilization. Scientific research enlightens us as much as spiritual intuition. Man's destiny is to create. Work is creative, liberating. Man fulfills himself in work.

Man's enslavement by the machine and the destruction of his crafts by industrialization have distorted the meaning and purpose of work. From John Ruskin to Rabindranath Tagore, reformers have denounced capitalism for its brutalizing use of the machine. Work has become odious because mechanization and especially Taylorism have degraded it by robbing it of creativity.

Pierre Hamp, in his epic writings on labor—*la peine des hommes*—has given this exact description: "The grandeur of man consists in doing his work well. Love of work, in spite of

---

[36] "A propósito de un cuestionairo sobre la reforma de la ley de instrucción." Collection of articles published by M. A. Dávila, 1914, p. 56. See also *La cultura superior en Italia* (Lima: E. Rosay, 1912), pp. 145 ff.

society, is the health of society. Man always takes pride in the skill of his hands, even when using them for the lowliest labor. If, like the idle rich, all men scorned labor, and if all men worked only because they were forced to, without any pleasure, slothfulness and corruption would destroy a desperate people."[37]

This is the principle that should be adopted by a society that is heir to the spirit and tradition of the Inca society, in which idleness was a crime, and work, performed with devotion, the highest virtue. The archaic thought of Dr. Deustua, rejected by even our fearful and confused bourgeoisie, descends directly from the viceroyal society, which a moderate *civilista* like Dr. Javier Prado described as a flabby society dedicated to sensual pleasures.

It is not just his concept of work that reveals the aristocratic and reactionary sentiment of Dr. Deustua and defines his ideological position in the debate on public education. Above all, his basic concept of teaching identifies his inspiration as feudalism.

Dr. Deustua was concerned almost exclusively with the education of the upper and ruling classes. For him, the whole problem of teaching was to educate the elite, which naturally was an elite of inherited privileges. Therefore, he cared only about university teaching.

No attitude could be more opposed to the modern approach to education. Dr. Villarán, from an orthodox, bourgeois standpoint, held up the example of the United States to Dr. Deustua. He reminded him that "there, primary school was the introduction to and the historical antecedent of the secondary school; and that college was the precursor of the university."[38] Today we could hold up to him, as an example closer to home, Mexico, a country where, as Pedro Henríquez Ureña says, culture is not understood in terms of the nineteenth century.

[37] F. Lefevre, *Une heure avec*, 2nd series, p. 172.
[38] Villarán, *Estudios sobre educación nacional*, p. 52.

No thought is given to the culture prevailing in the era of capitalism disguised as liberalism, the culture of a select group of dilettantes, an enclosed garden where artificial flowers are grown, an ivory tower where dead science is kept in museums. Mexico thinks of a social culture, offered and really given to all, based on work. To learn is not only to learn to know but also to learn to do. There should be no superior culture because it would be false and ephemeral where there is no popular culture.[39]

Need I say that I entirely agree with this concept, which is in open conflict with the thesis of Dr. Deustua.

Dr. Deustua placed the problem of education on a purely philosophical plane. Experience shows that on this plane, where reality and history are disregarded, the problem cannot be solved or understood. Dr. Deustua is indifferent to the relationship between education and the national economy. In fact, in this respect he is an absolute idealist in his lack of comprehension.

His argument, therefore, besides being antidemocratic and antisocial, is antihistorical. The problem of education cannot be understood in our time if it is not considered as an economic and social problem. The mistake of many reformers has been their abstract and idealistic methods and their exclusively pedagogical approach. Their proposals have ignored the close bond between economics and education, and they have tried to change the latter with no knowledge of the laws of the former. For that reason, they have not succeeded in reforming anything except to the extent permitted by the scorned or simply neglected socioeconomic laws. The controversy between classicists and modernists in education has been just as subject to the rate of capitalist development as the debate between conservatives and liberals in politics. The program and systems of public education in this era that now draws to a close have depended on the interests of

[39] Pedro Henríquez Ureña, *Utopia de América.*

the bourgeois economy. The realistic or modern approach has been imposed by the needs of industrialism. Industrialism is the phenomenon peculiar to this civilization which, under its influence, demands that schools produce more technicians than ideologists, more engineers than orators.

The unscientific and uneconomic approach in the discussion of teaching claims to represent a higher idealism. But it is actually the metaphysics of reactionaries, opposed and alien to the stream of history, and it therefore lacks any value as a force in human progress and reform. The lawyers and writers who come from the halls of the humanities, prepared by a rhetorical and pseudo-idealistic education, have always been far more immoral than the technicians who come from the faculties and institutes of science. Whereas the practical and theoretical or aesthetic activities of the latter have followed the path of economics and civilization, the practical and theoretical or aesthetic activities of the former, under the influence of the basest conservative interests and sentiments, have frequently blocked that path. Furthermore, the value of science as a stimulus to philosophical speculation cannot be disregarded or underestimated. The intellectual climate of this civilization owes much more to science than to the humanities.

Economics is specifically associated with education in the work of educators like Pestalozzi and Froebel, who have undertaken to reform the school system, bearing in mind that modern society tends to be a society of producers. The trade school represents a new concept of teaching, a principle peculiar to a civilization of workers. Although adopted and put into operation by the capitalist state, it has been limited to the primary schools, where it is presented as a class in "manual training." In Russia, the trade school is in the forefront of educational policy. In Germany it has been encouraged mainly by the rise of the Social Democrats during the revolutionary period.

Thus, the most significant reform has erupted in primary schools, whereas secondary schools and universities, dominated by the conservatism of their rectors, are still hostile to any attempt at reform and are indifferent to economic reality.

A modern concept of the school places manual and intellectual work at the same level, an equation that is not acceptable to the vanity of the aristocratic humanists. Contrary to the pretensions of these men of letters, the trade school is the authentic product of a civilization created by work and for work.

In the course of this essay I have not attempted to do more than outline the ideological and political basis of public education in Peru. I have omitted its technical aspect, which, besides not being within my competence, is subject to theoretical principles and to political and economic requirements.

I have stated, for example, that our Spanish and colonial heritage consisted not of a pedagogical method but of an economic and social regime. French influence later entered the picture, to the approval of those who regarded France as the Jacobin and republican fatherland as well as of those who admired the Restoration. North American influence finally prevailed as a result of our capitalist development together with the importation of American capital, technicians, and ideas.

In the last period of the conflict of ideologies and influences there can be distinguished the contrast between a growing capitalist affirmation and an obstinate feudalist and aristocratic reaction, the former advocating a practical approach in education and the latter defending a pseudo-idealistic orientation.

The emergence of a socialist movement and of a class conscience in the urban proletariat introduces a new factor in the debate that substantially modifies its terms. The creation of the popular universities "González Prada," the support by university youth of the principle of the socialization of culture, the

impact of the new educational philosophy on teachers, conclusively interrupt the erudite and academic dialogue between the
liberal-bourgeois spirit and the aristocratic-landholder spirit.[40]

The accounts of the first century of the republic are closed,
with an enormous liability in the field of public education. The
problem of Indian illiteracy has hardly been touched. To date
the government has failed to establish schools throughout the republic. The disproportion between resources and the size of the
undertaking is huge. There are not enough teachers for the im-
plementation of the modest program of popular education au-
thorized in the budget and given the present number of graduates from normal schools, there is little possibility of solving
this problem in the near future. A primary school teacher in
Peru is still harassed by the most overbearing and stupid *gamonalismo* and bossism. He has no assurance of even a relative
economic security. When a representative complains to Congress, which has come to regard the teacher as a servile instrument to round up votes, this complaint carries more weight in
official circles than the record of the services of an honorable
and dedicated teacher.

The problem of Indian illiteracy goes beyond the pedagogical
sphere. It becomes increasingly evident that to teach a man to
read and write is not to educate him. Primary school does not
redeem the Indian morally and socially. The first real step toward his redemption must be to free him from serfdom.[41]

[40] The renovative orientation of the normalists is expressed in publications
that have appeared in Lima and the provinces in recent years: *La Revista
Peruana de Educación*, Lima, 1926; *Revista del Maestro* and *Revista de Educación*, Tarma; *Ideario Pedagógico*, Arequipa; and *El Educador Andino*,
Puno.

[41] The Minister of Education, Dr. Oliveira, in a speech to the congress in
1927, recognized the connection between the problem of indigenous education and the land problem, accepting a reality that had invariably been
evaded by his predecessors in that post.

This is the thesis maintained by the authors of reform in Peru. Among their leaders are many young educators whose points of view are already far removed from those held a quarter of a century ago by Dr. Villarán when he was so ineffectual in his mild but categorical opposition to colonial ideology, as we have seen in our examination of the origin and development of the reform of 1920.

The Religious Factor

The Religion of Tawantinsuyo

W<small>E HAVE DEFINITELY LEFT BEHIND</small> the days of anti-clerical prejudice, when the "free-thinking" critic happily discarded all dogmas and churches in favor of the dogma and church of the atheist's free-thinking orthodoxy. The concept of religion has become broader and deeper, going far beyond a church and a sacrament. It now finds in religion's institutions and sentiments a significance very different from that which was attributed to it by those fervent radicals who identified religion with "obscurantism."

The revolutionary critic no longer disputes with religion and the church the services they have rendered to humanity or their place in history. We are therefore not surprised when a modern and perceptive writer like Waldo Frank explains the North American phenomenon by carefully tracing its religious origin and factors. According to him, the United States was created by the pioneer, the Puritan, and the Jew. The pioneer descends from and is the fulfillment of the Puritan, because the Puritan protest was rooted in his will for power. "The Puritan had begun by desiring power in England. This desire had turned him deviously into austere ways. He had soon learned the sweets of austerity. Now he became aware of the power over himself, over others, over physical conditions which the austere life brought with it. A virgin and hostile continent demanded whatever energy he could bring to bear upon it. A frugal, self-denying life released that energy far better than could another."[1]

The Anglo-Saxon colonizer did not find in North America an advanced culture or a powerful population; Christianity therefore did not proselytize. The Spaniard was not only different as a colonizer but also had a different mission. In Mexico, Peru, Colombia, and Central America the missionary was supposed to convert a large population with its own, deep-seated religious practices and institutions.

Because of this circumstance, the religious factor in these countries is more complex. The Catholic religion was superimposed on indigenous rites, only partially absorbing them. Any study of religious feeling in Spanish America therefore must begin with the cults found by the conquistadors.

This is not an easy task. The chroniclers of the colonial period could only consider these concepts and practices as a group of barbaric superstitions. Their accounts distort and blur the image of native cults. One of the most unusual Mexican rituals, which shows that in Mexico the idea of transubstantiation was known and applied, was for the Spaniard simply a demoniac artifice.

But no matter how little agreement there is today about Peruvian mythology, available information enables us to place it in the religious evolution of humanity.

The Inca religion lacked the spiritual power to resist conversion. Some historians deduce from philological and archeologi-

[1] Waldo Frank, *Our America* (New York: Boni and Liveright, 1919), p. 63.

cal evidence that the Inca mythology was related to the Hindu. But their belief rests on similarities of form, not on really spiritual or religious similarities. The basic characteristics of the Inca religion are its collective theocracy and its materialism. These characteristics differentiate it from the essentially spiritual Hindu religion. Without sharing the conclusion of Valcárcel that the man of Tawantinsuyo had virtually no idea of a "beyond," or behaved as though he had none, we cannot be oblivious to the tenuous and sketchy nature of his metaphysics. The Quechua religion was a moral code rather than a metaphysical concept, which brings us much closer to China than to India. State and church were absolutely inseparable; religion and politics recognized the same principles and the same authority. Religion functioned in terms of society. From this point of view, the Inca religion opposed the religions of the Far East in the same way that the latter, as pointed out by James George Frazer, opposed the Graeco-Roman civilization.

Greek and Roman society [writes Frazer] was built on the conception of the subordination of the individual to the community, of the citizen to the state; it set the safety of the commonwealth, as the supreme aim of conduct, above the safety of the individual whether in this world or in the world to come. Trained from infancy in this unselfish ideal, the citizens devoted their lives to the public service and were ready to lay them down for the common good; or if they shrank from the supreme sacrifice, it never occurred to them that they acted otherwise than basely in preferring their personal existence to the interests of their country. All this was changed by the spread of Oriental religions which inculcated the communion of the soul with God and its eternal salvation as the only objects worth living for, objects in comparison with which the prosperity and even the existence of the state sank into insignificance.[2]

Because of its identification with the social and political

---

[2] James George Frazer, *The Golden Bough*, abridged edition (London: Macmillan & Co., 1954), p. 357.

regime, the Inca religion could not outlive the Inca state. It had temporal rather than spiritual ends and cared more about the kingdom of earth than the kingdom of heaven. It was a social, not an individual, discipline. The blow that felled the pagan gods destroyed the theocracy. What survived of this religion in the Indian soul could not be a metaphysical concept, but agrarian rituals, incantations, and pantheism.[3]

All the accounts we have of the Inca ceremonies and myths make clear that the Quechua religion was much more than a state religion (in the sense that we know it today). The church was a social and political institution; it was the state itself. Religion was subordinate to the social and political interests of the empire. This aspect of the Inca religion is demonstrated in the treatment given by the Incas to the religious symbols of the people they conquered. The Inca church was more concerned with subjugating their gods than in persecuting or condemning them. The temple of the sun thus became the temple of a kind of federal religion or mythology.

The Quechua was neither proselytizer nor inquisitor. He used his efforts to unify the empire and, for this purpose, he was interested in abolishing cruel rituals and barbaric practices, not in the propagation of a new and unique faith. For the Incas it was more a matter of elevating than of replacing the religious habits of the people annexed to their empire.

The religion of Tawantinsuyo, furthermore, did not violate any of the feelings or customs of the Indians. It was not composed of complicated abstractions, but of simple allegories. All

[3] In an article published in no. 15 of *Amauta*, Antero Peralta disputes the generally accepted idea that the Indian is pantheist. Peralta maintains that the Indian's pantheism is unlike any pantheistic system of philosophy. We would like to point out to Peralta, whose research into the elements and characteristics of indigenous religion attests to his scholarly aptitude and vocation, that he places arbitrary limitations on the use of the word "pantheism." I believe that I have made clear that I attribute to the Indian of Tawantinsuyo a pantheistic sentiment and not a pantheistic philosophy.

its roots were nourished on the instincts and customs of a nation made up of agrarian tribes that had a healthy, rural pantheism and that were more inclined to cooperate than to wage war. The Inca myths rested on the primitive religious habits of the Indians, without opposing them except to the extent that the latter was considered obviously inferior to the Inca culture or dangerous to the social and political regime of Tawantinsuyo. The tribes of the empire believed, not in a religion or a dogma, but simply in the divinity of the Incas.

Therefore, the natural elements of the religion of the ancient Peruvians—animism, magic, totems, and tabus—are more interesting to investigate than the mysteries and symbols of their metaphysics and very rudimentary mythology. This investigation should yield sure conclusions about the moral and religious evolution of the Indian.

Abstract speculation on the Inca gods has frequently led the student to deduce from the correlation or affinity of certain symbols and names a probable relationship of the Quechua race with races that are spiritually and intellectually different. On the other hand, a study of the primary factors of this religion establishes the universality or near universality of innumerable magical rituals and beliefs and, therefore, the risk of looking in this field for proof of hypothetical common origins. In recent years, the comparative study of religions has made enormous strides that preclude use of the old premises for decisions about the singularity or significance of a cult. James George Frazer, who is responsible for so much of this progress, maintains that among all people the age of magic has preceded the age of religion; and he shows that groups of people totally unknown to one another have applied in a similar or identical fashion the Laws of "Similarity" and of "Contact or Contagion."[4]

4 Frazer, *The Golden Bough*, p. 11.

The Inca gods reigned over a multitude of minor deities who were destined to outlive them because they had been rooted in the soil and soul of the Indian long before the empire. The Indian's "animism" peopled the territory of Tawantinsuyo with local spirits and gods whose worship offered more resistance to Christian conversion than the Inca worship of the sun or of the god Kon. "Totemism," of the same substance as the *ayllu* and the tribe, which were more enduring than the empire, took refuge not only in tradition but in the very blood of the Indian. Magic, identified as a primitive art to cure the sick, had its own needs and vital impulses and was so deeply ingrained that it could survive for a long time under any religious belief.

These natural or primitive elements of worship fitted in perfectly with the character of the Inca monarchy and state. Moreover, these elements required the divinity of the Incas and of their government. The Inca theocracy is explained in all its details by the social condition of the Indian. There is no need to look for an easy explanation in the occult arts of the Incas. (This point of view assumes the existence of an oppressed mass to be overawed and humbled.) Frazer, who has made a masterful study of the magic origins of royalty, analyzes and classifies the various types of king-priests and human gods, more or less close to our Incas:

Among the American Indians [he writes, referring particularly to this case] the furthest advance towards civilization was made under the monarchical and theocratic governments of Mexico and Peru; but we know too little of the early history of these countries to say whether the predecessors of their deified kings were medicine-men or not. Perhaps a trace of such a succession may be detected in the oath which the Mexican kings, when they mounted the throne, swore that they would make the sun to shine, the clouds to give rain, the rivers to flow, and the earth to bring forth fruits in abundance. Certainly, in aboriginal America the sorcerer or medicine-man, surrounded by a halo of mystery and an atmosphere of awe, was a personage of great influence and importance, and he may well have developed into a chief or king in many tribes, though positive evidence of such a development appears to be lacking.

Although the author of *The Golden Bough* is overly cautious because of lack of historical material, he still reaches this conclusion: "In South America also the magicians or medicine-men seem to have been on the highroad to chieftainship or kingship." In a later chapter, he further defines his impression:

From our survey of the religious position occupied by the king in rude societies we may infer that the claim to divine and supernatural powers put forward by the monarchs of great historical empires like those of Egypt, Mexico, and Peru, was not the simple outcome of inflated vanity or the empty expression of a grovelling adulation; it was merely a survival and extension of the old savage apotheosis of living kings. Thus, for example, as children of the Sun the Incas of Peru were revered like gods; they could do no wrong, and no one dreamed of offending against the person, honour, or property of the monarch or of any of the royal race. Hence, too, the Incas did not, like most people, look on sickness as an evil. They considered it a messenger sent from their father the Sun to call them to come and rest with him in heaven.[5]

The Inca people knew no separation between religion and politics, between church and state. All their institutions, like all their beliefs, conformed strictly to their agricultural economy and to their sedentary spirit. Their theocracy rested on the ordinary and the empirical, not on the magical skills of a prophet or on his doctrine. Religion was the state.

Vasconcelos, who tends to depreciate the native cultures of America, thinks that without a supreme law they were con-

[5] Ibid., pp. 103–104.

demned to disappear because of their innate inferiority. These cultures, no doubt, had not altogether emerged intellectually from the age of magic. We know that the Inca culture was the work of a race more gifted in artistic creation than in intellectual speculation. For that reason, it has left us a magnificent popular art, if no Rig-Veda or Zend-avesta, which makes their social and political organization all the more remarkable. Religion, as only one aspect of this organization, could not survive it.

The Catholic Conquest

I have already said that the conquest was the last crusade and that the conquistadors were the last representatives of Spanish grandeur. As a crusade, the conquest was essentially a military and religious enterprise. It was carried out jointly by soldiers and missionaries. The triumvirate of the conquest of Peru would have been incomplete without Hernando de Luque, who acted as scholar and advisor of the company. Luque was the deputy of the church and of the faith. His presence protected the rights of the dogma and gave the expedition a doctrine. In Cajamarca, the faith of the conquest was invested in Father Valverde. Although the execution of Atahualpa was brought about solely by the crude political maneuverings of Pizarro, it was dressed up with religious reasons and made to appear as the first sentence passed by the Inquisition in Peru.

After the tragedy of Cajamarca, the missionary continued to dictate his law to the conquest. Spiritual power inspired and directed temporal power. On the ruins of the empire, in which church and state had been one, a new theocracy was built. In this theocracy, the latifundium, an economic mandate, was born of the *encomienda*, an administrative, spiritual, and religious mandate. The friars took solemn possession of the Inca temples. Perhaps a certain Thomist predestination decreed that the

Dominicans, masters in the scholarly art of reconciling Christianity with pagan tradition, should install themselves in the temple of the sun.[6]

Although the colonizer of Saxon America was the Puritan pioneer, the colonizer of Spanish America was not like the conquistador, the knight of the crusades. The reason is obvious: the Puritan represented a movement in ascent, the Protestant Reformation; the knight of the crusades personified an era that had ended, the Catholic Middle Ages. England continued to send Puritans to its colonies long after Spain had no more crusaders to send overseas. The species was extinct. The spiritual energies of Spain—aroused precisely by its reaction against the Reformation—produced an extraordinary religious renaissance, destined to waste its magnificent potential in a reaffirmation of intransigent orthodoxy: the Counter Reformation. "The true Spanish Reformation," writes Unamuno, "was the mystic Reformation. Unconcerned with the Protestant Reformation, mysticism was, nevertheless, Spain's strongest bulwark against it. Through the medium of the Spanish reform, Saint Teresa probably was as effective as Saint Ignatius of Loyola in the Counter Reformation."[7]

The conquest used up the last of the crusaders. And the crusade of the conquest, in most cases, was not a true crusade but a prolongation of its spirit. The noble was no longer interested in heroic deeds. The extent and wealth of Spanish possessions guaranteed him a courtier's life of opulence. The crusader of the conquest, when a nobleman, was poor; otherwise, he was a commoner.

Having come from Spain to occupy land for their king—

---

[6] The most zealous custodians of Latin tradition and Roman order—more pagan than Christian—take refuge in St. Thomas as in the strongest citadel of Catholic thought.

[7] Miguel Unamuno, *La mística española.*

whom the missionaries acknowledged first of all as a trustee of the Roman Catholic Church—the conquistadors appeared to be driven at times by a vague presentiment that they would be succeeded by lesser men. A confused and obscure instinct fomented their rebellion against the mother country, the same instinct that may have given Cortés the courage to burn his ships. The rebellion of Gonzalo Pizarro was kindled by a tragic ambition, a desperate and impotent nostalgia. With his defeat, the work and the race of the conquistators was finished. Conquest ended; colonization began. And if the conquest was a military and religious expedition, colonization was nothing but a political and ecclesiastical enterprise. It was begun by a man of the Church, Don Pedro de la Gasca. The priest replaced the missionary. The viceroyalty, dedicated to sensual pleasure and idleness, was to bring to Peru an educated nobility and learned men, people belonging to another Spain, the Spain of the Inquisition and of decadence.

During the colonial period, in spite of the Inquisition and the Counter Reformation, the civilizing process was largely religious and ecclesiastic. Education and culture were concentrated in the hands of the church. The friars contributed to the viceroyal organization, not only by converting heathens and persecuting heresy, but also by teaching arts and crafts and by establishing crops and factories. At a time when the City of the Viceroys was only a few rustic manor houses, the friars founded here the first university of the Americas. Together with their dogmas and rites, they imported seeds, vines, domestic animals, and tools. They studied the customs of the natives, recorded their traditions, and collected the first material on their history. Thanks to their ability to adapt and assimilate, Jesuits and Dominicans, but especially Jesuits, mastered many secrets of Indian history and spirit. And the Indians, exploited in the mines, the factories, and *encomiendas*, found their stoutest defenders in monasteries and even in parish priests. Fray Bartolomé de las Casas, who exemplified the best qualities of missionary and apostle, had predecessors and disciples.

Catholicism, with its sumptuous mass and its sorrowful devotion, was perhaps the only religion able to attact a population that could not easily rise to a spiritual, abstract religion. It was also aided by its astonishing ability to accommodate to any historical epoch or setting. The work of absorbing old myths and appropriating pagan dates, which had begun many centuries earlier in the West, was continued in Peru. Lake Titicaca, apparently the birthplace of the Inca theocracy, is the site of the most famous shrine of the Virgin.

The intelligent and scholarly writer Emilio Romero has interesting comments on the substitution of Catholic rites and images for Inca gods:

The Indians thrilled with emotion before the majesty of the Catholic ceremony. They saw the image of the sun in the shimmering brocade of the chasuble and cope and they saw the violet tones of the rainbow woven into the fine silk threads of the rochet. Perhaps they saw the *quipus* symbolized in the purple tassels of the abbot and the knotted cords of the Franciscan friar. . . . This explains the pagan fervor with which the multitude of Cuzco Indians fearfully trembled before the presence of "Our Lord of Earthquakes." This was the tangible image of their memories and their adorations, and far removed from the intent of the friars. Religious festivals vibrated with Indian paganism expressed in offerings taken to the churches of animals from their flocks and of the first fruits of their harvest. Later they themselves erected their ornate altars of Corpus Christi laden with mirrors framed in chased silver, raised their grotesque saints, and laid the products of their fields at the feet of the altars. Before the saints they nostalgically drank the same *jora* that they had used for their libations in honor of Cápac Raymi. Finally, shrieking in prayer, which for the Spanish priests were cries of penitence and for the Indians cries of terror, they danced the boisterous *cachampas* and the gymnastic *kashuas* before the fixed and glassy smile of the saints.[8]

The external trappings of Catholicism captivated the Indian, who accepted conversion and the catechism with the same ease and lack of comprehension. For a people who had never differentiated between the spiritual and temporal, political control incorporated ecclesiastic control. The missionaries did not instill a faith; they instilled a system of worship and a liturgy, wisely adapting them to Indian customs. Native paganism subsisted under Catholic worship.

Catholicism did not reserve this method exclusively for the Tawantinsuyo; historically, it has always taken on the coloring of its environment. The Roman Catholic Church is legitimate heir to the Roman Empire in its policy of colonization and assimilation of the people it subjugates. An investigation of the important dates of the Gregorian calendar has revealed amazing substitutions. Analyzing them, Frazer writes:

Taken altogether, the coincidences of the Christian with the heathen festivals are too close and too numerous to be accidental. They mark the compromise which the Church in the hour of its triumph was compelled to make with its vanquished yet still dangerous rivals. The inflexible Protestantism of the primitive missionaries, with their fiery denunciations of heathendom, had been exchanged for the supple policy, the easy tolerance, the comprehensive charity of shrewd ecclesiastics, who clearly perceived that if Christianity was to conquer the world it could do so only by relaxing the too rigid principles of its Founder, by widening a little the narrow gate which leads to salvation. In this respect an instructive parallel might be drawn between the history of Christianity and the history of Buddhism.[9]

Originally, this compromise spread from Catholicism to all

---

[8] Emilio Romero, "El Cuzco católico," *Amauta*, No. 10, December 1927.
[9] Frazer, *The Golden Bough*, p. 361.

Christianity. But it appears to be a special virtue or skill of the
Roman Catholic Church, not only because it is a compromise in
form only (Catholicism has been inflexible in the spheres of
dogma and theology), but because in the conversion of Americans and other peoples, only the Roman Catholic Church continued to use it systematically and effectively. From this standpoint, the Inquisition was strictly an internal affair: its aim was
the repression of heresy within the Catholic religion, not the
persecution of heathens.

But adaptability is, at the same time, the strength and weakness of the Roman Catholic Church. The religious spirit is only
tempered in combat, in suffering. "Christianity, or rather Christendom," says Unamuno, "as announced by Saint Paul, was not
a doctrine, although it expressed itself dialectically. It was a
way of life, it was struggle, it was agony. The doctrine was the
Gospel, the Glad Tidings. Christianity, Christendom, was a
preparation for death and resurrection, for life eternal."[10] By
passively accepting the catechism without understanding it, the
Indian spiritually weakened Catholicism in Peru. The missionary did not have to protect the purity of the dogma; his mission
was to serve as a moral guide, an ecclesiastical shepherd for a
rustic and simple flock, untouched by spiritual concerns.

In religion as in politics, the heroic times of the conquest were
followed by the viceroyal period, which was administrative and
bureaucratic. Francisco García Calderón pronounced this judgment on the era as a whole: "If the conquest was a mighty
endeavor, the colonial period was a prolonged moral debilita-
tion."[11] The first stage, symbolized by the missionary, cor-
responds spiritually to the flowering of mysticism in Spain.
Unamuno says that Spain used up on mysticism and the Counter Reformation the spiritual energies that other nations ex-

[10] Unamuno, *The Agony of Christianity*, trans. K. F. Reinhardt (New
York: Ungar, 1960), p. 28.
[11] Francisco García Calderón, *Le Pérou contemporain.*

pended on the Reformation. Unamuno defines Spanish mystics as follows:

They reject science as futile and seek knowledge for a pragmatic purpose, in order to love and work for and rejoice in God, not for the sake of knowledge alone. Whether or not they are aware of it, they are anti-intellectuals, and this distinguishes them from theologists like Eckhart. They favor voluntarism. What they look for is total and integral knowledge, a wisdom in which knowledge, feeling, and love unite and even merge as far as possible. We love truth because it is beautiful and, according to Father Avila, because we love truth we believe. Truth, goodness, and beauty blend and crystallize in this material wisdom. Mysticism naturally culminated in a woman, because woman's mind is less analytical than man's and her psychic powers are more closely attuned or perhaps less differentiated.[12]

We know that in Spain the spiritual blaze that kindled the Counter Reformation also illuminated the soul of Saint Teresa, Saint Ignatius, and other great mystics; but it later died down and ended tragically in the flames of the Inquisition. In Spain it flared up again in the struggle against heresy and the Reformation and for a while it cast an incandescent glow. Here, with Catholic rites easily superimposed on the pagan sentiment of the Indians, Catholicism lost its moral force. "A great saint like Rosa of Lima," observes García Calderón, "has little of the personality and creative drive of Saint Teresa, the great Spanish saint."[13]

On the coast and especially in Lima, another element arrived to sap the spiritual strength of Catholicism. The Negro slave brought to Catholic rites his fetishistic sensualism and his dark superstition. The Indian, a healthy pantheist and materialist, had reached the ethical level of a mighty theocracy; the Negro, on the other hand, exuded from every pore the primitivism of his African tribe. Javier Prado remarks: "Among Negroes the

[12] Unamuno, La mística española.
[13] García Calderón, Le Pérou contemporain.

Christian religion was turned into a superstitious, immoral cult. Completely inebriated by heavy drinking and inflamed by the carnality and licentiousness typical of their race, first African and then *criollo* Negroes would join the popular celebrations of 'devils and giants' and 'Moors and Christians.' Dancing with obscene movements and savage cries, they frequently would accompany religious processions to general applause."[14]

The clergy wasted most of its energies in internal quarrels or in the pursuit of heresy, as well as in constant and active rivalry with the representatives of temporal power. Professor Prado believes that even the apostolic fervor of Las Casas intensified this rivalry. But, at least in this case, ecclesiastic zeal served a noble and just cause that would not again find such stubborn defenders until long after the country's political independence.

Although Spanish Catholicism was able to impose itself on Indian paganism thanks to the singular appeal of its ceremonial pomp and majesty, as a concept of life and a spiritual discipline it was not qualified to create elements of work and wealth in its colonies. As I have observed in my essay on the Peruvian economy, this was the greatest weakness of Spanish colonization. But it would be arbitrary and exaggerated to assume from the entrenched medievalism that delayed Spain's evolution toward capitalism that Catholicism was solely responsible, when in other Latin countries it had been able to adjust intelligently to the principles of a capitalist economy. The religious orders, especially the Jesuits, operated in economic terrain more skillfully than the civil administration and its officials. Spanish nobility scorned work and commerce; the bourgeoisie, still immature, was infected by aristocratic values.

In general, the experience of the West furnishes concrete evidence of the close association of capitalism and Protestantism. Protestantism appears in history as the spiritual yeast of the

[14] Javier Prado, *Estado social del Perú durante la dominación española.*

capitalist process. The Protestant Reformation contained the essence, the seed, of the liberal state. Protestantism as a religious movement and liberalism as a political trend were related to the development of the factors of a capitalist economy. Facts support this argument. Capitalism and industrialism have flourished nowhere else as they have in the Protestant countries. The capitalist economy has reached its peak in England, the United States, and Germany. Within these countries, people of Catholic faith have instinctively clung to their rustic tastes and habits. (Catholic Bavaria is also rural.) No Catholic country has reached a high level of industrialization.

France, which should not be judged by the cosmopolitan financial market of Paris or by the Comité des Forges, is more agricultural than industrial. Italy, although population pressure has propelled it along the road to industry and created the capitalist centers of Milan, Turin, and Genoa, maintains its agrarian tendency. Mussolini often eulogizes rural and provincial Italy and in one of his most recent speeches he condemns excessive urbanism and industrialism for holding back population growth.

The country most steeped in Catholic tradition, Spain, which expelled the Jew, presents the most backward and feeble capitalist structure. To make matters worse, its underdeveloped industry and finance have not been compensated for by a prosperous agriculture, perhaps because the Spanish nobleman clings to his preconceptions about aristocratic professions whereas the Italian landholder has inherited a deep love of the soil from his Roman ancestors. In Spain, only a career in the church takes precedence over the choice between a military or a literary career.

The first stage in the emancipation of the bourgeoisie is, according to Engels, the Protestant Reformation. "Calvin's creed," writes the celebrated author of *Anti-Duhring*, "was fit for the boldest of the bourgeoisie of his time. His predestination doctrine was the religious expression of the fact that in the commercial world of competition, success or failure does depend, not upon a man's activity or cleverness, but upon circumstances uncontrollable by him."[15] The rebellion of the most advanced and ambitious middle class against Rome led to the institution of national churches intended to avoid all conflict between temporal and spiritual, between church and state. Free inquiry contained the embryo of all the principles of the bourgeois economy: free competition, free enterprise, et cetera. Individualism, essential to the development of a society based on these principles, was encouraged by Protestant ethics and practice.

Marx has explained several aspects of the relations between Protestantism and capitalism, and he makes this particularly penetrating observation:

The monetary system is essentially Catholic, the credit system essentially Protestant. . . . It is Faith that makes blessed. Faith in money-value as the imminent spirit of commodities, faith in the prevailing mode of production and its predestined order, faith in the individual agents of production as mere personifications of self-expanding capital. But the credit system does not emancipate itself from the basis of the monetary system any more than Protestantism emancipates itself from the foundations of Catholicism.[16]

Not only the dialectics of historical materialism attest to the connection between the two great phenomena. Today, in an era of reaction, both intellectual and political, Ramiro de Maetzu, a Spanish writer, discusses his countrymen's lack of economic sense. He interprets the moral factors of North American capitalism in this way:

North Americans owe their sense of power to Calvinism, which believes that God, from the beginning of time, has chosen some men for salvation and others for everlasting damnation; that salvation is known in each man's fulfillment of his duties in his work, from

[15] Frederick Engels, *Socialism Utopian and Scientific*, trans. E. Aveling (New York: Labor News Co., 1901), pp. xxiii–xxiv.
[16] Karl Marx, *Capital*, Vol. III, trans. E. Untermann (Chicago: Charles Kerr, 1909), p. 696.

which it is deduced that the prosperity attendant on fulfillment of these duties is a sign of the possession of divine grace and, therefore, must be preserved at all cost, which implies moralization of the manner of spending money. This theological doctrine is now only history. The people of the United States continue to progress, but like a stone hurled by an arm that no longer exists to renew the projectile's force after it has spent its momentum."[17]

Neoscholastics insist on disputing or minimizing the influence of the Reformation on capitalist development, claiming that Thomism already had laid down the principles of bourgeois economics.[18] Sorel has acknowledged the services rendered to Western civilization by Saint Thomas in his realistic approach to the dogma in science. He has especially stressed the Thomist concept that "human law cannot change the legal nature of things, which is derived from their economic content."[19] But if Saint Thomas brought Catholicism to this level of understanding economics, the Reformation forged the moral weapons of the bourgeois revolution, opening the way to capitalism. The neoscholastic concept can be easily explained. Neothomism is bourgeois but not capitalist. Just as socialism is not the same thing as the proletariat, capitalism is not the same thing as the bourgeoisie. Capitalism is the order, the civilization, the spirit born of the bourgeoisie, which existed long before and only later gave its name to an entire historical era.

During his period of pragmatism, Papini declared that religion could choose one of two roads: to possess or to renounce.[20] From the outset, Protestantism firmly chose the first. Waldo Frank correctly points to the will to power in the mystic drive of Puritanism. He tells us how "the discipline of the church be-

---

[17] Ramiro de Maeztu, "Rodó y el poder" in *Repertorio Americano*, Vol. VIII, No. 6, 1926.

[18] René Johannet, *Eloge du bourgeois français.*

[19] Georges Sorel, *Introduction à l'économie moderne* (Paris: Marcel Rivière, 1911), p. 289.

[20] Giovanni Papini, *Pragmatism.*

came a means of marshaling men against the material difficulties of unsubdued America; how the denial of the senses released greater energy for the hunt of power and wealth; and how the senses, mortified by ascetic precepts—which so well fitted the crude conditions of the country—had their revenge in an unleashed search for riches." Under these religious principles the North American university provided youth with a culture "all of whose meanings ran with the sense of the sanctity of property and the morality of 'success.' "[21]

Catholicism, on the other hand, straddled the two possibilities of possession and renunciation. Its will to power was expressed in military expeditions and above all in politics. It did not inspire any great economic venture. Spanish America, furthermore, did not offer to Catholicism an atmosphere conducive to asceticism. Instead of mortification, the senses found only pleasure, indolence, and self-indulgence on this continent.

Bringing the gospel to Spanish America must not be judged as a religious undertaking, but as the ecclesiastic enterprise it has been almost since the beginning of Christianity. Only a powerful ecclesiastic organization, able to mobilize militias of battle-hardened missionaries and priests, was capable of colonizing people in faraway and exotic lands for the Christian faith. Protestantism was never effective in spreading its doctrine, as a logical consequence of its individualism, which was designed to reduce the ecclesiastic framework of religion to a minimum. Its propagation in Europe was invariably due to political and economic reasons: the Catholic Church's conflicts with states and monarchs inclined to rebel against papal power and join the wave of secessionism; the growth of the bourgeoisie, which found in Protestantism a more convenient system and which resented Rome's support of feudal privileges. When Protestantism has undertaken to proselytize, it has wisely adopted a method that combines preaching with social service.

[21] Frank, *Our America*, p. 25.

In North America the Anglo-Saxon colonizer did not worry about converting the natives. He had to settle an almost virgin land and all his energies were absorbed by his harsh struggle to conquer nature. Here we see the inherent difference between the Anglo-Saxon and Spanish conquests. In its origin and process, the former was a completely individualist adventure that compelled the men who participated in it to live under great stress. (Individualism, pragmatism, and activism are still the mainsprings of North American development.)

Anglo-Saxon colonization did not need an ecclesiastical organization. Puritan individualism made each pioneer his own minister. The New England pioneer needed only his Bible (Unamuno calls Protestantism "the tyranny of the word"). North America was colonized with great economy of man's forces. Colonization did not use missionaries, priests, theologians, or monasteries; they were not required for the simple, crude possession of the land. A territory, rather than a culture and people, had to be conquered. Some might say that theirs was not an economy but a poverty, and they would be right provided that they recognized that from this poverty emerged the power and wealth of the United States.

The destiny of Spanish and Catholic colonization was much broader, its mission more difficult. In these lands, the conquistadors found people, cities, cultures; on the soil, roads and footprints that their passage could not erase. Proselytization had its heroic stage, when Spain sent us missionaries who still burned with the mystic fire and militant spirit of the crusaders. ("Together with the soldiers," I read in Julien Luchaire, "disembarked a multitude of Catholic monks and priests, chosen from the best.")[22] But once the Indian's rustic paganism had yielded to Catholic opulence, the conqueror was lulled by the slavery and exploitation of Indian and Negro, and by the abundance and wealth. The clergy was no longer a heroic and impassioned

[22] Julien Luchaire, *L'Eglise et le seizième siècle.*

militia but a pampered bureaucracy; well paid and well regarded.

Then came [writes Dr. M. V. Villarán] the second age in the history of colonial priesthood: the age of a placid life in magnificent monasteries, the age of sinecures, of profitable parishes, of social influence, of political control, of luxurious celebrations, which inevitably resulted in the abuse and corruption of customs. At that time, priesthood was the best career. It was an honorable and lucrative profession and those who devoted themselves to it lived like princes and dwelled in palaces. They were the idols of the worthy colonists, who loved them, respected them, feared them, made gifts to them, and willed them their properties. The monasteries were large and there was room for all. Bishoprics and other high church offices, canonries, curacies, chaplaincies, university chairs, private chapels, benefices of every kind abounded. The inhabitants were fervently pious and they lavishly provided for the upkeep of the ministers of the altar. Therefore, 'every second son of good family entered the priesthood.' "[23]

This church was no longer even that of the Counter Reformation and the Inquisition. The Holy Office had almost no heresies to persecute in Peru. It directed its action against citizens in bad repute with the clergy; against the superstitions and vices that furtively flourished in an atmosphere of sensuality and idolatry, heavy with the dregs of magic; and above all, against whatever it suspected might undermine or diminish its power. In this last respect, the Inquisition behaved more like a political than a religious institution. "The Holy Office," says Luchaire, "was powerful, but because the king wanted it to be. Its mission was to persecute political rebels as well as religious innovators. The weapon was in the hands of the king, not of the pope, and the king wielded it as much in his own as in the church's interest."[24]

Ecclesiastical science, furthermore, instead of keeping us

23 M. V. Villarán, *Estudios sobre educación nacional*, pp. 10, 11.
24 Luchaire, *L'Eglise et le seizième siècle*.

abreast of the intellectual currents of the time, separated us from them. The philosophy of scholasticism was kept alive and creative in Spain as long as it was warmed by the ardor of the mystics. But afterwards it congealed into pedantry and casuistry and turned into a stiff parchment of erudition and a creaky, rhetorical orthodoxy of Spanish theology. In *civilista* writings there is no lack of criticism of this phase of ecclesiastical work in Peru. "What science did the clergy offer?" asks Javier Prado in his thoughtful study. And he replies:

A vulgar theology, a formalist dogmatism, a confused and tiresome mixture of Aristotelian doctrine with the sophistry of scholasticism. Whenever the church has not been able to supply true scientific knowledge, it has resorted to distracting and wearying the mind with gymnastics of words and phrases and with an empty, extravagant, futile method. Here in Peru, speeches were read in Latin, which was not understood, and they were, nevertheless, discussed in the same language; here were scholars who, like Pico della Mirandola, had formulas to solve all scientific propositions; here the divine and human were decided by means of religious or scholarly authority, even though the most complete ignorance reigned not only about the natural sciences but also about philosophy and even about the teachings of Bossuet and Pascal.[25]

The struggle for independence, which opened a new road and promised a new dawn to the best spirits, revealed that religion, in the sense of mysticism and passion, was still to be found in a few criollo and Indian priests who in Peru, as in Mexico, furnished the liberal revolution with some of its first champions and great orators.

Independence and the Church

The War of Independence did not touch ecclesiastical privileges any more than it did feudal privileges. The upper clergy, conservative and traditional, was naturally loyal to the king and

[25] Prado, *Estado social del Perú.*

mother country. But like the landed aristocracy, it accepted the republic as soon as it realized that the latter was impotent against the colonial structure. The revolution in Spanish America was conducted by romantic and Napoleonic caudillos and given its theories by dogmatic and formalist orators. Although it was nourished on the principles and sentiments of the French Revolution, it neither inherited nor experienced the religious problem of France.

In France, as in other countries that did not undergo the Reformation, the bourgeois and liberal revolution could not be accomplished without Jacobinism and anti-clericalism. The battle against feudalism in these countries encountered an uneasy alliance between the Catholic Church and the feudal system. As much because of the conservative influence of its high officials as because of its doctrinal and emotional resistance to everything it saw in liberal thought of Protestant individualism and nationalism, the church foolishly bound up its fate with that of monarchical and aristocratic reaction.

But in Spanish America, especially in the countries where the revolution spent a long time in its political formulation (independence and the republic), the continuation of feudal privileges was accompanied logically by the continuation of ecclesiastical privileges. For this reason, when Mexico attacked the former in its revolution, it immediately found itself in conflict with the latter. In Mexico, because a large part of the property was in the hands of the church, ecclesiastical privileges were not only politically but materially identified with feudal privileges.

Peru had a liberal and patriotic clergy from the first days of its revolution. In a few isolated cases, civil liberalism was inflexibly Jacobin, and, in even fewer cases, anti-religious. Most of our liberals came from the Masonic lodges that were so active in preparing for independence, so they almost all professed the deism that made Freemasonry in these Latin countries a kind of spiritual and political substitute for the Reformation.

In France itself, the Revolution maintained good relations with Christianity even during the Jacobin period. Aulard wisely observes that in France the anti-religious or anti-Christian movement arose from circumstantial rather than doctrinal causes. "Of all the events," he says, "that wrought the frame of mind which resulted in the attempt to dethrone Christianity, the insurrection of La Vendée, by its clerical form, was the chief, the most influential. I might almost say that without La Vendée there would have been no worship of Reason."[26] Aulard refers to the deism of Robespierre, who argued that "atheism is aristocratic," whereas "the idea of a great Being who watches over oppressed innocence and punishes triumphant crime is entirely democratic." The worship of the goddess Reason only kept its vital impulse as long as it was a cult of the fatherland threatened and plotted against by foreign reaction with the approval of papal power. Moreover, "the cult of Reason," Aulard added, "was almost always deist and not materialist or atheist."[27]

The French Revolution resulted in separation of church and state; and later Napoleon used the concordat to subordinate the church to the state. But the Restoration periods jeopardized his work by renewing the conflict between clergy and laymen, in which Lucien Romier claims to see a resumé of the history of the republic. Romier starts out from the premise that feudalism was already conquered when the Revolution broke out. Under the monarchy, according to Romier—and here he is joined by all reactionary writers—the bourgeoisie had already assumed control.

Victory over the nobility was already achieved. The kings had put feudalism to death. An aristocracy remained which had no force of its own and which owed all its privileges and titles to the central authority. It was a body of gallooned officials with more or less

---

[26] Alphonse Aulard, *Christianity and the French Revolution*, trans. Lady Frazer (London: Ernest Benn, 1927), p. 98.
[27] Ibid., pp. 111 and 113.

hereditary functions, the fragile remains of a power that was top-pled by the first republican wave. After easily carrying out this de-struction, the republic had only to maintain an accomplished fact without exerting any particular effort. On the other hand, the mon-archy had failed with the church. In spite of the secular domestica-tion of the higher church officials, in spite of a conflict with the Curia that was revived with every reign, in spite of many threats of rupture, the struggle against Roman authority had not given the state any more control over religion than in the times of Philip the Handsome. Therefore, it is against the church and the ultramontane clergy that the republic directed its main activities for a century.[28]

The situation was very different in the Spanish colonies of South America. In Peru in particular, the revolution found feu-dalism intact. The clashes between civil and ecclesiastical power had no doctrinal basis. They reflected a domestic quarrel, a la-tent power struggle typical of countries where colonization felt it had a religious mission and where spiritual authority tended to prevail over temporal. From the outset, the republican consti-tution proclaimed Catholicism as the national religion. Locked within Spanish tradition, these countries lacked the elements of a Protestant Reformation. The worship of Reason would have been still more alien to a people who engaged in little intellec-tual activity or philosophical speculation. The reasons for a sec-ular state that existed in other historical latitudes did not exist in Peru. Nurtured on Spanish Catholicism, the Peruvian state was bound to be semifeudal and Catholic.

The republic continued the policy of Spain in this as in other spheres. García Calderón says:

By means of religious foundations, the tithing system, and ecclesias-tical benefices, a civil constitution was established for the church, following the French example. In this sense, the revolution was tra-ditionalist. From the time of the first absolute monarchs, the Span-

[28] Lucien Romier, *Explication de notre temps* (Paris: Bernard Grasset, 1925), pp. 119–121.

ish kings had the right to intervene and protect the church; in their hands, the defense of Catholicism turned into a civil and legislative action. The church was a social force, but the weakness of its hierarchy impaired its political ambitions. It could not, as in England, enter into a constitutional agreement and freely define its frontiers. The king protected the Inquisition and was more Catholic than the pope; in his role as guardian, he prevented conflicts and he proved to be sovereign and unique.[29]

In this statement, García Calderón points out the basic contradiction existing within Latin American countries that have not separated church and state. If its Catholicism is alive and active, the Catholic state cannot practice a secular policy which, taken to its logical conclusion, would end in a theocracy. From this point of view, the thought of ultramontane conservatives like García Moreno appears to be more consistent than that of the moderate liberals who are determined to reconcile the state's official Catholicism with a liberal and national secular policy.

Peruvian liberalism, ineffective and formalist on the economic and political levels, could not be less so on the religious. It is not true, as some claim, that clerical and ecclesiastical influence fought to prevent Jacobin radicalism. The personal attitude of Vigil, an impassioned free thinker sprung from the ranks of the church, does not really belong to our liberalism, which never tried to secularize any more than it tried to defeudalize the state. Jorge Guillermo Leguía writes authoritatively on José Gálvez, the most representative and responsible of the liberal leaders:

His ideology revolved around two precepts: equality and morality. Therefore, it is wrong to assume from his criticism of the ecclesiastical tithes that he is a Jacobin. Gálvez never denied the church and its dogmas. He respected and believed in them. The abbess was misguided who, when told on May 2 of the tragic explosion of the Torre de la Merced, exclaimed: "What a good use of gunpowder!" A deputy could hardly be anticlerical who invoked the Trinity in

[29] García Calderón, *Le Pérou contemporain.*

the introduction to the constitution. When Gálvez stripped the church of an income that incarnated the survival of feudalism, his purpose was not anti-clerical but an economic and democratic reform. Nor was he, as is commonly believed, the author of that proposal, which had been initiated by Vigil.[30]

Forced by its role as a governing class, the landed aristocracy adopted bourgeois ideas and attitudes and partially assimilated the remains of liberalism. The rise of the *civilista* party was indicative of its liberal evolution and growing capitalist awareness. This movement was rejected by the ecclesiastical element, which coincided more, and not only in the publication of a newspaper, with conservative and plebiscitary Pierolism. In this period of our history, as I mention elsewhere, the aristocracy took on a liberal air; the demos, in reaction, although they protested against the business clique, acquired a conservative and clerical tone. The *civilista* hierarchy included some moderate liberals who tried to guide the state toward capitalism, breaking as much as possible with feudal tradition. But the feudal class's domination of *civilismo*, together with the lag in our political development caused by the war, prevented these *civilista* lawyers and jurists from making any progress. Before the power of clergy and church, *civilismo* generally responded with a passive pragmatism and conservative positivism which, with a few individual exceptions, characterized its mentality.

The first really effective anti-clerical activity was the Radical movement, which undertook to denounce and condemn the three elements of Peruvian politics in the recent past: *civilismo*, Pierolism, and militarism. Directed by men of a more literary than philosophical temperament, it devoted its energies to this battle, which did produce, especially in the provinces, a certain increase in religious indifference. This was no gain, because it had no effect whatsoever on the socio-economic structure in

[30] Jorge Guillermo Leguía, "La convención de 1856 y don José Gálvez," *Revista de Ciencias Jurídicas y Sociales*, no. 1, p. 36.

which the anathemized system was deeply rooted. The Radical or "González-Pradist" protest lacked effectiveness because it offered no social and economic program. Its two chief slogans, anti-centralism and anti-clericalism, were by themselves no threat to feudal privileges. Only the movement of Arequipa, recently vindicated by Miguel Angel Urquieta,[31] tried to enter social and economic terrains, although this effort did not go beyond the drafting of a program.

In the South American countries where liberal thought has freely followed its course, inserted into a normal capitalist and democratic evolution, it has been recognized—although only as an intellectual exercise—that Protestantism and a national church are logical requirements for a liberal, modern state.

But capitalism has lost its revolutionary spirit and so this thesis has been overtaken by events.[32] Socialism, according to the conclusions of historical materialism, not to be confused with philosophical materialism, considers that ecclesiastical forms and religious doctrines are produced and sustained by the socio-economic structure. Therefore, it is concerned with changing the latter and not the former. Socialism regards mere anti-clerical activity as a liberal bourgeois pastime. In Europe, anti-clericalism is characteristic of countries where the Protestant Reformation has not unified civil and religious conscience and where political nationalism and Roman universalism live in either open or latent conflict, which compromise can moderate but not halt or resolve.

Protestantism does not penetrate Latin America as a spiritual and religious power, but through its social services (Y.M.C.A., Methodist missions in the sierra, et cetera). This and other signs

[31] See the article "González Prada y Urquieta" in *Amauta*, no. 5.

[32] Julio Navarro Monzo, leader of the Y.M.C.A. and proponent of a new reformation, acknowledges in his book *El problema religioso en la cultura latinoamericana* that, "inasmuch as the Latin countries unfortunately remained outside of the Reformation of the seventeenth century, it is now too late to think of converting them to Protestantism."

indicate that it has exhausted its possibilities for normal expansion. Furthermore, it suffers from Latin America's anti-imperialism, which suspects the Protestant missions of being strategic outposts of British or North American capitalism.

Rationalist thought of the nineteenth century sought to explain religion in terms of philosophy. More realistically, pragmatism has accorded to religion the place from which rationalism conceitedly thought to dislodge it. As Sorel predicted, the historical experience of recent years has proven that present revolutionary and social myths can occupy man's conscience just as fully as the old religious myths.

Regionalism and Centralism

Basic Premises
Hᴏᴡ ɪꜱ ᴛʜᴇ ǫᴜᴇꜱᴛɪᴏɴ of regionalism presented in our time? In some departments, especially in the south, there is an obvious regionalist sentiment. But regionalist aspirations are not defined in explicit and vigorous protests. In Peru, regionalism is a vague feeling of unrest and dissatisfaction, rather than a movement or a program.

This can be explained by our economic and social situation and by our historical development. The question of regionalism can no longer be approached in terms of the radical or Jacobin ideology of the nineteenth century.

I believe that our study of regionalism should start from the following premises:

(1) The dispute between federalists and centralists is as anachronistic as the controversy between conservatives and liberals. In theory and practice the battle has moved from an exclusively political to a social and economic terrain. The new generation is no longer interested in the form, the administrative

mechanism, of our regime, but in its substance, the economic structure.

(2) Federalism does not appear in our history as a popular cause, but rather as a justification of *gamonalismo* and its clientele. The mass of Indians do not participate in it and its converts are limited to the bourgeoisie of the old colonial cities.

(3) Centralism is supported by regional bossism and *gamonalismo*, prepared on occasion to say or feel that they are federalist. Federalism recruits its followers among the caciques or *gamonales* in disfavor with the central power.

(4) One of the defects of our political organization is its centralism; the solution, however, does not lie in a federalism rooted and inspired in feudalism. Our political and economic organization needs to be completely revised and transformed.

(5) It is difficult to define the limits of regions historically existing in Peru as such. The departments originated in the artificial *intendencias* of the viceroyalty. They therefore have no tradition or reality derived from the Peruvian people and their history.

The idea of federalism has no deep roots in our history. The only ideological conflict, the only doctrinal difference in the first half-century of the republic, was that of Conservatives and Liberals. It did not reflect opposition between the capital and the regions but antagonism between large landholders, descended from colonial feudalism and aristocracy, and the mestizo demos of the city, heirs to the rhetorical liberalism of independence. This struggle spread, naturally, to the administrative system. By eliminating municipalities, the conservative constitution of Huancayo expressed the conservative position on self-government. But neither Conservatives nor Liberals of that time considered administrative centralization or decentralization to be a cardinal issue. Later, when the old landholders and aristocrats, allied with merchants made wealthy by contracts and business deals with the government, turned into a capitalist class, they recognized that the Liberal program was more suited to their interests and requirements than the aristocratic. Conservatives and Liberals, without distinction, declared themselves favorable or opposed to decentralization. In this new period, conservatism and liberalism, which were now not even given those names, no longer corresponded to class interests. In that curious period, the wealthy became somewhat liberal and the masses became somewhat conservative.

But, in any case, the *civilista* caudillo Manuel Pardo designed a decentralization policy with the creation of departmental councils in 1873. Years later, the Democratic caudillo Nicolás de Piérola, a politician and statesman of conservative mentality and spirit, although his demagoguery would appear to indicate the contrary, wrote in the "declaration of principles" of his party the following statement: "Our diversity of race, language, climate, and terrain, no less than the distances between our population centers, demand that a federal system be established as a means of satisfying our needs of today and tomorrow; but in conditions that take into account the experience of countries similar to ours with this system, as well as the peculiarities of Peru."[1]

After 1895, declarations against centralism multiplied. The Liberal party of Augusto Durand came out in favor of a federal system. The Radical party lost no opportunity to attack and criticise centralism. And suddenly there appeared, as if by magic, a Federal party. Centralism was then defended solely by the *civilistas*, who in 1873 had demonstrated their willingness to practice a policy of decentralization.

But all this was theoretical speculation. Actually, the parties were not anxious to abolish centralism. Sincere Federalists were not only few in number and scattered among the different parties, but they exercised no real influence on opinion. They did not represent a popular cause. Piérola and the Democratic party

---

[1] *Declaración de principios del partido demócrata* (Lima, 1897), p. 14.

had governed for several years. Durand and his friends had shared the honors and responsibilities of power with the Democrats for some time. Neither group had used the occasion to deal with the problem of changing the administrative system or of reforming the constitution.

After the decease of the unstable Federal party and the spontaneous dissolution of González-Pradist radicalism, the Liberal party continued to wave the banner of federalism. Durand realized that the federalist idea, which the Democratic party had exhausted in a platonic and cautiously written declaration, could serve to strengthen the Liberal party in the provinces by attracting forces hostile to the central authority. Under or rather against the government of José Pardo, he published a federalist manifesto. But his subsequent policy clearly revealed that the Liberal party, notwithstanding its profession of federalist faith, only brandished the idea of federation for propaganda purposes. The Liberals formed part of the cabinet and of the majority in congress during Pardo's second administration. And they did not show, either as cabinet ministers or as members of congress, any intention of renewing the federalist battle.

Billinghurst, perhaps with a more passionate conviction than other politicians who used this platform, also wanted decentralization. Unlike the Democrats and the Liberals, he cannot be reproached for forgetting his principle when in power; his experience in the government was too brief. But it must be stated objectively that Billinghurst took presidential office as an enemy of centralism and that this was of no benefit to the campaign against centralism.

At first glance some may infer from this rapid review of the attitude on centralism taken by Peru's political parties that from the date of the Democratic party's declaration of principles to Dr. Durand's federalist manifesto there has been an effective federalist movement in Peru. But appearances are deceiving.

This review really proves that the federalist idea has aroused neither energetic resistance nor ardent support. A worthless slogan, it could not alone signify the program of a movement or a party.

This is not to ratify or recommend in any way bureaucratic centralism. But it is evidence that the diffuse regionalism of southern Peru has not yet materialized into an active federalist affirmation.

Regionalism and Gamonalismo

Any keen observer of our historical development, whatever his point of view, must be struck by the fact that Peruvian thought is at present concerned less with politics—and in this case "politics" has the broad connotation of "old-time politics" or "bourgeois politics"—than with social and economic issues. The "problem of the Indian" and the "agrarian question" are much more interesting to modern Peruvians than the "principle of authority," "universal suffrage," the "reign of intelligence," and other subjects discussed by Liberals and Conservatives. This is not because the political mentality of previous generations was more abstract, more philosophical, more universal, and that, to the contrary, the mentality of today's generation may be, and is, more realistic, more Peruvian. It is because the controversy between Liberals and Conservatives was derived on both sides from the interests and aspirations of a single social class. The proletariat lacked any program or ideology of its own. Liberals and Conservatives looked down on the Indian as an inferior, different class. They either tried to ignore the problem of the Indian or they did their best to reduce it to a philanthropical and humanitarian problem.

Today, with the appearance of a new ideology that expresses the interests and aspirations of the masses, who gradually have acquired a class consciousness, a national movement has arisen that sympathizes with the lot of the Indian and makes the solution of his problem basic to a program for the reform and reconstruction of Peru. The problem of the Indian has ceased to be, as in the time of the discussions between Liberals and Conservatives, a secondary or subordinate theme and has become a paramount issue.

The foregoing demonstrates that, contrary to what superficial, self-styled nationalists suppose and suggest, the spirit of this generation has conceived a program that is a thousand times more nationalist than that which in the past was nourished only on aristocratic sentiments and superstitions or on Jacobin concepts and formulas. A spirit that considers the problem of the Indian to be of supreme importance is simultaneously very humane and very nationalist, very idealist and very realist. And its timeliness is proven by the identical approaches of both those who support it from within and those who judge it from without. Eugenio d'Ors is a Spanish professor who is extravagantly admired by Peruvians who associate nationalism with conservatism. On the occasion of Bolivia's centennial, he has written:

In some American countries especially, I see very clearly what the justification of independence should be according to the law of Good Works. I see what should be the work, the task, the mission in your country. Bolivia, like Peru and Mexico, has a great local problem, which at the same time signifies a great universal problem. It has the problem of the Indian, of his situation in the national culture. What to do with this race? There have traditionally been two contrasting methods. The Saxon method has been to drive it back, decimate it, and slowly to exterminate it. The Spanish method, on the contrary, tried to approach it, redeem it, and mix with it. I do not want to say now which of these methods is preferable. What has to be established in all fairness is the obligation to work with one or the other method. It is morally impossible to follow a line of conduct that simply evades the problem and tolerates the existence of a teeming mass of Indians beside the white population, without worrying about its situation except to exploit it—selfishly, greedily, cruelly—for the most wretched and back-breaking labor.[2]

This is not the moment to argue with Eugenio d'Ors about his contrast of the presumed humanitarianism of the Spanish method with the relentlessly destructive will of the Saxon method. Probably the author identified the Spanish method with the noble spirit of Father de las Casas and not with the policy of the conquest and the viceroyalty, which was impregnated with prejudice against not only the Indian but even the mestizo. I just want to point out that the opinion of Eugenio d'Ors is a recent testimony of the way in which both the enlightened combatants and the intelligent spectators of our historical drama agree in their interpretation of the message of the times.

Assuming that "the problem of the Indian" and the "agrarian question" take priority over any problem relative to the mechanism of the regime if not to the structure of the state, it is absolutely impossible to consider the question of regionalism or, more precisely, of administrative decentralization from standpoints not subordinate to the need to solve in a radical and organic way the first two problems. A decentralization that is not directed toward this goal is not even worth discussion.

And decentralization in itself, simply as a political and administrative reform, would not signify any progress toward solution of the "problem of the Indian" and the "problem of land," which fundamentally are one and the same. On the contrary, decentralization carried out for no other reason than to authorize a degree of autonomy to the regions or departments would increase the power of *gamonalismo* against any solution in the interest of the Indian masses. To become convinced of this, it is enough to ask oneself what caste, what class, what category opposes the redemption of the Indian. There is only one, categorical, answer: *gamonalismo*, feudalism, bossism. Therefore, is

[2] Eugenio d'Ors, in a letter written on the occasion of the centennial of Bolivian independence, published in *Repertorio Americano*.

there any doubt that the more autonomous a regional administration of *gamonales* and caciques, the more they would sabo-
tage and resist any effective attempt to redress the wrongs done
to the Indian?

There can be no illusions. The decent groups in the cities will
never prevail against *gamonalismo* in regional administration.
The experience of more than a century has taught us what to
expect of the possibility that in the near future a democratic
system will function in Peru that will fulfill, at least on paper,
the Jacobin principle of "popular sovereignty." The rural masses, or the Indian communities in any case, would remain outside
suffrage and its results. Therefore, even if only because the absent are never right—*les absents ont toujours tort*—the organ-
isms and authorities that would be created "through election,"
but without their vote, would have neither the ability nor the
knowledge to do them justice. Who would be so naive as to imag-
ine that, within the present economic and political situation, the
regions would be governed by "universal suffrage"?

Both the system of "departmental councils" of President Manuel Pardo and the federal republic proclaimed in the manifesto
of Augusto Durand and other proponents of federation have not
represented nor could they represent anything but the ambition
of *gamonalismo*. In practice, the "departmental councils" would
transfer to the caciques of the departments a series of powers
independent of central authority. The federal republic would
have performed more or less the same function and had the same
effect.

The regions and provinces are absolutely right to condemn
centralism, its methods, and its institutions. They are also right
to denounce an organization that concentrates the administration of the republic in the capital. But they are completely
wrong when, deceived by a mirage, they believe that decentralization will suffice to solve their basic problems. *Gamonalismo* is
an accessory to and responsible for all the evils of the central re-

gime. Therefore, if decentralization only serves to place regional administration and the local regime directly under control of the *gamonales*, the substitution of one system for the other does not correct or promise to correct any deep-seated injustice.

Luis E. Valcárcel endeavors to demonstrate the survival of "Inca-ism without the Inca." Here is a subject that is far more significant than the outdated topics of political studies in the past. It also confirms my statement that contemporary concerns are not exclusively political, but principally economic and social. Valcárcel probes the question of the Indian and his land, and seeks the solution not in *gamonalismo* but in the *ayllu*.

The Region in the Republic

We come to one of the serious problems of regionalism: the definition of regions. I find that our regionalists of the old school have never approached the problem realistically, which indicates the abstract and superficial nature of their arguments. No intelligent regionalist would claim that the boundaries of regions coincide with our political organization, that is, that "regions" are "departments." Department is a political term that does not designate a reality, much less an economic and historical unit. The department is primarily a convention that only satisfies a functional need or criterion of centralism. I cannot conceive of a regionalism that abstractly condemns a centralist regime without objecting concretely to its peculiar territorial division. Regionalism logically is translated into federalism. In any case, it is expressed in a specific plan for decentralization. No true regionalism is satisfied with municipal autonomy. As Herriot says in the chapter of his book *Créer* that he devotes to administration, "regionalism superimposes on the department and the commune a new organ, the region."[3]

But it is not a new organ except in its political and administrative function. A region is not created by a government stat-

---

[3] Edouard Herriot, *Créer* (Paris: Payot, 1919), vol. II, p. 191.

ute. Its biology is more complicated and it can trace its origin farther back than the nation itself. In order to claim autonomy from the latter, it must already exist as a region. No one can doubt the right of Provence, Alsace-Lorraine, and Bretagne to feel and call themselves regions; not to mention Spain, where the national unit is less stable, and Italy, where it is less old. In Spain and Italy, the regions are clearly differentiated by tradition, character, people, and even language.

According to its physical geography, Peru is divided into three regions: the coast, the sierra, and the *montaña*. (In Peru only nature is well defined.) And this division is not altogether physical. It is related to all our social and economic reality. Sociologically and economically, the *montaña* or, better, the tropical forest, is still not significant; it can be thought of as a colonial possession of the Peruvian state. The coast and the sierra, on the other hand, are the two regions in which it is possible actually to distinguish the differences in terrain and people.[4] The sierra

---

[4] Miguelina Acosta tells me that the value of the *montaña* in the Peruvian economy cannot be measured by recent data. These years are exceptional in that they mark a period of depression. Exports from the *montaña* today are negligible in Peru's trade statistics, but they were very significant until the World War. Loreto is now in the situation of a region that has suffered a disaster.

This is an accurate observation. The importance of Loreto cannot be appreciated by looking only at the present. The production of the *montaña* played a leading role in our economy until a few years ago. During the period when rubber appeared to be of immense value, the *montaña* began to be thought of as El Dorado. About twenty years ago, Francisco García Calderón wrote in *Le Pérou contemporain* that rubber was the wealth of the future. Everyone shared this illusion.

In reality, the fortune of rubber was aleatory, depending on temporary circumstances. We did not realize this at the time because we are easily carried away by a Panglossian optimism when we tire of our superficially frivolous skepticism. Logically, rubber could not be put in the same category as a mineral resource produced almost exclusively by our country.

The depression in Loreto is not the result of a temporary industrial crisis. Miguelina Acosta knows very well that industrial activity is only beginning in the *montaña*. Rubber was a forest resource that was exploited, actually devastated, because it was located in an area accessible to transportation.

The economic past of Loreto does not, therefore, invalidate the substance

is Indian; the coast is Spanish or mestizo (in this case, the adjectives "Indian" and "Spanish" acquire a very broad meaning). I repeat here what I wrote in an article about a book by Valcárcel:

The dualism in Peruvian history and the Peruvian soul is expressed in our time as a conflict between the historical development on the coast and the Indian sentiment that survives in the sierra and that is deeply rooted in nature. Modern Peru is a product of the coast and modern Peruvianism was formed in the lowlands. Neither the Spaniard nor the criollo could conquer the Andes. In the Andes the Spaniard was always a pioneer or a missionary, which are also the roles of the criollo until the Andes extinguishes the conquistador in him and little by little creates an Indian.[5]

The Indian race and language, displaced from the coast by the Spaniard and his language, have fearfully taken refuge in the

---

of my statement. When I write that the *montaña* still lacks economic importance, I refer to the present; and I compare its importance to that of the sierra and the coast. It is a relative judgment.

I use the same standard of comparison to judge the sociological significance of the *montaña*. I recognize two fundamental elements, two main forces, in Peruvian society. I do not deny the existence of other elements, but I believe them to be secondary.

I prefer not to be satisfied with this explanation. I want to give fair consideration to Miguelina Acosta's observations and her basic argument that too little is known about the sociology of the *montaña*. The Peruvian of the coast, like the Peruvian of the sierra, is unaware of the Peruvian of the *montaña*. In the *montaña*, or more exactly in the department of Loreto, there are people with customs and traditions almost unrelated to the customs and traditions of the people of the coast and the sierra. Loreto has evolved differently in our sociology and history; its biological layers are not the same.

In this respect, it is impossible not to agree with Dr. Acosta Cárdenas, who is the person most qualified to explain Peruvian reality with a thorough study of the sociology of Loreto. Discussion of regionalism must regard Loreto as a region, because Loreto is the *montaña*. The regionalism of Loreto more than once has risen up in protest. Although it has not produced theory, it has produced action, which means that it has to be taken into account.

[5] José Carlos Mariátegui, "De la vida incaica," *Mundial*, September 1925.

sierra. Therefore, in the sierra are combined all the elements of a region, if not of a nationality. The Peru of the coast, heir of Spain and the conquest, controls the Peru of the sierra from Lima; but it is not demographically and spiritually strong enough to absorb it. Peruvian unity is still to be accomplished. It is not a question of the communication and cooperation of former small states or free cities within the boundaries of a single nation. In Peru the problem of unity goes much deeper. Instead of a pluralism of local or regional traditions, what has to be solved is a dualism of race, language, and sentiment, born of the invasion and conquest of indigenous Peru by a foreign race that has not managed to merge with the Indian race, or eliminate it, or absorb it.

The regionalist movement in the cities or districts where it is most active, if it does not reflect simply the dissatisfaction of *gamonalismo*, is obviously although unconsciously promoted by this contrast between coast and sierra. When this is its motivation, it indicates a conflict not between capital and province but between the Spanish Peru of the coast and the Indian Peru of the sierra.

The above definition of regions does not advance us in our examination of decentralization. On the contrary, this goal is lost to view in order to fix on a much greater goal. The sierra and the coast are two regions geographically and sociologically; but they cannot be two regions politically and administratively. Distances within the Andes are greater than distances from the sierra to the coast. The natural movement of the Peruvian economy is trans-Andean and demands that roads of penetration be given preference over longitudinal roads. Development of centers of production in the sierra depend on an outlet to the sea. Any positive program of decentralization has to be inspired chiefly by the needs and directions of the national economy. The historical purpose of decentralization is to encourage not secession but union, not to separate and divide regions but to assure

and perfect their unity within a more functional and less forced
association. Regionalism does not mean separatism.

These statements lead, therefore, to the conclusion that Peruvian regionalism and its program are imprecise and nebulous
solely because there are no well-defined regions.

One of the facts that forcefully supports this belief is the sincere and profound sentiment of regionalism in the south, specifically in the departments of Cuzco, Arequipa, Puno, and Apurí-
mac. These departments constitute our most clear-cut and integrated region. Trade and other relations between them keep
alive an old unity inherited from the Inca civilization. In the
south, the "region" rests solidly on its historical foundations
with the Andes as its bastions.

The south is basically of the sierra. Here, where the coast
shrinks to a slender strip of land, coastal and mestizo Peru has
not been able to establish itself. The Andes advance to the sea,
converting the coast into a narrow cornice dotted with ports and
coves and forcing the cities into the sierra. The south has been
able to maintain its sierra, if not its Indian, character in spite of
the conquest, the viceroyalty, and the republic.

To the north the coast widens and becomes economically and
demographically dominant. Trujillo, Chiclayo, and Piura are
cities with a Spanish spirit and flavor. Commerce between these
cities and Lima is easy and frequent, but what really links them
to the capital is their common tradition and sentiment. A map
of Peru explains Peruvian regionalism better than any complicated, abstract theory.

The centralist regime divides the national territory into departments; but it accepts and at times employs a more general
classification that assigns the departments to three groups:
North, Center, and South. The Peru-Bolivia Confederation of
Santa Cruz split Peru into two halves, a division basically no
more arbitrary and artificial than the boundaries set by the centralist republic. Departments and provinces that have no contact

with one another are grouped under the labels North, South, and Center. The term "region" appears to be mainly a convention.

However, neither state nor parties have ever been able to define Peruvian regions in any other way. The Democratic party, to whose theoretical federalism I have already referred, practiced its federalist principle within its own system by placing a central committee over regional committees for North, South, and Center. (This might be called a federalism for internal consumption.) When the constitutional reform of 1919 instituted regional congresses, it set up the same division.

But this delimitation of departments conforms solely to a centralist criterion. Regionalists cannot adopt it without appearing to base their regionalism on premises and concepts peculiar to the metropolitan mentality. All attempts at decentralization have suffered from precisely this original defect.

Centralist Decentralization

Decentralization, no matter what form it has taken in the history of the republic, has always represented an absolutely centralist concept and design. Parties and caudillos have occasionally adopted, for reasons of convenience, the idea of decentralization; but when they have tried to apply it, they have not had the knowledge or the ability to break away from centralist practice.

This centralist tendency is easily explained. Regionalist aspirations do not constitute a concrete program or propose a definite method of decentralization and autonomy because they express a feudalist sentiment instead of a popular cause. The *gamonales* were concerned only with increasing their feudal power. Regionalism was incapable of drawing up its own program. In most cases it only managed to mouth the word "federation." Therefore, the decentralization program turned out to be a product typical of the capital.

On a theoretical plane, the capital has never defended the centralist system with too much ardor or eloquence; on a practical plane, it has skillfully conserved its privileges intact. It has had little difficulty in making a few concessions in theory to the idea of an administrative decentralization, but the solutions sought to this problem have been moulded by centralist standards and interests.

The first effective attempt to decentralize was the experiment of departmental councils instituted by the 1873 law of the municipalities. (The federalist experiment of Santa Cruz is not included in this study, not so much because it was shortlived, as because it was a supranational concept imposed by a statesman whose ideal was the union of Peru and Bolivia.)

The departmental councils of 1873 were centralist not only in form but in inspiration. The model for the new institution originated in France, citadel of centralism. Our legislators tried to adapt to Peru a system enacted by the Third Republic, which was manifestly anchored to the centralist principles of the Consulate and the Empire.

The reform of 1873 was a typically centralist decentralization. It did not satisfy any of the specific grievances of regional sentiment. Furthermore, by strengthening the artificial political division of the republic into departments or districts according to the needs of the centralist regime, it opposed or discouraged all effective regionalism.

In his study of local government, Carlos Concha states that "the organization given to these bodies, modeled on the French law of 1871, did not conform to the political culture of the period."[6] This is a *civilista* judgment on a *civilista* reform. The departmental councils failed because they were in no way related to the historical reality of Peru. They were designed to transfer from central authority to regional *gamonalismo* part of the former's responsibilities—primary and secondary education, the

[6] Carlos Concha, *El régimen local*, p. 135.

administration of justice, and law enforcement. Regional *ga-monalismo* was as little interested in assuming these responsibilities as it was capable of discharging them. Furthermore, the operation and mechanism of the system were too complicated. The councils were like small parliaments chosen by the electoral colleges of each department and representing the provincial municipalities. The caciques would have liked a less unwieldy machine, something simpler in composition and easier to manage. Such annoying obligations as public education were not their concern, but the central government's. The departmental council did not rest on either the people—above all the peasants, who took no part in the game of politics—or on the feudal lords and their clientele; it was, therefore, a completely artificial institution.

The War of 1879 ended the experiment, but the departmental councils had already failed. In their few years of existence they had demonstrated that they could not fulfill their mission. After the war, when the administration was reorganized, the law of 1873 was forgotten.

The law of 1886, which created the departmental juntas, was oriented in the same way, only this time centralism took less trouble to give it the appearance of decentralization. The juntas operated until 1893 under the presidency of the prefects and, in general, they were entirely subordinate to the central government.

This apparent decentralization did not propose to gradually give administrative autonomy to the departments nor did it establish juntas in order to attend to regional aspirations. Its purpose was to reduce or eliminate the central government's responsibility in the distribution of funds available for education and road construction. All administration continued to be strictly centralized. The only administrative independence granted the departments was the independence of their poverty. Without recourse to the central government, every department was supposed to maintain its own schools and roads out of its income from excise taxes. The departmental juntas were used to allocate the budget for education and public works among the various departments.

That this was their real purpose is proven by the way in which the departmental juntas declined and disappeared. As its finances recovered from the consequences of the War of 1879, the central government began to reclaim the functions it had entrusted to the departmental juntas. It took over public education completely and extended its authority in proportion to the expansion of its overall budget. Departmental revenues became so insignificant compared to national revenues that centralism was further reinforced. The departmental juntas were finally left with only a few supervisory and bureaucratic activities, at which time they were abolished.

The constitutional reform of 1919 had to give some kind of token recognition to regionalist sentiment. The most important of its decentralizing measures, municipal autonomy, has yet to be implemented. The principle of municipal autonomy has been incorporated into the national constitution, but the mechanism and structure of local government have not been touched, except in a negative way; the government appoints municipal authorities.

On the other hand, no time was lost in organizing regional congresses. These parliaments of North, Center, and South are offshoots of the national parliament; they incubate for the same period, in the same electoral climate; they are born of the same womb, on the same day; their legislative mission is subsidiary and complementary; and by now their own parents are certainly convinced that they are useless. In any event, six years of experience show them to be an absurd parody of decentralization.

Actually, there was no need to wait for proof of their ineffectiveness. Regionalism wants an administrative, not a legislative, decentralization. It is not possible to conceive of a regional diet or parliament without a corresponding executive body. To create more legislatures is not to decentralize. The regional congresses have not even served to relieve the pressures on the national congress. Many local issues continue to be debated in both congresses. The problem, in short, remains unchanged.

The New Regionalism

I have examined the theory and practice of past regionalism. I must now express my own points of view on decentralization and define the terms in which, in my opinion, this problem is presented to the new generation.

First of all, it is necessary to make clear the alliance or agreement between regional *gamonalismo* and the centralist government. *Gamonalismo* could declare itself more or less federalist and anti-centralist as long as it was negotiating this alliance. But ever since it agreed to become the centralist government's most useful agent, it has renounced any program that would displease its allies in the capital.

It is time to announce the end of the old opposition between centralists and federalists of the ruling class, an opposition which, as I have observed in the course of my study, never was very dramatic. Theoretical opposition has turned into a practical understanding. Only the *gamonales* in disfavor with the central government are disposed to take a regionalist attitude, which, of course, they are prepared to abandon as soon as their political fortune improves.

Government form is no longer our paramount concern. We live in an era when economics only too obviously dominates and absorbs politics. In every country in the world, discussion of the economic bases of the state now takes precedence over reform of its administrative machinery.

The remains of Spanish feudalism are more deeply and firmly embedded in the sierra than in the rest of the republic. If Peru is to progress, it is imperative that this feudalism, which represents a survival of the colonial period, be liquidated. The redemption and salvation of the Indian, here are the program and goal of Peruvian reform. The new generation wants Peru to stand on its natural biological foundations. It feels in duty bound to create a more Peruvian, more autochthonous Peru. There can be no doubt that the historical and logical enemies of this program are the heirs to the conquest, the descendants of the colony, that is, the *gamonales*.

It is necessary to absolutely repudiate and to utterly discourage a regionalism that originates in feudal sentiments and interests and therefore aims at increasing the power of *gamonalismo*. Peru has to choose between the *gamonal* and the Indian; it has no other alternative. In the face of this dilemma, all questions of the system's structure become secondary. The new generation's primary concern is that Peru proclaim itself against the *gamonal* and for the Indian.

As a consequence of the ideas and events that daily confront us with this dilemma, regionalism begins to separate into two distinct and toally different tendencies. In other words, it begins to shape into a new regionalism. This regionalism is no mere protest against the centralist regime. It is an expression of the sierra conscience and of the Andean sentiment. The new regionalists are, above all, pro-Indian and they cannot be confused with the old-style anticentralists. Valcárcel sees the roots of Inca society intact under the flimsy layer of colonialism. His work belongs to Cuzco, to the Indian, to the Quechua, not to a region. It is nourished on Indian sentiment and autochthonous tradition.

For these regionalists the primary problem is the problem of the Indian and of land. And here they are in agreement with the new generation in the capital. Today it is no longer possible to speak of the contrast between capital and regions, but of the conflict between two mentalities, between two ideologies, one that declines and the other that ascends, both spread throughout sierra and coast, province and city. Those of our youth who continue to speak the vaguely federalist language of the past are mistaken. It will fall to the new generation to build Peruvian unity on a solid foundation of social justice.

Acceptance of these principles and goals does away with the possibility of any dissension arising out of regionalist or centralist self-interest. To condemn centralism is to condemn *gamonalismo* and the two condemnations are motivated by the same hope and the same ideal.

Municipal autonomy, "self-government," and administrative decentralization cannot be discussed alone but only from the standpoint of a radical reform. They must be considered and judged in the light of their relationship to the social problem. No reform that strengthens the *gamonal* against the Indian, no matter how much it appears to satisfy regionalist sentiment, can be a good and just reform. Any formal triumph of decentralization and autonomy is subordinate to the cause of the Indian, which must be defended and given first place in the revolutionary program of the vanguard.

The Problem of the Capital

Regionalists have often expressed their feelings against centralism by denouncing Lima. But here, as elsewhere, they have never gone beyond flowery speeches. They have made no serious and thoughtful effort to put the capital on trial, although they would have had more than sufficient evidence for holding such a trial.

This task, undoubtedly superior to the objectives and motives of *gamonalista* regionalism, can and should be undertaken by the new regionalism. Meanwhile, I shall complete my explanation of the old topic "regionalism and centralism" by posing the problem of the capital. How far is Lima's privileged position justified by national history and geography? Here is a question that needs to be cleared up. Lima's hegemony rests on less solid ground than mere mental intertia would lead us to believe. It belongs to a period of national historical development and is subject to age and termination.

The spectacle of the development of Lima in recent years moves our impressionable *limeños* to deliriously optimistic predictions about the future of the capital. The new suburbs and the asphalt avenues down which automobiles race at sixty or seventy kilometers per hour easily persuade a *limeño*—under his skin-deep and cheerful skepticism—that Lima is not far behind Buenos Aires and Río de Janeiro.

All their predictions are based on the physical impression of the growth of the urban area. They see only the opening of new surburbs and point out that, given its rate of urbanization, Lima will soon be connected with Miraflores and Magdalena. "Urban developments" actually now cover, on paper, a city of at least one million inhabitants.

But by itself the rate of urbanization proves nothing. Without a recent census, we cannot calculate the population increase of Lima from 1920 to date. The 1920 census set Lima's population at 228,740.[7] Although the percentage of growth in the last eight years is not known, available data indicate that neither increase in births nor increase in immigration have been very high. Therefore, it is only too apparent that Lima has expanded much more in area than in population. Urbanization proceeds on its own.

The *limeño's* optimism concerning the future of the capital is nourished largely by his confidence that Lima will indefinitely enjoy the advantages of a centralist government, assuring its place as the center of power, pleasure, fashion, et cetera. The development of a city, however, does not depend on political and administrative privileges; it depends on economic privileges. Therefore, the issue is whether or not the natural development of the Peruvian economy guarantees that Lima will continue to

[7] *Extracto estadístico del Perú* (1926), p. 2.

play the role necessary for its predicted or, rather, hoped-for future.

Let us rapidly examine the biological laws of cities and see how favorable they are to Lima. The essential factors in a city are the geographic factor, the economic factor, and the political factor. Of these three factors, Lima maintains its supremacy only in the political.

Lucien Romier writes on the development of French cities: "Whereas secondary cities grow out of local changes, large cities are formed by national and international connections and movements; their fortune is bound up in a network of vaster activities; and their destiny crosses administrative and even territorial borders to follow the general trade routes."[8]

In Peru, these national and international connections and movements are not concentrated in the capital. Lima is not geographically the center of the Peruvian economy. It is not, above all, the outlet for Peru's commercial traffic.

In an article on "the capital of *esprit*," published in an Italian journal, César Falcón makes some wise remarks on this subject. Falcón states that the reasons for the impressive growth of Buenos Aires are basically economic and geographic. Buenos Aires is the port and market for Argentina's agriculture and livestock. It is the crossroads of Argentine trade.[9] Lima, on the other hand, can be only one of the outlets for Peruvian products. The products of North and South have to use other ports on the long Peruvian coastline.

All this evidence is incontrovertible. In customs statistics, Callao will long remain the leading port. But the growing exploitation of land and its resources will not be principally to the advantage of Callao. It will promote the expansion of several

[8] Lucien Romier, *Explication de notre temps* (Paris: Bernard Grasset, 1925), p. 50.
[9] César Falcón, *Le vie d'Italia dell'America Latina* (1925).

other ports. For example, Talara has become in a few years the second port of the republic in volume of exports and imports.[10] The direct benefits of the oil industry are lost to the capital. This industry exports and imports without using either the capital or its port as intermediary. Other industries that emerge in the sierra or on the coast will follow the same course.

A glance at the map of any nation whose capital is a large city of international importance will show, first of all, that the capital is the focal point of the country's railways and highways. A great capital in our time is a great railway center and its function as an axis is most clearly marked on a railway map.

Although political privilege partly determines the organization of a country's railway grid, the primary factor is still an economic one. All production centers naturally and logically connect with the capital, the most important station, the richest market. The economic factor coincides with the geographic factor. The capital is not a product of chance. It has been formed thanks to a series of circumstances that have favored its hegemony; but none of these circumstances would have operated if its location had not been suitable.

The political factor does not suffice. It is said that without the papal seat, Rome would have died in the Middle Ages. This may or may not be true. In any event, it is just as true that Rome was chosen to receive the papal seat because it was the capital of the greatest empire in the world. The history of the Terza Roma precisely demonstrates that political privilege is not enough. Notwithstanding the magnetic force of the Vatican and the Quirinal, the seat of the church and the seat of the government, Rome has not prospered at the same rate as Milan. (The *Risorgimento* optimism about the future of Rome ended in the

[10] According to *Extracto estadístico del Perú*, the port of Talara follows Callao, with the value of imports at *Lp.* 2,453,719 and of exports at *Lp.* 6,171,983.

failure told about in the novel by Emile Zola. The business enterprises that enthusiastically rushed into construction of an
enormous subdivision were ruined. Their undertaking was premature.) The economic development of northern Italy has
assured the predominance of Milan, which owes its growth to
its position in the traffic of this industrial and commercial Italy.

Any great modern capital has had a complex formation,
deeply rooted in tradition. Lima, however, has had a somewhat
arbitrary beginning. Founded by a conquistador, a foreigner,
Lima appears to have originated as the military tent of a com-
mander from some distant land. Lima did not compete with
other cities to win its title as capital. The creature of an aristocratic age, Lima was born into nobility and was baptized City
of Kings. It was created by the colonizer or, rather, the conquistador, not by the native. Then the viceroyalty consecrated it as
the seat of Spanish power in South America. Finally, the War
of Independence—an uprising of the criollo and Spanish population, not of the Indian population—proclaimed it the capital
of the republic. The Peru-Bolivia Confederation temporarily
threatened its hegemony. But this state, when it reestablished
the dominion of the Andes and the sierra, looked too far south for
its axis, in an instinctive, subconscious effort to restore the Tawantinsuyo. And, for this among other reasons, it fell. Lima,
armed with political power, reclaimed its privileges as capital.

The work of the Central Railroad in this period was not only
on behalf of the mineral wealth of Junín but, above all, on behalf of Lima. Peru, heir of the conquest, had to leave the dwell-
ing place of the conquistador, the seat of the viceroyalty and the
republic, in order to fulfill its mission of scaling the Andes.
Later, after the Andes had been spanned by rail and the montaña lay beyond, a railroad was similarly envisaged to connect
Iquitos with Lima. The time was 1895 and the president was the
man who in his declaration of principles a few years earlier had
professed his federalist faith. More mindful of Lima than of

eastern Peru, he approved the route from Pichis, thereby once again behaving as a typical centralist.

To date the Central Railroad is one of Lima's greatest sources of economic power. The minerals of the department of Junín which, thanks to this railway, are exported through Callao were our leading mineral export. Although they are now second to the petroleum in the North, this does not indicate any decline in the Center's mining activities. The central railway also brings down the products of Huánuco, Ayacucho, Huancavelica, and Chanchamayo. The railroad to Pachitea, the railroad to Ayacucho and Cuzco, and in general the overall design of the state's railway program combine to make it the trunk of our transportation system.

But the future of this railway is threatened. The Central Railroad climbs the Andes at one of the steepest points. Because of its very high operation costs, freight charges are expensive. Therefore, the railway that is planned for construction from Huacho to Oyón will become to some extent a rival of this line. The new railway, which will transform Huacho into a first-ranking port, will carry a substantial part of the production of the Center to the coast. But in any case, a railroad into the sierra, even if it is the principal one, is not enough to assure Lima a dominant position in the transportation system of the country.

Although centralism may continue for a long time, Lima can never become the nucleus of the network of roads and railways. The nature of the territory forbids it. In order to develop their resources, the sierra and *montaña* require roads into the interior, that is, roads that will provide various outlets along the coast for their products. Maritime transport will not for some time need coastal roads. Lengthwise roads will be inter-Andean. A coastal-plain city like Lima cannot be the central station in this complicated network, which inevitably will look for cheaper and closer ports.

Industry is one of the primary factors in the formation of modern cities. London, New York, Berlin, and Paris owe their size chiefly to industry. Industrialism is a phenomenon characteristic of western civilization. A great city is basically a market and a factory. Industry has created first the force of the middle class and then the force of the working class. As many economists have observed, industry today does not follow consumption; it precedes and overflows the market. It is not satisfied with meeting demand; it sometimes creates it. Industrialism appears to be all-powerful. And although mankind, weary of machines and other devices, occasionally declares itself willing to return to nature, there is still no sign that machines and manufacturing will disappear. Russia, the motherland of a burgeoning socialist civilization, works feverishly to develop its industry. Lenin dreamed of the day his entire country would have electric power. In short, whether a civilization is rising or ebbing, industry remains mighty. Neither the bourgeoisie nor the proletariat can conceive of a civilization that is not based on industry. There are some who predict the decay of the city, but there is no one who predicts the decline of industry.

No one denies the power of industry. If Lima combined the conditions necessary for a great industrial power, it would undoubtedly become a great city. But the possibilities of industry in Lima are limited. This is not only because they are limited all over Peru—a country which for some time will have to remain a producer of primary materials—but also because the formation of great industrial centers is also governed by laws, as often as not the same laws that govern the formation of cities. Industry springs up in capitals because, among other reasons, the latter are at the heart of the country's transportation system. A centralized network of highways and railroads is as indispensable to industry as it is to trade. We have already seen in preceding essays that the physical geography of Peru runs counter to centralization.

Industry is also attracted to a city because certain raw materials are produced in the vicinity. This law operates especially for heavy industry like smelting. The great iron and steel mills arise near mines that can supply them. The location of coal and iron deposits determines this aspect of the economic geography of the West.

And in these days of worldwide electric power, a third factor that attracts industry to a site is the proximity of hydraulic resources. "White coal" can work the same miracles as black coal to create industry and cities. Lima has none of these factors; its surroundings do not attract industry.

It should be mentioned that the industrial possibilities based on natural resources—raw materials, hydraulic power—would not have much immediate value. Because of its disadvantageous position in terms of geography, human resources, and technology, Peru cannot dream of becoming a manufacturing country in the near future. For many years it will have to continue its role in the world economy as exporter of primary products, foodstuffs, et cetera. Another disadvantage is its present condition as a country with a colonial economy subject to the trade and financial interests of the industrial countries of the West.

Today there is no indication that Peru's emerging industrial activities are concentrating in Lima. The textile industry, for example, is widely scattered; although Lima has the most factories, a high percentage is in the provinces. It is probable that the manufacture of wool cloth, as can be seen already, will develop in the ranching regions where there is also a supply of cheap native labor due to lower living costs.

Finance and the banking system are another factor in a great city. The recent experience of Vienna has shown the value of this element in the life of a capital. After the war, Vienna was impoverished by the dissolution of the Austro-Hungarian Empire. It was reduced from the capital of a mighty nation to the capital of a tiny state. Its commerce and industry, drained and weakened, were prostrate. It no longer could lure tourists with the promise of pleasure and luxury. In the middle of this crisis, Vienna was saved from final disaster by its situation as a financial market. The Balkanization of Central Europe, which ruined it commercially and industrially, benefited it financially. Vienna, because of its geographical location in Europe, was uniquely qualified to be an important center of international finance. International bankers were the profiteers of the bankruptcy of the Austrian economy. The darkened, empty halls of Vienna's cabarets and cafes were turned into banking and foreign exchange offices. Here is another object lesson that a great financial market must be at the crossroads of international traffic.

The political capital may be distinct from the economic capital. I have already mentioned the contrast between Milan and Rome in the history of democratic and liberal Italy. The United States avoided this problem with a solution which may be very wise, but which is especially adapted to the federal structure of that country. Washington, the political and administrative capital, is aloof from all conflicts and competition between New York, Chicago, San Francisco, et cetera.

The fate of the capital depends on significant political changes, as is demonstrated in the history of Europe and of America itself. A political order has never been able to establish itself in a seat hostile to its spirit. The Europeanization policy of Peter the Great moved the Russian court from Moscow to Petrograd. Perhaps a presentiment of its mission in the East made the Bolshevik revolution feel more secure, in spite of its Western ideology, in the Kremlin in Moscow.

The Spanish conquest in Peru ended the power of Cuzco, capital of the Inca empire.[11] Lima was the capital of the colony. It

[11] In his book *Por la emancipación de América Latina* (pp. 90–91) Haya de la Torre contrasts and compares the colonial histories of Mexico and Peru. "In Mexico," he writes, "the races have mixed together and the new capital

was also the capital of the independence, although liberty was first proclaimed from Tacna, Cuzco, and Trujillo. It is the capital today, but will it be the capital tomorrow? This is not an irrelevant question in terms of a bold search into the future. The answer depends on whether first place in Peru's social and political reform is given to the rural Indian masses or to the coastal proletariat. The future of Lima, in any case, is inseparable from the mission of Lima, or even the will of Lima.

---

was built in the same place as the old. Mexico City and all of the country's large cities are located in the heart of the country, in the mountains, on the high plateaus that are crowned with volcanoes. The tropical coast serves for communication with the sea. The conquistador in Mexico fused with the Indian, became one with him in the very heart of his sierras, and forged a race which, though not absolutely a race in the strict sense of the word, is one nevertheless because of the homogeneity of its customs, the tendency toward a complete mingling of blood, and the continuity, without violent solutions, of the national ambience. That never happened in Peru. Indigenous, mountain Peru, the real Peru, lay beyond the western Andes. The old national cities—Cuzco, Cajamarca, et cetera—were disregarded. New and Spanish cities were built on the tropical coast where it never rains, where there are no changes of temperature, where that sensual, Andalusian atmosphere of our gay and submissive capital could develop." It is significant that these observations—more strongly worded than almost all of the usual complaints and boasts by Lima's critics—come from a native of Trujillo, that is, of one of "those new and Spanish cities" whose predominance he considers responsible for many things he detests. This and many other signs of the present revising of attitudes should be pondered by those who say that the revolutionary and regenerative spirit is exclusively of the sierra.

Literature on Trial

THE WORD "TRIAL" in this case is used in its legal sense. I do not propose to present a discourse on Peruvian literature, but only to testify in what I consider to be an open trial. It seems to me that so far in this trial the witnesses have been almost entirely for the defense and that it is time to call some witnesses for the prosecution. My testimony is admittedly partisan. Any critic, any witness, has a responsibility that he must consciously or unconsciously discharge. Despite dark suspicions to the contrary, I am positive and constructive by temperament and I condemn the iconoclastic and destructive bohemian as unethical; but my responsibility to the past compels me to vote against the defendant. I do not exempt myself from discharging it nor do I apologize for its partiality.

Piero Gobetti, with whom I feel great spiritual affinity, writes in one of his essays: "True realism is devoted to the forces that produce results and it has no use for results intellectually admired *a priori*. The realist knows that history is reform and that the process of reform is not limited to a diplomacy of the initiated but is carried out by individuals who operate as revolutionaries by setting different standards."[1]

I do not pretend to be an impartial or agnostic critic, which in any event I do not believe is possible. Any critic is influenced by philosophical, political, and moral concerns. Croce has proved that even the impressionistic and hedonistic criticism of Jules Lemaitre, which is supposed to be free of philosophical content, is related, no less than the criticism of Sainte Beuve, to the thought and philosophy of its times.[2]

Man's spirit is indivisible and it must be so to achieve plenitude and harmony. I declare without hesitation that I bring to literary exegesis all my political passions and ideas, although in view of the way this word has been misused, I should add that my politics are philosophy and religion.

---

[1] Piero Gobetti, *Opera critica*, I, 88. This idea is entirely in accord with Marxist dialectics and in no way excludes those *a priori* syntheses so cherished by intellectual opportunism. Outlining the personality of Domenico Giulotti, Papini's companion in the cultural adventure of the *Dizionario dell uomo salvatico*, Gobetti writes: "Individuals must take clear-cut positions. Compromise is the work of history and of history alone; it is a result." (ibid., p. 82). In the same book, concluding some observations about the Greek concept of life, he states: "The new test of truth is a task in harmony with the responsibility of each person. Ours is an era of struggle (struggle between men, between classes, between states) because only through struggle can abilities be tempered and can each person, by stubbornly defending his position, collaborate in the life process."

[2] Benedetto Croce, *Nuovi saggi di estetica*, pp. 205–207. With relentless logic, this same collection disqualifies the aestheticist and historicist trends in artistic historiography. It declares that "the true criticism of art is certainly aesthetic criticism, not because it scorns philosophy as a pseudo-aesthetic criticism, but because it functions as a philosophy or concept or art; and it is historical criticism, not because it is concerned with what is extrinsic to art, like pseudo-historical criticism, but because, having availed itself of historical data for an artistic reproduction (and at this point it is still not history), once the artistic reproduction is accomplished, history is made by deciding what has been reproduced, that is, by characterizing it according to the concept and establishing precisely what has happened. Therefore, the two trends that conflict in the undercurrents of criticism coincide in criticism; and historical criticism of art and aesthetic criticism of art are one and the same."

This does not mean that I judge literature and art without reference to aesthetics, but that in the depths of my consciousness the aesthetic concept is so intimately linked to my political and religious ideas that, although it does not lose its identity, it cannot operate independently or differently.

Riva Agüero judged literature with the criterion of a *civilista*. His essay on "the nature of literature in independent Peru"[3] is unmistakably colored, not only by political beliefs, but also by the sentiments of a class system. It is at the same time a piece of literary historiography and a political apologia.

The class system of the colonial *encomendero* underlies his

---

[3] Although or perhaps because it was written in his youth, *Carácter de la literatura del Perú independiente* is a vivid and sincere reflection of Riva Agüero's spirit and feelings. His later literary criticism does not basically alter this thesis. In its praise of the talented criollo and his *Comentarios reales*, his *Elogio del Inca Garcilaso* could have presaged a new attitude. But, in fact, neither his erudite curiosity about Inca history nor his ardent efforts to interpret the sierra landscape have diminished Riva Agüero's loyalty to the colony. His stay in Spain, as we all know, has intensified his conservative and viceroyal sympathies. In a book written in Spain, *El Perú histórico y artístico: Influencia y descendencia de las montañeces en él* (Santander, 1921), he shows a deeper concern with the Inca society, but this is only a sign of a scholarly interest that has been influenced by the opinions of Garcilaso and of the most objective and cultured of the chroniclers. Riva Agüero states that "at the time of the conquest, the social regime of Peru aroused enthusiasm in observers as scrupulous as Cieza de León and in men as learned as the Licenciado Polo de Ondegardo, the Oidor Santillán, the Jesuit author of *Revelación anónima*, and Father José de Acosta. The social content and agrarian regulations of the vagaries of the illustrious Mariana and of Pedro de Valencia (disciple of Arias Montano) may have been influenced not only by Platonic tradition but by the contemporary data of the Inca organization that made such an impression on all who studied it." Riva Agüero does not try to excuse his mistakes, as when he acknowledges that in his early criticism of *Ollantay* he had greatly exaggerated the Spanish inspiration of the present version in his essay on the "character of literature in independent Peru" and that, in the light of recent studies, even if *Ollantay* still appears to have been reconstructed by a colonial writer, "it must be admitted that its design, poetic techniques, all its songs and many of its passages are in the Inca tradition and only slightly modified by the editor." Nevertheless, none of these demonstrations of scholastic integrity nullifies the purpose and criteria of his work, which is intensely Spanish in tone and which pays homage to the motherland by championing the "deep-rooted" Spanish heritage of Peru.

opinions, which invariably are expressed in terms of Hispanism, colonialism, and social privilege. Riva Agüero departs from his political and social preoccupations only to the degree that he adopts the standards of a professor or a scholar, and then the departure is merely apparent, because never does his spirit move more securely in the academic and conservative sphere. Nor does Riva Agüero bother to conceal his political prejudices when his literary evaluations are mixed with anti-historical observations about the presumed error of the founders of independence in their choice of a republic over a monarchy or when he violently attacks the tendency to form parties around principles in opposition to the traditional oligarchical parties, on the grounds that such opposition would incite sectarian conflict and arouse social enmities.

Riva Agüero could not openly admit to the political bias of his exegesis: first, because it is only long after the time of his writing that we have learned to dispense with many obvious and useless deceptions; second, because, as a member of the aristocratic *encomendero* class, he was obliged to profess the principles and institutions of another class, the liberal bourgeoisie. Even though it felt itself to be monarchist, Hispanist, and traditionalist, that aristocracy had to reconcile its reactionary sentiment with the practice of a republican and capitalist policy and with respect for a democratic and bourgeois constitution.

With the end of uncontested *civilista* authority in the intellectual life of Peru, the scale of values established by Riva Agüero, together with all affiliated and related writings, has undergone revision.[4] I confront his unacknowledged *civilista* and colonialist

---

[4] I prefer to discuss and criticize Riva Agüero's thesis because I consider it to be the most representative and predominant. Further proof of Riva Agüero's pre-eminence and influence is the fact that later studies aspiring to critical impartiality and untouched by his political motives are attached to his opinions and evaluations. In the first volume of *La literatura peruana*, Luis Alberto Sánchez admits that García Calderón wrote in *Del roman-*

bias with my avowed revolutionary and socialist sympathies. I do not claim to be a temperate and impartial judge; I declare myself a passionate and belligerent adversary. Arbitrations and compromises take place in history, provided that the opponents engage in long, drawn-out disputes.

The Literature of the Colony

Language is the raw material that unites literature. The Spanish, Italian, and French literatures began with the first ballads and tales, artistic works of enduring value written in those languages. Directly derived from Latin and still not entirely differentiated from it, they were for a long time considered dialects. The national literature of the Latin peoples was born, historically, with the national language, which was the first element to delineate the general limits of a literature.

In the history of the West, the flowering of national literatures coincided with the political affirmation of the nation. It formed part of the movement which, through the Reformation and the Renaissance, created the ideological and spiritual factors of the liberal revolution and the capitalist order. The unity of European culture, maintained during the Middle Ages by Latin and by papal authority, was shattered by the nationalist movement, which individualized literature. "Nationalism" in literary historiography is therefore purely political in its origins and extraneous to the aesthetic concept of art. It was most vigorously defined in Germany, where the writings of the Schlegel brothers profoundly influenced literary criticism and historiography. In his justly celebrated *Storia della letteratura italiana*—praised by

---

ticismo al modernismo, dedicated to Riva Agüero, what is really a gloss of the latter's book. Although years later García Calderón was to do more research for his synthesis of *La literatura peruana*, he did not add much information to that already noted by his friend and colleague, the author of *La historia en el Perú*, nor did he attempt a new interpretation or go to the indispensable popular sources.

Brunetiére as a "history of Italian literature which I constantly quote and which is never read in France"—Francesco de Sanctis characterizes the criticism of the 1800's as "the cult of nationality, which so impresses modern critics and for which Schlegel exalts Calderón, a very nationalistic Spaniard, and disparages Metastasio, who was not in the least Italian."[5]

National literature in Peru, like Peruvian nationality itself, cannot renounce its Spanish ties. It is a literature written, thought, and felt in Spanish, although in many instances and to varying degrees the language is subject to indigenous influence in intonation and even in syntax and pronunciation. Indian civilization did not have a written language and therefore it did not acquire a literature; or rather, literature remained in the realm of ballads, legends, and choreography. Quechua writing and grammar are the work of the Spaniard, and Quechua literature belonged entirely to bilingual men of letters like El Lunarejo until the appearance of Inocencio Mamani, the young author of *Tucuipac Manashcan*.[6] The Spanish language, more or less Americanized, is the literary language and intellectual tool of Peru's still undefined nationality.

In literary historiography, the concept of a national literature is neither timeless nor very precise. No systematization can keep

[5] Francesco de Sanctis, *Teoria e storia della letteratura*, I, 186. Having already cited Croce's *Nuovi saggi di estetica*, I should mention that in reproving Adolf Bartels and Richard M. Meyer for their preoccupation with nationalism and modernism respectively in their histories of literature, Croce asserts that "it is not true that poets and other artists are the expression of the national conscience, of the race, of the stock, of the class, or of anything similar." Croce's reaction against the inordinate nationalism that characterized the literary historiography of the nineteenth century—with the exception of the exemplary European, George Brandes—is, like all reactions, extreme; but the vigilant and generous universalism of Croce responds to a need to resist the exaggerations of works imitating the imperial German models.

[6] See in nos. 12 and 14 of *Amauta* the news and comments of Gabriel Collazos and José Gabriel Cossío on the Quechua comedy by Inocencio Mamani, who had probably been exposed to the influence of Gamaliel Churata when he wrote it.

up with changing events. The nation itself is an abstraction, an allegory, a myth that does not correspond to a reality that can be scientifically defined. Commenting on Hebrew literature as an exception, De Sanctis states: "The idea of a national literature is an illusion. Its people would have to be as isolated as the Chinese are supposed to be (although the English have also penetrated China). The imagination and style now known as orientalism are not peculiarly of the Orient but of all the East and of all barbaric, primitive literatures. Greek poetry has Asiatic elements, Latin poetry has Greek, and Italian poetry has both Greek and Latin."[7]

The Quechua-Spanish dualism in Peru, still unresolved, prevents our national literature from being studied with the methods used for literatures that were created and developed without the intervention of the conquest. Peru is different from other countries of America where dualism is absent or does not constitute a problem. The individuality of Argentine literature, for example, expresses a strongly defined national personality.

The first stage of Peruvian literature could not escape its Spanish origin, not because it was written in the Spanish language, but because it was conceived with Spanish spirit and sentiment. Here, I see no discrepancy. Gálvez, high priest of the cult of the viceroyalty in literature, recognized as a critic that "the colonial period produced servile and inferior imitators of Spanish literature and especially of Góngora, from whom they took only the bombastic and the bad. They had no understanding of or feeling for the Peruvian scene, except Garcilaso [de la Vega, el Inca], who was moved by its natural beauty, and Caviedes, who in his acute observations of certain aspects of national life and in his criollo malice should be considered the forefather of Segura, Pardo, Palma, and Paz Soldán."[8]

The two exceptions, the first much more than the second, are

[7] De Sanctis, *Teoria e storia della letteratura*, I, 186–187.
[8] José Gálvez, *Posibilidad de una genuina literatura nacional*, p. 7.

indisputable. Garcilaso was a solitary figure in the literature of the colony. He was the meeting ground of two cultures and two eras. But he was more Inca than conquistador, more Quechua than Spaniard. It is this circumstance, also exceptional, that accounts for his originality and greatness.

Garcilaso was born of the first fruitful embrace of conquistador and Indian woman. He was historically the first Peruvian, if by "Peruvianness" we mean a social formation determined by the Spanish conquest and colonization. The name and work of Garcilaso fill an entire period of Peruvian literature. The first Peruvian, he nonetheless remained Spanish. From a historical-aesthetic standpoint his work belongs to the Spanish epic. It cannot be separated from Spain's most heroic undertaking: the discovery and conquest of America.

The early period of Peruvian literature was colonial and Spanish even in style and subject matter. All literature normally begins with the lyric,[9] as did the oral literature of the Peruvian Indian. The conquest transplanted to Peru, together with the Spanish language, an advanced literature that continued to evolve in the colony. The Spaniard had already developed the narrative from epic poem to novel. The novel is typical of the literary phase that begins with the Reformation and the Renaissance. It is basically the history of the individual in a bourgeois society and, from this point of view, Ortega y Gasset is not far wrong when he refers to the decline of the novel. The novel will be reborn, no doubt, as realistic art in the proletarian society. For the moment, however, the proletarian tale, as an expression of revolutionary deeds, is more epic than novel.

[9] In his *Teoria e storia della letteratura* (p. 205), De Sanctis says: "In art as in science, man's departure point is subjectivity and, therefore, lyricism is the earliest form of poetry. But subjectivity later turns into objectivity and subjective emotion in a narrative is secondary and incidental. Lyricism is the terrain of the ideal, narration is the terrain of the real. In the first, impression is purpose and action is occasion; in the second, the contrary is true. The first does not dissolve into prose except by destroying itself; the second is resolved in prose, which is its natural tendency."

The medieval epic, which was disappearing from Europe at the time of the conquest, was revived in Peru. The conquistador could feel and describe the conquest in epic writing. The work of Garcilaso falls between epic and history. The epic, as De Sanctis remarks belongs to the heroic days.[10] After Garcilaso, the hopelessly mediocre literature of the colony offers no original epic creation. Although the writers of the colony generally repeated or continued the themes of Spanish authors, they lagged behind because of distance. The titles in colonial literature betray the pedantry and outdated classicism of the authors. It is a list that collects and copies, when it does not plagiarize. The only personal voice is that of Caviedes, who expressed the *limeño* bent for mockery and mischief. El Lunarejo, despite his Indian blood, was above all an admirer of Góngora. This attitude is typical of an old literature which, having exhausted its renaissance, becomes baroque and overly cultivated. The *Apologético en favor de Góngora* therefore follows the tradition of Spanish literature.

The Survival of Colonialism

Our literature did not cease being Spanish when the republic was founded. For many years it continued to be, if not Spanish, colonial—a tardy echo of the classicism and then of the romanticism of the mother country.

Because of the special character of Peruvian literature, it cannot be studied within the framework of classicism, romanticism, and modernism; nor of ancient, medieval, and modern; nor of popular and literary poetry, et cetera. I shall not use the Marxist classification of literature as feudal or aristocratic, bourgeois

[10] De Sanctis writes: "In times of struggle, mankind ascends from one idea to another and the intellect does not triumph unless fantasy is shaken. When an idea has prevailed and developed into a peaceful exercise, the epic is replaced by history. Epic poetry, therefore, can be defined as the ideal history of mankind in its passage from one idea to another." (Ibid., p. 207.)

or proletarian. In order not to strengthen the impression that I have organized my case along political or class lines, I shall base it on aesthetic history and criticism. This will serve as a method of explanation rather than as a theory that *a priori* judges and interprets works and their authors.

A modern literary, not sociological, theory divides the literature of a country into three periods: colonial, cosmopolitan, and national. In the first period, the country, in a literary sense, is a colony dependent on its metropolis. In the second period, it simultaneously assimilates elements of various foreign literatures. In the third period, it shapes and expresses its own personality and feelings. Although this theory of literature does not go any farther, it is broad enough for our purposes.

The colonial cycle is clearly defined in Peruvian literature. Our literature is colonial not only because of its dependence on Spain but especially because of its subservience to the spiritual and material remnants of the colony. Felipe Pardo, arbitrarily designated by Gálvez as one of the precursors of literary Peruvianness, repudiated the republic and its institutions not simply out of aristocratic feelings but more out of royalist feelings. All his satire, second rate at best, reflects the mentality of a magistrate or *encomendero* who resents a revolution that, at least in theory, declares the mestizo and Indian to be his equals. His jeers are inspired by his class consciousness. Pardo y Aliaga does not speak as a Peruvian. He speaks as a man who feels Spanish in a country conquered by Spain for the descendants of its captains and educated class.

This same spirit, to a lesser degree but with the same results, characterizes almost all our literature until the *colónida* generation which, rebelling against the past and its values, declares its allegiance to González Prada and Eguren, the two most liberal writers in Spanish literature.

What kept this nostalgia for the colony alive so long in our literature? It was not the individual writer's attachment to the past. The reason must be sought in a world more complex than that usually glanced at by the critic.

The literature of a country is maintained by its economic and political substratum. In a country dominated by the descendants of *encomenderos* and magistrates of the viceroyalty, nothing could have been more natural than serenades under balconies. The mediocre writers of a republic that considered itself heir to the conquest could only labor to embellish the viceroyal heraldry. A few superior intellects—forerunners of future events in any country—were able to elude the fate imposed by history on the lackeys of the latifundium.

Without roots, our colonial literature was meager, sickly, and weak. Life, says Wilson, comes from the land. Art is nourished on the sap of tradition, history, and people. In Peru, literature did not grow out of the indigenous tradition, history, and people. It was created by the importation of Spanish literature and sustained by imitation of that literature. An unhealthy umbilical cord has kept it tied to the mother country.

For this reason, during the colonization we had nothing but baroque and pedantic clerics and magistrates whose great-grandchildren became the romantic troubadours of the republic.

Colonial literature, despite an occasional pale evocation of the empire, lacked any aptitude or imagination for reconstructing the Inca past. Its historiographer, Riva Agüero, precluded from criticizing this incapacity, hastens to justify it and cites in his support a writer of the metropolis. "The events of the Inca empire," he writes, "according to a famous literary critic (Menéndez y Pelayo), can be of no more interest to us than are the tales of the Turdetanos and the Sarpetanos to the Spaniards." He ends his essay with these words:

There is a theory, which I find limited and unproductive, that literature can be Americanized by going back to before the conquest and bringing to life the Quechua and Inca civilizations with the ideas and feelings of the natives. Menéndez y Pelayo, Rubio, and Juan Valera all agree that this is not to Americanize but to romanticize. Those civilizations and semi-civilizations are dead and extinct. There is no way to revive their tradition because they left no literature. For criollos of Spanish blood they are foreign and strange and nothing links us to them; they are just as foreign and strange to the mestizos and Indians who have been Europeanized by education. Garcilaso de la Vega is unique among the latter.

The mentality of Riva Agüero is typical of the descendants of the conquest, the heirs to the colony, for whom the views of the scholars of the Corte were articles of faith. In his opinion, "there is much more material to be found in the Spanish expeditions of the sixteenth century and in the adventures of the conquest."[11]

Even when the republic reached maturity, our writers never thought of Peru as anything but a Spanish colony. Their domesticated imagination sent them to Spain in search of models and even themes. The *Elegía a la muerte de Alfonso XII*, for example, was written by Luis Benjamín Cisneros, who was, nonetheless, within the graceless and heavy romantic style, one of the most liberal spirits of the 1800's.

The Peruvian writer has almost never felt any ties with the common people. Even had he so desired, he was not capable of interpreting the arduous task of forming a new Peru. The new Peru was vague; only the Inca empire and the colony were clearly defined, and he chose the colony. And between this fledgling Peruvian literature and the Inca empire and the Indian came the conquest, isolating them from each other.

After Spain destroyed the Inca civilization, the conquistador established a new state that excluded and oppressed the Indian. With the native race enslaved, Peruvian literature had to be-

[11] José de la Riva Agüero, *Carácter de la literatura del Perú independiente* (Lima, 1905).

come more criollo and coastal as it became less Spanish. For this reason, no vigorous literature could emerge in Peru. The mixture of invader and Indian did not produce a homogeneous type in Peru. To the Spanish and Quechua blood was added a torrent of African blood and later, with the importation of coolie labor, a little Asiatic blood. In addition, the tepid, bland climate of the lowland where these diverse ethnic elements were blended could not be expected to produce a strong personality.

It was inevitable that our motley ethnic composition should affect our literary process. Literature could not develop in Peru as it did in Argentina, where the fusion of European and Indian produced the gaucho. The latter has permeated Argentine literature and made it the most individualistic in Spanish America. The best Argentine writers have found their themes and characters in folklore. Santos Vega, Martín Fierro, Anastasio el Pollo were all folk heroes long before they became literary creations. Even today, Argentine literature, which is open to the most modern and cosmopolitan influences, reaffirms its gaucho heritage. Poets in the vanguard of the new generation proclaim their descendance from the gaucho Martín Fierro and from his bizarre family of folksingers. Jorge Luis Borges, saturated in westernism and modernism, frequently adopts the accent of the countryside.

In independent Peru, writers like Listas and Hermosillas and their disciples almost invariably disdained the common people. Their fantasy of provincial nobility was impressed only by the Spanish, the viceroyal. But Spain was far away. Although the viceroyalty survived in the feudal regime established by the conquistadors, it belonged to the past. All the literature of these authors, therefore, appears to be flimsy and weak, dangling in the present. It is a literature of undeclared emigrants, nostalgic relics.

The few writers with vitality in this weary procession of wornout dignitaries of rhetoric are the ones who somehow portrayed the people. When it ignores the authentic, living Peru, Peruvian literature is a heavy, indigestible miscellany of Spanish literature. The "ay" of the Indian and the pirouette of the *zambo* are the only notes of animation and veracity in this flaccid literature. The fabric of *Tradiciones* sparkles with the thread of Lima's gossipy lower class, which is one of the vital forces in traditionalist prose. Melgar, scorned by scholars, will outlive Althaus, Pardo, and Salaverry, because his melancholy songs will always give the people a glimpse of their sentimental tradition and genuine literary past.

Ricardo Palma, Lima, and the Colony

Colonialism—nostalgic evocation of the viceroyalty—seeks to appropriate the figure of Ricardo Palma. This servile, mawkish literature claims to be of the same substance as *Tradiciones*. The "futurist" generation, which I have often described as the most backward of our generations, has dedicated most of its eloquence to assuming the glory of Palma. Here, for once, it has maneuvered adroitly and Palma officially appears as the foremost representative of colonialism. But a serious examination of the work of Palma, comparing it with the political and social process of Peru and with the inspiration of the colonialist genre, reveals that this appropriation is completely artificial. To classify the writing of Palma as colonialist literature is to diminish if not to distort it. *Tradiciones* cannot be identified with a literature that, in a tone and spirit peculiar to the academic clientele of the feudal class, reverently exalts the colony and its events.

Felipe Pardo and José Antonio de Lavalle, both avowed conservatives, are unctuous in their recollections of the colony. Ricardo Palma, on the other hand, reconstructs it with rollicking realism and an irreverent and satiric imagination. Whereas the interpretation of Palma is rough and lively, that of the prose and poetry writers of the serenade under the balconies of the viceroyalty, so pleasing to the ears of the people of the *ancien ré-*

gime, is devout and lyrical. The two versions do not resemble each other either in substance or in approach.

The reason for their very different fates lies basically in a difference in quality, but also in a difference in spirit. Quality is always spirit. The heavy, academic work of Lavalle and other colonialists is forgotten because it cannot be popular; the work of Palma lives on because it can be and is popular.

The spirit of *Tradiciones* is evidenced throughout the book. Riva Agüero, true to the interests of his group and class, identifies it with colonialism in his study of the literature of independent Peru. He recognizes that Palma, "belonging to the generation that broke with the mannerisms of the writers of the colony," was an author who was "a liberal and a son of the republic." But deep down, Riva Agüero is disturbed by the irreverent and unorthodox spirit of Palma.

Riva Agüero tries to subdue this feeling, but it emerges more than once in his study. He states that when Palma "speaks of the church, the Jesuits, the nobility, he smiles and he makes the reader smile." He hastens to add that it is "a delicate smile that does not wound." He says that he will not be the one to reproach Palma for his Voltairean attitude. But he ends by confessing his true feelings: "Sometimes the jests of Palma, no matter how kindly and gentle, destroy his historical sensibilities. We observe that, in freeing himself of the traditional pretensions, he has become unsympathetic and indifferent to his material."[12]

If a commentator and historiographer of Peruvian literature who manages to praise Palma and at the same time to defend the colony explicitly differentiates Palma from Pardo and Lavalle, how has it been possible to create and maintain the error of lumping them together? The explanation is easy. This error originated in the personal disagreement between Palma and

[12] Ibid.

González Prada and it has been perpetuated by the conflicting attitudes of the "Palmistas" and the "Pradistas." Haya de la Torre, in a letter on "Peruvian Mercutio" to the magazine *Sagitario* of La Plata, makes the following comment: "Between Palma, who mocked, and Prada, who lashed, the sons of that doubly censured past and social class preferred the razor edge to the whip."[13] Haya goes on to make a point that is extremely well taken on the historical and political meaning of *Tradiciones*:

Personally, I believe that Palma was interested in but not attached to traditions. Palma sank his pen into the past in order to shake it on high and laugh at it. No institution or man of the colony or even of the republic escaped the unerring aim of the irony, the sarcasm, and, always, the ridicule of his witty criticism. It is well-known that Palma was the literary enemy of the Catholic clergy and that his *Tradiciones* was abhorred by monks and nuns. By a curious paradox, Palma found himself surrounded, adulated, and nullified by a troupe of distinguished intellectuals, Catholics, wealthy heirs, and highly placed admirers.[14]

It should not be wondered at that this penetrating analysis of the meaning and affiliation of *Tradiciones* comes from a writer who has never practiced literary criticism. Mere literary erudition does not suffice for a profound interpretation of the spirit of literature. Political acumen and historical perspective are more important. The professional critic considers literature by itself without relating it to politics, economics, the totality of life. Therefore, his investigation does not reach the essence of literary events by exploring their beginnings and subconscious.

A history of Peruvian literature that takes into account its

---

[13] In *Sagitario*, no. 3 (1926), and in *Por la emancipación de la América Latina* (Buenos Aires, 1927), p. 139.
[14] Ibid., p. 139.

social and political roots will end the convention against which today only a vanguard protests. It will then be seen that Palma is closer to González Prada than has appeared until now.[15]

The *Tradiciones* of Palma is politically and socially democratic; Palma interprets the common people. His ridicule, which reflects the mocking discontent of the criollo demos, undermines the prestige of the viceroyalty and its aristocracy. The satire of *Tradiciones* does not probe very deeply nor does it hit very hard. Precisely for this reason it is identified with the sugar-coated humor of the bland, sensual demos. Lima could not produce any other kind of literature and *Tradiciones* exhausts and sometimes exceeds its possibilities.

If the revolution of independence in Peru had been the undertaking of a relatively solid bourgeoisie, republican literature would have adopted another tone. The new ruling class would have expressed itself simultaneously in the work of its statesmen and in the words, style, and attitude of its poets, novelists, and critics. But in Peru the advent of the republic did not herald the advent of a new ruling class.

The revolution was continental in scope and barely Peruvian. There was only a handful of Peruvian liberals, Jacobins, and revolutionaries. The best blood and the greatest energy were expended in battles and in times of struggle. Because the republic was based on the army of the revolution, we had a stormy interim of military rule during which a revolutionary class could not consolidate itself and the conservative class automatically emerged again. The *encomenderos* and landholders, who during the revolution wavered between being patriots and being royalists, openly took charge of the republic. The colonial and monarchical aristocracy transformed itself officially into a republican bourgeoisie. Although the socio-economic system of the colony superficially adapted itself to the institutions created by the

[15] In a letter to *Amauta*, no. 4, Haya, carried away by his enthusiasm, undoubtedly exaggerates this vindication.

revolution, it was saturated in the colonial spirit. Underneath a coldly formal liberalism, this class yearned for the lost vice-royalty.

The criollo or, rather, demos of Lima was neither consistent nor original. From time to time he was aroused by the clarion call of some budding caudillo; but once the spasm had passed, he fell once again into voluptuous somnolence. All his impatience and rebelliousness were converted into a joke, an impertinent remark, or an epigram, which found their literary expression in the biting satire of *Tradiciones*.

Palma belongs to a middle-class elite which, by a complex combination of historical circumstances, was not permitted to turn into a bourgeoisie. Like this composite, larval class, Palma nursed a latent resentment against the oldtime, reactionary aristocracy. The satire of *Tradiciones* frequently sinks its sharp teeth into the men of the republic. But in contrast to the reactionary satire of Felipe Pardo y Aliaga, it does not attack the republic itself. Palma, together with the demos in Lima, is conquered by the anti-oligarchical oratory of Piérola. And, above all, he remains faithful to the liberal ideology of independence.

Colonialism or *civilismo*, using Riva Agüero and other intellectuals as its spokesmen, takes over Palma, not only because this appropriation presents no threat to its policies, but mainly because of the hopeless mediocrity of its own literary personnel. Critics from this class know that it is useless to try to inflate the work of Felipe Pardo or José Antonio Lavalle. The *civilista* literature has produced nothing but small, dry exercises in classicism or graceless, vulgar attempts at romanticism. Therefore, it needs to acquire Palma in order to display, rightfully or not, an authentic prestige.

But I should make clear that colonialism is not solely responsible for this error. It is partly due—as I have already said—to "González-Pradism." In an essay on the literature of Peru by Federico More, I find the following judgment on the author of

Tradiciones: "Ricardo Palma, representative, exponent, and sentinel of colonialism, tells historical anecdotes and has a repertory of amusing stories. He writes with an eye to the Royal Academy and, in order to recount the nonsense and gossipy remarks of the little marchionesses with their kinky hair and thick lips, he tries to use the Spanish of the Golden Age."[16] More claims that only the "coarse snicker" of Palma will remain.

For some people this judgment is no more than a reflection of the notorious rancor of More, whose loves are not taken seriously but whose enmities cannot be discounted. For two reasons his views should be given consideration: first, the special belligerence with which More supports González Prada; second, the thoughtfulness of the essay that contains these sentences.

In this essay More makes a conscientious effort to analyze the spirit of national literature. His argument, although not totally acceptable, deserves to be carefully examined. More starts from a premise that is shared by every profound criticism: "Literature," he writes, "is only the translation of a political and social state." The judgment on Palma, in brief, belongs to a study containing valuable ideas, not to an impoverished after-dinner dissertation. And this compels us to take notice of it and to comment on it. But, while doing so, the essential lines of More's argument should be pointed out.

More looks for the elements of race and land in Peruvian literature. He studies its colors and outline, but he disregards its complementary tints and contours. This is a method that a pamphleteer, not a critic, would use. Whereas his argument gains emphasis, it loses flexibility, and it gives us a very static image of Peruvian literature.

Although his conclusions are not always correct, they are based on true concepts. More is aware of Peruvian dualism. He avers that in Peru "one is either colonial or Inca." Having

[16] Federico More, "De un ensayo sobre las literaturas del Perú" in *El Diario de la Marina* (Havana, 1924) and in *El Norte* (Trujillo, 1924).

written over and over again that Peru is son of the conquest and creation of the coast, I must agree with More regarding the origin and process of the conflict between Incaism and colonialism. Like More, I am inclined to think that that conflict, that antagonism, is and will be for many years the decisive factor, sociologically and politically, in Peruvian life.

Peruvian dualism is reflected and expressed in literature.

Literature [More writes] presents a divided Peru, as is logical. A basic fact emerges: the Andean is rural, the *limeño* is urban. And the same is true of the two literatures. For those who act under the influence of Lima, everything has an Ibero-African flavor, everything is romantic and sensual. For those of us who act under the influence of Cuzco, the most beautiful and profound part of life is realized in mountains and valleys where everything has an indecipherable subjectivity and is touched with drama. The *limeño* is susceptible to color, the *serrano* to music. The heirs to the colony regard love as a challenge. The children of the fallen race hear in love a choir that transmits the voice of destiny.

But this literature of the sierra which More describes so vehemently, contrasting it with colonial or Lima literature, has only just begun to exist. It has no history and almost no tradition. The two outstanding writers of the republic, Palma and González Prada, belong to Lima. I am a great admirer, as will be seen further on, of Abelardo Gamarra; but I think that More tends to overestimate him, although in one passage of his study he concedes that "Gamarra, unfortunately, was not a fully rounded, many-sided artist, clear and sparkling, the complete man of letters that is needed."

More himself recognizes that the "Andean regions, Incaism, still have no great writer to synthesize in thundering, coruscating pages the anxieties, temper, and moods of the Inca soul." He thereby confirms the thesis that until Palma and González Prada, Peruvian literature is colonial or Spanish. The literature of the sierra, with which More compares it, did not acquire a personality of its own before Palma and González Prada. Lima imposed its models on the provinces. Worse yet, the provinces came to Lima for their models. The polemic prose of provincial regionalism and radicalism descends from González Prada, whom More justifiably reproaches for his love of rhetoric.

More believes that Gamarra represents an integral Peru and that he opens a new chapter in our literature. In my opinion, the new chapter begins with González Prada, who marks the transition from pure Hispanism to the beginning of a Europeanism that will have decisive consequences.

But Ricardo Palma, whom More mistakenly designates as "representative, exponent, and sentinel of colonialism," is also, despite his limitations, of this integral Peru that begins to take shape in us. Palma interprets the criollo, the mestizo, and the middle-class elite of a republican Lima which, even if it is the one that acclaims Piérola—who is more of Arequipa than of Lima in temperament and style—is no less the one that in our time criticizes its own tradition, rejects its colonial lineage, denounces its centralism, supports the claims of the Indian, and extends both hands to the rebels of the provinces.

More sees only colonial Lima—conservative, somnolent, frivolous. "There is no ideological or emotional issue," he says, "that has produced a reaction in Lima. Neither modernism in literature, nor Marxism in politics, nor symbolism in music, nor expressionism in painting has stirred the sons of this sedative city. Voluptuousness is the tomb of an inquiring mind." But this is not correct. Lima, where the first nucleus of industrialism has been established, is the Lima where, in perfect accord with the historic development of the nation, the first resounding word of Marxism has been pronounced. More, somewhat disconcerted by his country, may not know this, but he can sense it. In Buenos Aires and La Plata there are many who are qualified to inform him of the protests of a vanguard that represents a new national spirit in Lima, as in Cuzco, Trujillo, and Jauja.

The accusations against colonialism, or *limeñismo* as More prefers to call it, have originated in Lima. Here in the capital we are putting the capital on trial—in open battle with what Luis Alberto Sánchez calls *perricholismo* and with a passion and severity that Sánchez himself finds alarming.[17] In Lima some of us had evolved from the aesthetic values of D'Annunzio, imported by Valdelomar, to the social criticism of the journal *España*. Ten years ago we founded *Nuestra Epoca*, in which, without reservation and without compromising with any group or caudillo, we called to account the old politics.[18] In Lima some student spokesmen for the new spirit created the popular universities five years ago and inscribed the name of González Prada on their banner.

Henríquez Ureña says that there are two Americas: one good and one bad. The same can be said of Lima. Lima has no roots in an autochthonous past. Lima is daughter of the conquest. But from the moment that it intellectually and spiritually becomes less Spanish in order to become a little cosmopolitan, from the moment it shows concern for contemporary ideas and issues, Lima no longer appears exclusively as the home of colonialism and Hispanism. The new Peruvianness will be created, using the Indian as its historic cement. Its axis will probably rest on Andean stone rather than on the clay of the coast. But Lima, restless and reformist, wants to participate in this creative work.

González Prada

In our literature, González Prada heralds the transition from the colonial to the cosmopolitan period. Ventura García Cal-

---

[17] See the essay "Regionalism and Centralism" in this book.

[18] Only two issues of *Nuestra Epoca* (July, 1918) were published and they were rapidly sold out. Both issues followed a tendency strongly influenced by *España*, Araquistain's journal, a tendency that was to reappear a year later in the short-lived newspaper *La Razón*, which is best remembered for its campaign for university reform.

derón describes him to be "the least Peruvian" of our writers. But we have already seen that until González Prada, the Peruvian element in this literature is still not Peruvian, but only colonial. The author of *Páginas libres* appears as an author whose spirit is Western and whose culture is European. But within a Peruvianness that is not yet distinct and positive, why should he be considered the least Peruvian of the writers who interpret it? Because he is the least Spanish? Because he is not colonial? The reason turns out to be paradoxical. Because he is the least Spanish and because he is not colonial, his writing announces the possibility of a Peruvian literature. It represents liberation from the mother country and the final rupture with the viceroyalty.

This Parnassian, this Hellenist, marmorean and pagan, is historically and spiritually much more Peruvian than all those in our literary process who, before and after him, collected and repeated Spanish literature. In this generation there surely does not exist a single heart that feels that the bad-tempered and nostalgic disciple of Lista is more Peruvian than the pamphleteering iconoclast who attacked the past that commanded the loyalties of the former together with hack writers of the same stamp and ancestry.

González Prada did not interpret this country; he did not examine its problems; he did not bequeath a program to the generation that followed. Nonetheless, he represents an instant, the first lucid instant, in the conscience of Peru. Federico More calls him a forerunner of the new Peru, of the integral Peru. But in this respect, Prada has been more than a forerunner. The devious and rhetorical prose of *Páginas libres* contains the seed of the new national spirit. In his famous speech at the Politeama in 1888, González Prada says: "The real Peru does not consist of the criollos and foreigners who live in the strip of land between the Pacific and the Andes; the nation is formed by the multi-

tudes of Indians scattered along the eastern stretch of the cor-
dillera.[19]

Despite his grandiloquent style, González Prada never scorned
the common people. On the contrary, he always championed
their humble cause. He warned his followers against the futility
and sterility of a literature for the elite. "Plato," he reminded
them in a lecture at the Ateneo," said that the populace was an
excellent language teacher. Languages are invigorated and re-
freshed in the fount of popular speech, much more than in the
dead rules of the grammarians and in the prehistoric exhuma-
tions of the erudite. Original words, graphic expressions, daring
constructions spring from the songs and sayings of the common
people. In the same way that infusorians change continents, the
masses transform languages." "The true poet," he stated in another part of the same speech, "resembles a tree growing on a
mountain top: with its branches, which are the imagination, it
reaches toward the clouds; with its roots, which are the feelings,
it clings to the earth." And in his notes on language, he repeated
the same thought in other words:

Masterpieces are noted for their accessibility; they are not the heritage of a chosen few but of all men of good sense. Homer and
Cervantes are democratic geniuses: a child understands them. The
talents that claim to be aristocratic and incomprehensible to the
multitude use abstruse form to conceal emptiness. If Herodotus had
written like Gracián, if Pindar had composed like Góngora, would
they have been listened to and applauded at the Olympic games?
Look at the great writers who shook men's souls in the sixteenth
and eighteenth centuries, especially Voltaire, whose prose was as
natural as breathing, as clear as distilled alcohol.[20]

At the same time, González Prada condemned colonialism.
In the Ateneo conference, after making clear the consequences

[19] Manuel González Prada, *Páginas libres.*
[20] Ibid.

of silly, senile imitation of Spanish literature, he openly advocated breaking this bond. "Let us leave behind our childish ways and look to other literatures for new elements and inspirations. We prefer the free and democratic spirit of this century to the conservative spirit of monarchical nations. Let us study the masterpieces of Spanish authors and enrich their melodious language; but let us always remember that intellectual dependence on Spain will prolong our infancy."[21]

In the writing of González Prada our literature begins to have contact with other literatures. González Prada represents in particular the French influence. But in general he has the merit of having opened the way to various foreign influences. His poetry and prose show an intimate knowledge of Italian literature. His prose often rails against academicians and purists and unorthodoxly delights in neologisms and gallicisms. His verse found new moulds and exotic rhythms in other literatures.

Clearly perceiving the hidden although not unknown link between conservative ideology and academic literature, González Prada attacked the one and denounced the other. Now that we are aware of the close relationship between the serenades to the viceroyalty in literature and the domination of the feudal class in economics and politics, this aspect of his thought acquires new significance.

As González Prada declares, all literature attitudes, consciously or unconsciously, reflect political feelings and bias. Literature is not independent of other categories of history. Who does not recognize, for example, the political purpose behind the ostensibly literary definition of González Prada as the "least Peruvian of our writers"? To deny Peruvianness to his personality is simply a way of denying the validity of his protest in Peru. It is a disguised attempt to disqualify his rebellion. The same label of exoticism is used today against the ideas of the vanguard.

[21] Ibid.

Since the death of Prada, those who were not able to undermine his influence or his example have changed tactics. They
have tried to distort and diminish his figure by praising him and
claiming to be his heirs and disciples. González Prada has run
the risk of becoming an official academic figure. Fortunately,
the new generation has been on guard against this strategem.

Youth distinguishes between what is topical and temporary
in the writing of González Prada and what is timeless and
eternal. They know that in Prada it is the spirit, not the letter,
that matters. The false González-Pradists repeat the letter; the
genuine ones repeat the spirit.

A study of González Prada belongs to literary criticism rather
than to political reporting. The fact that his work has greater
political than literary significance does not contradict or conflict
with the fact that, first and foremost, his work in itself was
more literary than political.

Everyone considers González Prada a man of words, not of
action. But this is not what makes him more literary than political. It is the words themselves.

The word can be a program or a doctrine. No doctrines or
programs as such are presented in *Páginas libres* or in *Horas de
lucha*. In the speeches and essays that compose these books, González Prada does not use the language of a statesman or sociologist to try to define Peruvian reality. He only suggests it in the
language of an author. He does not express his thought in concrete proposals or ideas; he envelopes them in phrases that are
effective as propaganda and rhetoric but of little practical and
scientific value. "Peru is a mountain crowned with a cemetery."
"Peru is a sick body: where a finger is pressed, pus bursts
forth." The most memorable phrases of González Prada reveal
the man of letters, not the statesman. They are an indictment,
not a call to action.

The radical movement itself originated as a literary and not
as a political phenomenon. The Unión Nacional or Radical

party began as a "Literary Circle" and turned into a political group, thereby obeying the mandate of its era. The biological process of Peru called for politicians rather than authors. Literature is not bread but a luxury. The writers around González Prada vaguely felt the vital needs of this lacerated and impoverished nation. "The 'Literary Circle,' a pacific society of poets and dreamers," said González Prada in his speech at the Olimpo in 1887, "is changing into a militant propaganda center. Where is the source of radicalism in literature? We receive gusts from the hurricanes that sweep over European capitals and echoes of the voice of a republican and free-thinking France. Our youth openly battles to put a violent end to what seems likely to die a lingering death; it is impatient to clear the way and raise the red flag over the crumbling towers of national literature."[22]

González Prada did not resist the forces of history that drove him from tranquil Parnassian contemplation into harsh political combat. But he could not draw up a battle plan for his troops. His individualistic, anarchical, solitary spirit was not suited to the direction of a vast collective enterprise.

When the Radical movement is studied, it is said that González Prada did not have the temperament of a leader, a caudillo. It should also be pointed out that his temperament was basically literary. If González Prada had not been born in a country that urgently needed to be reorganized and revitalized both politically and socially, in which a strictly artistic work could not bear fruit, he would never have been tempted to form a party.

His culture, like his temperament, was mainly literary and philosophical. His speeches and articles reveal that he lacked any formal training in economics and politics. His judgments, imprecations, and aphorisms are unmistakably literary in in-

22 Ibid.

spiration. I have quoted some of the penetrating observations on sociology and history that are frequently discovered in the setting of his elegant and sparkling prose. But as a whole, his work is literary in style and structure.

Nourished on nationalism and positivism, González Prada exalted the value of science. This attitude is peculiar to the modern literature of his time. Science, Reason, Progress were the myths of the nineteenth century. González Prada, who followed the road of liberalism and Encyclopedism to arrive at the utopia of anarchism, fervently adopted these myths. Even his verses express his rationalist spirit: "Down with foolish sentiment! Let us worship divine Reason!"

It fell to González Prada to announce only what men of another generation ought to do. He preached realism. Denouncing the vaporous verbosity of tropical rhetoric, he urged his contemporaries to get their feet back on the ground. "Let us end our millenial trip through tenuous idealism and let us return to the seat of reality, recalling that outside Nature there is nothing but illusory symbolism, mythological fantasy, and metaphysical shadow. At these rarified heights, we are becoming nebulous and ethereal. Let us harden ourselves. It is better to be iron than mist."[23]

But he himself never succeeded in becoming a realist; in his time, realism was historical materialism. Although the beliefs of González Prada never constrained his audacity or his freedom, he left to others the work of creating Peruvian socialism. After the Radical party failed, he gave his loyalty to the distant and abstract utopianism of Kropotkin. And in the dispute between Marxists and Bakuninists, he supported the latter. In this, as in all his conflicts with reality, he reacted according to his literary and aristocratic affinities.

[23] Ibid.

Because the spirit and culture of González Prada were literary, the Radical movement has not willed to us a series of even elementary studies on Peruvian reality or a body of specific ideas on the problems of Peru. The program of the Radical party, which in any event was not drawn up by González Prada, is an exercise in the political prose of a "literary circle," none other than that of the Unión Nacional, as we have already seen.

González Prada, although influenced by all the great myths of his time, is not uniformly positivist. He burns with the fire of the eighteenth-century rationalist. His Reason is passionate and revolutionary. The positivism and historical materialism of the nineteenth century represent a domesticated rationalism. They reflect the temper and the interests of a bourgeoisie which, with power, has turned conservative. The rational, scientific spirit of González Prada is not satisfied with the mediocre, timid conclusions of bourgeois reason and science. In González Prada the intrepid Jacobin lives on, intact.

Javier Prado, García Calderón, and Riva Agüero reveal a conservative positivism as opposed to the revolutionary positivism of González Prada. The ideologists of *civilismo* were true to their social prejudices when they submitted us to the authority of Taine. The ideologist of radicalism claimed always to have beliefs superior to and different from those which in France were identified with a movement of political reaction and which here in Peru were used by the educated oligarchies as an apologia.

Notwithstanding his rationalist and scientific affinities, González Prada was saved from exaggerated intellectualism by his artistic sensibilities and his devotion to justice. Deep inside this Parnassian, there is a romantic who never despairs of the power of the spirit.

One of his penetrating opinions on Renan, who *ne dépasse pas le doute*, proves to us that González Prada was well aware of the risks of excessive criticism:

All the defects of Renan are explained by his overly critical spirit. His fear of being deceived and his preoccupation with keeping himself pure and passionless made him affirm everything with certain reservations or deny everything with certain limitations; that is, he did not affirm or deny and he even contradicted himself, for on occasion he would submit an idea and, immediately qualifying it, go on to defend the contrary. This accounts for his lack of popularity; the masses only understand and follow men who are frank and violent in their affirmation—with words, like Mirabeau, with deeds, like Napoleon.

González Prada always prefers affirmation to negation or doubt. He is bold and courageous in thought and he shuns uncertainty. He feels acutely the need to *dépasser le doute*. Vasconcelos has a phrase which could have been written by González Prada: "pessimism regarding the realities, optimism regarding the ideal." His words are frequently pessimistic, but they are almost never skeptical.

In his study of the ideology of González Prada that forms part of his book *El nuevo absoluto*, Mariano Ibérico Rodríguez well defines the thinker of *Páginas libres* in the following words:

In tune with his times, he has great faith in the efficacy of scientific work. He believes in the existence of inflexible and eternal universal laws, but his belief in science and determinism does not lead him to a narrow, moral eudaemonism or to Spinoza's resigned acceptance of cosmic necessity. On the contrary, his restless, free spirit transcended the logical consequences of his ideas to advocate action and struggle, to affirm liberty and life. Prada's anarchical declarations obviously recall some of Nietzsche's vast philosophy, and, as in Nietzsche, the determinist concept of reality opposes the exultant drive of the inner force.[24]

For these and other reasons, we feel close to González Prada in spirit, if not in many of his ideas. González Prada deceived himself, for example, when he preached anti-religion. Today

[24] Mariano Ibérico Rodríguez, *El nuevo absoluto*, p. 45.

much more is known than in his time about many matters, including religion. We know that a revolution is always religious. The word "religion" has a new value and it no longer serves only to designate a ritual or a church. It is of little importance that the Soviets write on their propaganda posters that "religion is the opium of the people." Communism is essentially religious, but not in the old sense of the word, which still misleads so many. González Prada preached the passing of all religious beliefs without realizing that he himself was the bearer of a faith. This rationalist is to be most admired for his passion; this atheist, almost pagan, must be respected for his moral asceticism. His atheism is religious, especially when it appears to be most vehement, most absolute. González Prada is found in his creed of justice, in his doctrine of love, and not in the rather vulgar anti-clericalism of some pages of *Horas de lucha*.

The ideology of *Páginas libres* and *Horas de lucha* is now largely out of date. But what is fundamental and enduring in González Prada does not depend on the validity of his beliefs and judgments. His beliefs do not even characterize his work. As Ibérico remarks, González Prada is distinguished "not only by a rigid systemization of concepts—provisional symbols of a state of mind—but by a certain spirit, a resoluteness of the entire personality, which are expressed in his literary artistry and in his virile exaltation of effort and struggle."[25]

I have said that what endures in González Prada is his spirit. We of the new generation admire his austere moral example and, above all, we respect his intellectual honesty and his noble and vigorous rebellion.

I myself feel that in the new Peruvian generation González Prada would recognize as disciples and heirs only those men with the will and enterprise required to surpass his own work. He would disdain the mediocrity who repeated his phrases. He

[25] Ibid., pp. 43–44.

would cherish the youth who was capable of translating his ideas into action and he would be renewed and reborn in the man who could make a truly original and contemporary statement.

González Prada can be described in the words that he used for Vigil in his *Páginas libres*: "Few lives have been so pure, so full, so worthy of imitation. It is possible to attack the form and substance of his writings, to brand his books as old-fashioned and inadequate, to demolish his entire intellectual structure; but the man will remain standing, invulnerable."

Melgar

During the colonial period, Peruvian literature appears, in its most prominent incidents and figures, as a phenomenon of Lima. No matter that its catalog includes the provinces. The model, style, and direction have been set by the capital. And this is understandable. Literature is an urban product and all literary processes gravitate toward the city. In Peru, furthermore, Lima has not had to compete with other cities of similar rank. Its domination has been guaranteed by an extreme centralism.

Because of the absolute hegemony of Lima, our literature has not been able to nourish itself on indigenous soil. Lima has been first of all the Spanish capital and then the criollo capital. Its literature has reflected this.

Nevertheless, indigenous sentiment was not totally unexpressed in this period of our literary history. Its first worthwhile exponent was Mariano Melgar. The critics of Lima treat him rather scornfully. They consider him to be too popular and without elegance. They are bothered by the fact that his verses employ a rather colloquial syntax and slang expressions. Basically, these critics do not like the *yaraví* type of poetry and they prefer any soporific ode of Pando.

I do not react by overestimating Melgar as an artist. I judge him on a relative basis in the context of his time, when Peruvian literature was just beginning.

Melgar is a romantic not only in his art but also in his life. Romanticism had not officially reached our literature. In Melgar, therefore, romanticism was not an imitation, as it was to be later in others; it was a spontaneous outburst, indicating his artistic sensitivity. It has been said that part of his literary fame is due to his heroic death, but this opinion barely disguises the disdain that inspires it. Melgar died very young. Although it is always risky to speculate on the probable career of an artist cut off prematurely, it is not too much to suppose that a mature Melgar would have produced an art purged of rhetoric and classical mannerisms and, therefore, more native and pure. The rupture with the mother country would have had a special effect on his spirit and, in any case, a very different one from the effect it had on the spirit of the literary men of a city as Spanish and colonial as Lima. Mariano Melgar, following his romantic impulses, would have found his inspiration increasingly in the rural and indigenous.

Those who are offended by the coarseness of his speech and of his imagery suffer from the prejudices of the aristocrat and the academician. The artist who writes a poem of lasting emotion in the language of the people is, in any literature, infinitely superior to the poet who writes a refined piece in academic language fit for an anthology. Furthermore, as Carlos Octavio Bunge points out in his study of Argentine literature, popular poetry has always preceded artistic poetry. Some *yaravíes* of Melgar survive only as fragments of popular poetry and by this token they have achieved immortality.

Sometimes his simple imagery has a pastoral ingenuousness that reveals his indigenous strain and autochthonous background. Oriental poetry is characterized by its rustic pantheism in metaphor. Melgar is very Indian in his primitive, peasant imagination.

This romantic ended by devoting himself passionately to the revolution. For him the revolution was not the liberalism of the Encyclopedists; it was fundamentally a patriotic fervor. The revolutionary feeling of Melgar, like that of Pumacahua, was fed by our own blood and our own history.

For Riva Agüero, the poet of the *yaravíes* was only "a singular moment in Peruvian literature." Let us correct his judgment by saying that he was the Peruvian moment in this literature.

Abelardo Gamarra

Abelardo Gamarra still has no place in the anthologies. Critics rank his work as secondary and relegate it to popular literature, which, for their refined tastes, is worthless. He is not even given a prominent place in criollo literature. The first name cited in any history of criollo literature is always that of Felipe Pardo, a confirmed colonialist.

Nevertheless, Gamarra is one of our most typical writers. Within the literature of the capital, he is the writer who gives the province its purest expression and who recalls the indigenous strain. Ricardo Palma is a criollo of Lima; El Tunante is a criollo of the sierra. The Indian race is alive in his jovial art.

El Tunante has the Indian's stubbornness and resignation, his pantheistic unconcern with the hereafter, his bucolic gentleness, his rustic common sense, and his realistic and austere imagination. He has the criollo's witty speech, his mocking laughter, his keen intelligence, and his adventurous and rollicking spirit. Coming from a village in the sierra, El Tunante adapted himself to the capital and coast without losing his integrity. The feeling and tone of his work make it the most authentically Peruvian in a half-century of imitations and babble.

It is also Peruvian in spirit. From his youth, Gamarra was in the vanguard. He participated in Radical protest with genuine devotion to its revolutionary patriotism. What was only an intellectual and literary attitude in other Radicalists was a profound and vital impulse in El Tunante. In flesh and spirit Gamarra was deeply repelled by the *encomendero* aristocracy and its corrupt and ignorant clientele. He always understood that these people did not represent Peru, that Peru was something else. He guarded this sentiment against *civilismo* and its intellectual and ideological expressions. His unerring instinct protected it from the "democratic" illusion. El Tunante was not deceived by Piérola. He perceived that the government of 1895 was not a democratic revolution but only a restoration of *civilismo*. Although he remained until his death a fervent admirer of González Prada, whose Catilinarian rhetoric he translated into popular language, he could not conceal his longing for a more enterprising and constructive spirit. He sensed the historical lack of an Alberdi or a Sarmiento in Peru. Especially in his later years, he realized that idealistic and reformist politics must be solidly grounded in reality and history.

His work is not merely social satire. A generous political and social idealism underlies his lively portrayals of people and customs; and it is this idealism that distinguished his writing from Segura's.

Furthermore, El Tunante's criollo character is more complete, more profound than that of Segura. His interpretation of personalities and objects is more authentic and alive. Gamarra's work—which is the most widely read in the provinces—is full of penetrating comments and triumphs of description. El Tunante is a Pancho Fierro of our literature. He is a popular genius, a spontaneous and intuitive writer.

Heir to the revolutionary spirit of independence, he logically had to feel different from and opposed to the heirs to the conquest and the colony. Therefore, no title or diploma has been conferred on his work by academic or literary authorities. (El Tunante, like Rubén Darío, must have thought, "Deliver us, O

Lord, from academies.") He is disdained for his syntax, his spelling, and, above all, for his spirit.

Life joyfully mocks the carpings of his critics by bestowing on Gamarra's books the immortality it denies to books that have been officially honored. Although it is the people and not the critics who remember Gamarra, this suffices to assure for him his place in the history of our literature, even though it is formally disputed.

The work of Gamarra appears as a scattered collection of outlines and sketches. That it has no central theme and is not a refined artistic creation is not altogether the fault of the author, but is also the result of the inchoate literature it represents.

El Tunante wanted to record the language of the street as an art form. He was not mistaken in his intention, for this is the tradition that has produced the early classics of all literatures.

Chocano

It is my belief that José Santos Chocano belongs to the colonial period of our literature. His grandiloquent poetry betrays its Spanish origins. Critics who present him as an interpreter of the autochthonous soul use a logic that is as simplistic as it is false: Chocano is exuberant; therefore, he is autochthonous. This is the principle on which critics incapable of understanding the autochthonous have based almost all their theory of the essential Americanism and tropicalism of the poet of *Alma América*.

This theory could not be contested when the authority of colonialism was absolute. Now an iconoclastic generation holds it up to the light of their disbelief. The first question posed is: Is the autochthonous really exuberant?

A critic as wise and as distinguished as Pedro Henriquez Ureña, on examining the matter of exuberance in Spanish American literature, observes that the greater part of this literature does not appear to be a product of the tropics. It proceeds, rather, from cities of a temperate and even autumnal climate. He very correctly points out that "in America we continued to respect intensity as long as it was prescribed for us from Europe; even today we have three or four 'vibrant poets,' to use the term of the romantics. Are we not attributing to the influence of the tropic what is really the influence of Victor Hugo, or Byron, or Espronceda, or Quintana?" Henríquez Ureña does not believe in the theory of a spontaneous exuberance in American literature. This literature is less exuberant than it appears, and verbosity is mistaken for exuberance. "If there is an abundance of words, it is because there is a paucity of culture and discipline, and not because of any exuberance peculiar to us."[26] Verbosity is not to be ascribed to geography or to environment.

To study the case of Chocano, we have to begin by locating it in Peru. In Peru, the autochthonous is the indigenous or, more precisely, the Inca; and the indigenous, the Inca, is basically austere. The art of the Indian is the antithesis and the contradiction of the art of Chocano. The Indian systematizes and stylizes everything according to a hieratic primitivism.

No one claims to find the emotion of the Andes in Chocano's poetry. Critics like Riva Agüero, who pronounce his poetry autochthonous, think of it only as expressing the emotion of the *montaña*, that is, the jungle. If, with no idea of what the *montaña* really is, they rush to discover or recognize it in the bombast of Chocano, they only repeat the poet's own assumption that he is "the bard of autochthonous and savage America."

The *montaña* is exuberance, plus many other things that do not appear in the poetry of Chocano. Chocano is merely an eloquent spectator of its landscapes and scenic pageantry. All his images represent an exterior fantasy. It is not the man of the tropical forest who is heard but, at most, an imaginative and ardent stranger who thinks he possesses and expresses the jungle.

[26] Pedro Henríquez Ureña, *Seis ensayos en busca de nuestra expresión*, pp. 45–47.

This is understandable. The *montaña* exists almost exclusively as nature, as landscape, as scenery. It still has not produced a people or a civilization. Chocano, in any case, has not been nourished on its soil. By race, mentality, and education the poet of *Alma américa* belongs to the coast. He comes from a Spanish family. He was formed intellectually and spiritually in Lima. And his intensity, which in the final analysis is the only proof of his artistic and esthetic Americanism, descends directly from Spain.

The techniques of, and models for, Chocano's eloquence are in Spanish literature. Stylistically he has been influenced by Quintana and spiritually by Espronceda. Byron and Hugo are cited by Chocano, but it is the poets of the Spanish language who have most directly influenced his writing. He has the romantic egoism, as well as the arrogance and conceit, of Díaz Mirón; and his romanticism verges on a modernism and decadence that are derived from Rubén Darío.

These traits clearly define the artistic loyalties of Chocano, who, in spite of the successive waves of modernism that have reached his writing without essentially changing it, has preserved in his work the tone and temperament of a survivor of Spanish romanticism in all its grandiloquence. His spiritual loyalties, moreover, coincide with his artistic. The "bard of autochthonous and savage America" is the scion of conquistadors. He himself acknowledges this in his poetry, which, although not lacking in literary and rhetorical admiration for the Incas, overflows with love for the heroes of the conquest and the magnates of the viceroyalty.

Unlike the specifically colonialist writers, Chocano is not a member of the Lima plutocracy. For example, he cannot be identified with Riva Agüero. He is a spiritual descendant of the conquest rather than of the viceroyalty. Socially and economically, the conquest and the viceroyalty are two phases of the same phenomenon, but spiritually they are not in the same cate-

gory. The conquest was a heroic undertaking; the viceroyalty
was a bureaucratic enterprise. The conquistadors belonged, as
Blaise Cendrars would say, to a mighty race of adventurers; the
viceroys and the magistrates came from a flabby nobility or an
educated mediocrity.

In his early poetry the minstrel of *Iras santas* revealed his
debt to Espronceda and to Byronic romanticism. As a youth,
Chocano's attitude was one of rebellion, sometimes suggesting
anarchy, other times hinting at social protest, but always vague.
He launched a delirious and bizarre offensive against the military government of the period, but it never became more than a
literary gesture.

Chocano later appeared to be politically involved in Pierolism.
His revolutionary beliefs acquiesced in the revolution of 1895,
which abolished a military regime in order to restore a regime
of *civilismo* under the provisional direction of Nicolás de Piérola.
Afterwards, Chocano joined the intellectual clientele of the
plutocracy. He did not abandon Piérola and his pseudo-democra-
cy to associate himself with González Prada but to hail Javier
Prado y Ugarteche as the thinker of his generation.

The political direction of a writer is almost always his spiritual, if not his artistic, direction. Literature, on the other hand,
is known to be permeated with politics, even when it seems
most remote and estranged from political influences. At the moment, we do not want to classify Chocano as an artist; we want
to ascertain his spiritual and ideological position. Because this
position is not clearly indicated in his poetry, we must look for
it in his prose, which is not only more explicit than his poetry
but is neither contradicted nor weakened by it.

In the poetry of Chocano we find the heightened and self-
centered individualism so typical of the romantic ranks. All of
Chocano's anarchism is summed up in this individualism, which
in later years he reduces and limits. Although he does not absolutely renounce his sensual egoism, he does renounce much of

his philosophical individualism. The cult of "I" is linked to the cult of "hierarchy." The poet considers himself an individualist, not a liberal, and his individualism becomes a "hierarchical individualism" that, far from cherishing liberty, almost despises it. On the other hand, the hierarchy it respects is not the eternal hierarchy created by the Spirit; it is the precarious hierarchy imposed by might, money, and tradition in the mutable present.

In the same way, the poet comes to dominate his early spiritual outbursts. At its peak, his art exhibits a rather pagan pantheism in its exalted although rhetorical love of nature. This pantheism, as reflected in his animistic imagery, sounds the only note of an "autochthonous and savage America." (The Indian is pantheist, animist, materialist.) Chocano, nevertheless, has tacitly abandoned pantheism to adopt the principle of hierarchy, which has taken him back to the Roman Catholic Church. Ideologically, Rome is the historical citadel of reaction. Those who journey to its hills and shrines in search of the Christian faith return disillusioned. Those who are satisfied to find, instead, fascism and the Church—the authority and the hierarchy in the Roman sense—reach their goal and discover their truth. The poet of *Alma américa* is one of the latter pilgrims. He who has never been a Christian finally turns Catholic. The weary romantic, the heretical convert, takes shelter in the secure fold of tradition and order which he once thought he had left forever in order to conquer the future.

Riva Agüero and His Influence on the "Futurist" Generation

The "futurist" generation—as it is paradoxically known— marks the restoration of colonialism and *civilismo* in the literary thought of Peru.

The emotional and ideological authority of the heirs to colonialism had been undermined by fifteen years of Radical teachings. After a period of military caudillos similar to the one that followed the wars of independence, the latifundium class had reestablished its political control but not its intellectual dominion. Radicalism had been strengthened by the moral reaction to defeat, for which the people blamed the plutocracy, and had found a favorable climate for spreading its revolutionary gospel. Its propaganda had especially stirred the provinces and a wave of progressive ideas had swept the republic.

The old guard of *civilismo* intellectuals had become elderly and enfeebled, and they could not react effectively against the Radical generation. The restoration had to be carried out by a regiment of young men. *Civilismo* was sure of the university and expected to recruit there an intellectual militia that would extend its action beyond the university to a total reconquest of intellect and emotion. One of its natural and primary objectives was to recover ground lost in literature; at that time, the work of a single popular writer, González Prada's disciple, El Tunante, was more widely read and understood than the work of all the university writers together.

Historical circumstances favored the restoration. *Civilismo* appeared to be firmly consolidated in the economic and political order—essentially a *civilismo* order—inaugurated by Piérola in 1895. Many professionals and men of letters who had been attracted to the Radical movement during the chaotic period following our war, now moved toward the *civilismo* camp. The Radical generation had dispersed. González Prada had withdrawn into an aloof asceticism and had lost contact with his scattered disciples. So the "futurist" generation encountered almost no resistance.

Civilistas and Democrats, separated in the party struggle, were mingled in its ranks. Its advent, therefore, was welcomed by the leading newspapers of Lima. *El Comercio* and *La Prensa* sponsored the "new generation" that seemed destined to effect the reconciliation between *civilistas* and Democrats which the coalition of 1895 had barely initiated. Its leader and captain, Riva Agüero, who combined the tradition of *civilismo* and plutocracy with an almost filial devotion to the Democratic "caliph," revealed this tendency from the beginning. Attacking radicalism in his study of "the literature of independent Peru," he said that "the parties of principle not only do not produce goods but they do irreparable damage. In the present system, party differences are not very great nor are party divisions very deep. Alliances are easily formed and collaboration is frequent. Wise governments can, without much effort, invite the participation of all useful men."

This opposition to parties of principle betrayed the class feelings and motives of Riva Agüero's generation. He only too clearly announced his intention of strengthening and consolidating a class system. To deny principles and ideas the right to govern the country was to sanction rule by "decent people," the "educated class." In this respect as in others, Riva Agüero was in complete agreement with Javier Prado and Francisco García Calderón, and this was because Prado and García Calderón also represented restoration. Their ideology was basically the same conservative positivism. Idealistic and progressive phrases disguised traditional beliefs. As I have commented, Riva Agüero, Prado, and García Calderón all revered Taine. In order to make clear his loyalties, Riva Agüero stated in his already cited study —which was undoubtedly the first political and literary manifesto of the "futurist" generation—that he was a follower of Brunetière.

Riva Agüero began his political career with a revision of literary values that was absolutely in keeping with the aims of a restoration. He idealized and glorified the colony, attributing to it the origin of our nationality. He traced the roots of our nationality back to an idealized and glorified colony. He overrated colonialist literature by acclaiming its mediocrities. He was

scornful of the romanticism of Mariano Melgar and he reproached González Prada for the most valid and fruitful part of
his work, which was his protest.

The "futurist" generation represented the university and was
both academic and rhetorical. It made use of modernism only
for the elements it needed to condemn the unrest of romanticism.

One of its most typical undertakings was its organization of a
counterpart of the Academy of the Spanish Language. One of
its most conspicuous artistic efforts was its return to Spain in
prose and verse.

The most characteristic trait of the "futurist" generation was
its *pasadismo*. From the outset, its writers dedicated themselves
to idealizing the past. In his study, Riva Agüero stoutly defended
established privileges and traditions.

For this generation, the past was neither very remote nor very
near, but coincided precisely with the era of the viceroyalty, on
which it lavished all its affection and tenderness. Riva Agüero
was categorical in his belief that Peru was descended from the
conquest and that its infancy was the colony. From this moment,
Peruvian literature became markedly colonialist and produced a
phenomenon that Luis Alberto Sánchez calls *perricholismo* and
that still continues.

This phenomenon—in its origins, not in its consequences—
combines two sentiments: love of Lima and love of the past.
Translated into political terms, they were centralism and conservatism, because the *pasadismo* of Riva Agüero's generation
was not just a romantic gesture inspired by literature. This generation was traditionalist, not romantic, and its literature, tinged
with "modernism," was a reaction against the literature of romanticism. Romanticism condemned the present in the name of
the past or the future. Riva Agüero and his contemporaries, on
the other hand, accepted the present, although, in order to direct
and govern it, they invoked and evoked the past. They were

characterized, spiritually and ideologically, by a positivist conservatism, an opportunistic traditionalism.

Of course, there are various shades within this overall color. Individually, for example, José Gálvez does not answer the above description. His *pasadismo* was essentially romantic. Haya calls him the "only sincere disciple of Palma," undoubtedly referring to the literary and sentimental nature of his *pasadismo*. This distinction is not clearly expressed, but it is based on an obvious fact. Gálvez, whose poetry was a pale, attenuated repetition of Chocano's verbosity, had a romantic streak. His *pasadismo* was therefore less localized in time than that of the rest of his generation; it was a total *pasadismo*. Although in love with the viceroyalty, he was not exclusively absorbed by that era. For him, "all the past was better." On the other hand, his *pasadismo* was more localized in space. The scene of his evocations was almost always Lima. But I attribute this to his romantic streak.

Gálvez, on the other hand, sometimes differs with the thesis of Riva Agüero. His opinions on the possibility of a genuinely national literature are unorthodox within the "futurist" movement. He declares himself, with a number of reservations and qualifications, in agreement with the leader of his generation and of his party about Americanism in literature. He is not convinced that it is impossible to revive poetically the ancient American civilizations.

No matter how remote the civilizations, the material itself has not disappeared; no matter how deep the Spanish influence, even those of us of purest Spanish descent feel bonds with that race whose golden tradition deserves recollection and whose majestic and mysterious ruins overawe us. Precisely because we are so intermingled and our historical roots so intertwined and because for those very reasons our culture is not as profound as it appears, we are impressed by the literary material of those dead epochs even though we do not consider it fundamental. If the tremulous *yaraví* music still can pierce our soul with a strange anguish, we must carry within us some residue of the Inca empire and of the struggle between the two races. Furthermore, our history cannot have begun with the Conquest and no matter how nebulous the psychic legacy we have received from the Indian, we have something of that conquered race whose living ruins wander disowned and neglected in our sierras, constituting a serious social problem that painfully throbs in our life. Why can this race not have a place in our literature, which has abounded in historical feelings for other races that are strange and foreign to us?[27]

Gálvez, however, is not correct in his definition of a national literature. "It is a matter of turning the soul toward the sound of the vibrations around us." But in the next line he reduces its elements to "history, tradition, and nature." Here reappears the lover of the past. In his concept, a really national literature should be nourished on history, legend, and tradition, all of the past. Although the present is also history, Gálvez certainly did not think so when he chose the sources of our literature. For him, history was nothing but the past. Gálvez does not demand that national literature should interpret Peru in its entirety or that it should perform a really creative function. He denies it the right to be a literature of the people. Arguing with El Tunante, he maintains that "the artist should scorn slang expressions, which are often useful in an article on popular customs but are far removed from the fine, aristocratic form that an artistic work should take."[28]

The "futurist" generation follows the ideas of Riva Agüero. When Gálvez votes against or, rather, leaves his vote blank in these and other debates, his dissent has only an individual value. Meanwhile, the "futurist" generation makes use of his nostalgia and romanticism in the serenade under the balconies of the vice-

---

[27] Gálvez, *Posibilidad de una genuina literatura nacional*, pp. 33–34.
[28] Ibid., p. 90.

royalty, which is intended politically to revive a legend indispensable to the supremacy of the heirs to the colony.

The feudal caste has no titles other than those of colonial tradition, nothing that advances its interests more than a traditionalist literary current. At the core of colonialist literature are found only the urgent requirements for the life force of a class, a "caste." Any doubts about the basically political origin of the "futurist" movement may be dispelled by considering that when this group of lawyers, writers, men of letters, et cetera reached maturity, they were no longer satisfied with being only a movement and wanted to become a party.

Colónida *and Valdelomar*

Colónida represented not so much a revolution, which would exaggerate its importance, as an insurrection against academicism and its oligarchies, its emphasis on rhetoric, its conservative taste, its old-fashioned gallantry, and its tedious melancholy. The *colónidos* called for sincerity and naturalness. As a movement it was too irregular and anarchical to be condensed into a trend or defined in a formula. It expended its energy in iconoclastic shouting and spasms of snobbery.

A short-lived journal put out by Valdelomar gave its name to the movement. *Colónida* was not a group or a school, but an attitude and a mood; and *colonidismo* was produced by writers both within and outside the circle of Valdelomar. It was a fleeting literary meteor that had no precise outlines, no true aesthetic pattern to impose on its followers. Rather than an idea or a method, *colonidismo* was egocentrism, individualism, a vague iconoclasm, a hazy reformism. *Colónida* was not even an association of kindred temperaments or, strictly speaking, a generation. Its ranks included not only Valdelomar, More, and Gibson, but youthful writers like myself who were just beginning.

The *colónidos* coincided only in their revolt against all academic values, reputations, and temperaments. Their bond was protest, not affirmation. Nonetheless, as long as they participated in the same movement, they had some spiritual traits in common. They tended to have a rather morbid taste for the decadent, the elite, the aristocratic. Valdelomar brought the seeds of the D'Annunzio manner from Europe and sowed them in our voluptuous, rhetorical, and meridional soil.

Although the *colónidos* were eccentric, aggressive, unfair, and even immoderate, they were useful. They renewed and stirred up national literature, which they denounced as a vulgar imitation of second-rate Spanish literature. They attacked its fetishes and icons and proposed new and better models. They began what many writers referred to as "a revision of our literary values." *Colónida* was a negative, disintegrative, belligerent force, expressing the opposition of those writers who objected to the domination of national reputation by an antiquated, official, and pretentious art.

On the other hand, the *colónidos* did not always behave correctly. They sympathized with all the heretical, unorthodox, solitary figures of our literature. They gathered around González Prada, taking from him what they needed least. They cherished the aristocratic, Parnassian individualist in González Prada and ignored the agitator and the revolutionary. More defined González Prada as "a Greek born in a country of *zambos*." However, they appreciated and esteemed Eguren, who was disdained by the undiscerning taste of the critics and public of that time.

Colónida was a brief phenomenon. After a series of polemics, *colonidismo* fades into obscurity. Each of the *colónidos* went his own way and the movement was liquidated. It is unimportant that some of its echoes remain and that more than one youth is still stirred by some of its ideas. As a spiritual attitude, *colonidismo* is not of our time. The appetite for renewal that generated the *colónida* movement could not be satisfied by small doses of decadence and exoticism. The disappearance of *Colónida* went unnoticed because it was never a faction, but only a temporary gesture.

Colonidismo ignored politics. Its individualism and elitism isolated it from the common people and insulated it against emotions. The *colónidos* regarded politics as a bourgeois function, bureaucratic and prosaic. The journal *Colónida* was written for the Palais Concert and the Unión. Federico More was compulsively dedicated to conspiracy and to pamphleteering, but his political beliefs were anti-democratic, anti-social, and reactionary. More dreamed of an aristocracy of critics or even of writers. He had no experience with social reality and he despised the masses.

But once the experiment was over, the writers who had participated in it, especially the younger ones, became interested in new political currents. This interest has its origins in the political literature of Unamuno, Araquistain, Alomar, and other writers for the magazine *España*; in Wilson's eloquent and professorial speeches advocating a new freedom; and in the philosophy of Víctor M. Maúrtua, whose influence on the Socialist orientation of some of our intellectuals is almost unknown. It was marked by the appearance of *Nuestra Epoca*, a journal of even shorter duration than *Colónida*. Among contributors to *Nuestra Epoca*, which was published for the masses and not for the Palais Concert, were Félix del Valle, César Falcón, César Ugarte, Valdelomar, Percy Gibson, César A. Rodríguez, César Vallejo, and myself. Structurally very different from the *Colónida* writers, the group included a disciple of Maúrtua and future professor at the university, Ugarte, as well as a labor leader, Del Barzo. In this movement, more political than literary, Valdelomar took second place to writers younger and less famous than himself.

Valdelomar, nevertheless, had evolved. A great artist is almost always a man of great sensitivity. His preference for a tranquil, easy life prevented him from being an agitator; but, like Oscar Wilde, Valdelomar would have come to love socialism. Valdelomar was not locked up in an ivory tower. He did not deny his demagogic and stormy past as a supporter of Billinghurst nor was he ashamed of this episode. In spite of his aristocratic leanings, Valdelomar admired humble and simple people, as is evidenced in the civic conscience found in some of his writing. Valdelomar wrote his prayer to St. Martin for the school children of Huaura. During his lecture tours in the north, he spoke before an audience of workers in praise of labor. I recall that in our last talks together he listened with interest and respect to my early ramblings on socialism. In this moment of maximum maturity and promise, he was felled by death.

I understand why there has been no exact, clear, accurate definition of the art of Valdelomar. He died at thirty, before he had found or defined himself. His disorganized, versatile, and somewhat incoherent production contains only the constituents of the work that death frustrated. Although Valdelomar did not succeed in fully developing his vigorous and exuberant personality, he has nonetheless left us many magnificent pages.

His personality not only influenced a generation of writers, but it initiated a trend in our literature that has since intensified. Valdelomar, who brought cosmopolitan elements from abroad, was attracted by criollo and Inca elements. He relived his childhood in a fishing village and he discovered, albeit intuitively, the quarry of our autochthonous past.

One of the essential ingredients of the art of Valdelomar is his humor. Almost everything that the public took seriously, Valdelomar said in jest, *pour épater le bourgeois*. If the bourgeoisie had laughed with him about his egocentric poses, Valdelomar would not have been so determined to use them. His writing was imbued with an elegant, airy humor that was new to us, and his newspaper articles, his "maximum dialogues," were full of wit. This prose, which could have been more refined and enduring if Valdelomar had had time to polish it, was improvised and journalistic.[29]

There was nothing biting or vicious in Valdelomar's humor. He caricatured men gently and he looked at life with a fond smile. Evaristo, employed in a village pharmacy and twin brother to a bilious, unhappy weeping willow tree, is one of those melancholy caricatures that Valdelomar liked to draw. In this Pirandellian novel one feels Valdelomar's tenderness for his unlucky, pale, sickly character.

Valdelomar seems to fall into despair and pessimism. But these are passing moods and temporary depressions. He was too pantheistic and sensual to be a pessimist. Like D'Annunzio, he believed that "life is beautiful and worthy of being lived magnificently." This spirit is revealed in his tales and vignettes of village life. Valdelomar always looked for happiness and pleasure and, on the rare occasions when he found them, he knew how to enjoy them fully.

In his "Confiteor," which is possibly the most noble, pure, and beautiful erotic poetry of our literature, Valdelomar reaches the height of Dionysian exaltation. In the grip of erotic emotion, Valdelomar thinks that nature, the universe, cannot be indifferent to his love. His love is not egoistic: it has to feel itself surrounded by cosmic joy. Here is the supreme note of "Confiteor":

[29] Valdelomar's humor fed on vulgar pretentiousness. One evening in the Palais Concert, Valdelomar said to me: "Mariátegui, they offend the light and fine dragonfly here by calling it a hummingbird." At that time as decadent as he, I urged him to defend the noble and injured rights of the dragonfly. Valdelomar asked the waiter for some paper and in the midst of the mellifluous mumur of the cafe, he wrote on a table one of his "maximum dialogs." His humor was always like this—innocent, childlike, lyrical. It was the reaction of a refined and pure soul against the vulgarians and a dull, provincial atmosphere. He disliked "fat, drunken men," gold stickpins, detachable cuffs, and elasticized shoes.

My Love Will Animate the World

What will I do on the day that your eyes
look at me with love?
My soul will fill the world with joy,
Nature will vibrate with the beating of my heart,
all will be happy:
sky, sea, trees, the landscape . . . My passion
will sound divinely-colored notes of gladness
for the sad universe;
the birds will carol, the treetops
sing a song; the happiness in my soul
will reach the graveyard,
and the dead will feel the cool breeze of my love.

Is It Possible to Suffer?

Who says that life is sad?
Who speaks of pain?
Who complains?   Who suffers?   Who weeps?

"Confiteor" is the naïve, lyrical confessions of a lover exulting
in his love and happiness. In the presence of his loved one, the
poet "trembles like a frail reed," and he is convinced that not
everyone can understand his passion. The image of his loved one
is Pre-Raphaelite, presented only for those who have "contem-
plated the angel of the Annunciation in the canvas by Burne-
Jones." This absolute lyricism in love had never been reached by
any of our poets. There is something of the "allegro" of Beethoven in the above verses.

In spite of "El hermano ausente," "Confiteor," and other
verses, Valdelomar is denied the title of poet that is granted, on
the other hand, to Felipe Pardo. Valdelomar does not fit into the
arbitrary classifications of old-fashioned criticism. The noblest
nuances and the most delicate notes of this great lyricist's temperament can never be grasped by those definitions. In tune
with his times, Valdelomar was versatile and restless, "very

modern, bold, and cosmopolitan." His humor and his lyricism occasionally foreshadow modern avant-garde literature.

Valdelomar does not herald a new era in our literature because too many decadent influences acted on him. Together with Faith, the Sea, and Death, he places Twilight among the "ineffable and infinite" elements that entered into the development of his Inca legends. From his youth, his art was influenced by D'Annunzio. The twilight emotions of *Il fuoco* were intensified in Italy by the Roman dusk, the voluptuous sunset on the Janiculum, the autumn grape harvest, and amphibian Venice—maritime and malarial.

But his vivid and pure lyricism keeps Valdelomar from becoming poisoned by too much decadence. Humor saves him from the universe of D'Annunzio, as in his story of "Hebaristo, the willow who died of love." This was a Pirandellian tale, although Valdelomar scarcely knew Pirandello, who was an unknown playwright at the time of his visit to Italy. His method was Pirandellian: the pantheistic paralleling of the lives of a pharmacist and a weeping willow tree. His characterization was Pirandellian: a slightly caricatured *petit-bourgeois* clerk. His drama was Pirandellian: an attempt to break out of a monotonous existence, which ends with a ridiculous snap.

A pantheistic, pagan sentiment drove Valdelomar to the village, to nature. The impressions of his childhood, which had been spent on a peaceful bay, sink melodiously into his subconscious. Valdelomar is unusually sensitive to rustic settings. The emotion of his childhood is composed of home, beach, and field. The "heavy, perfumed sea breeze" impregnated him with a briny melancholy: "And what it said to me remains in my soul; my father was silent and my mother was sad, and no one knew how to teach me happiness" ("Tristitía").

Valdelomar, nevertheless, has the cosmopolitan feelings of the modern man who travels. New York and Times Square attract him just as much as the enchanted village and the "caramel-colored gamecock." From the fifty-fourth floor of the Woolworth Building he passes effortlessly to the mint and purslane of the solitary paths of his childhood. His stories exhibit the kaleidoscopic mobility of his fantasy. The dandy-ism of his Yankee and cosmopolitan stories, the exotic flavor of his Chinese and oriental images ("my soul trembles like a frail reed"), the romanticism of his Inca legends, the impressionism of his criollo tales, follow one another like seasons and repeat and alternate in the author's artistic journey without transitions and without spiritual ruptures.

His work is essentially fragmentary and reflects criollo exuberance and lack of discipline. Valdelomar combined to a high degree the qualities and defects of the coastal mestizo. He would go from an extreme of creative frenzy to an Asiatic and fatalistic renunciation of all desire. His mind would be simultaneously occupied by an essay on art, a humorous sketch, a pastoral tragedy ("Verdolaga"), and a romance ("La Mariscala"). He was so creative that any theme—the turkey buzzards of Marinete, the Plaza del Mercado, the cockfights—could kindle his imagination. Valdelomar was the first of our writers to perceive the tragic beauty of the bullfight and, at a time when this subject was relegated to the pedestrian prose of bullfight fans, he wrote *Belmonte, el trágico*.

Valdelomar introduced the *greguería* into our literature. I can testify that he delighted in the first books of Gómez de la Serna to reach Lima. Because he loved originality and investigation of the microcosm, he had a natural predilection for the *greguería*. On the other hand, Valdelomar still did not suspect in Gómez de la Serna the discoverer of the dawn. His impressionist criollo retina was expert in enjoying voluptuously from the golden riverbank the ambiguous colors of twilight. It is impressionism, within its local variety, that most precisely defines his artistic affinities.

Our "Independents"

Outside the movements, the trends, and even the generations themselves, there has been no lack of more or less independent, solitary cases of literary vocation. But the literary process slowly erases the memory of the writer who does not leave descendants. He can work alone, but his work cannot escape oblivion if it does not have a message for posterity. Only the forerunner and the originator survive. For the purpose of my study, the intrinsic value of an individual lies not in himself but in his influence.

We have seen how a generation or rather a Radical movement that recognized González Prada as its leader succeeded a neo-*civilista* or colonialist movement that proclaimed Palma as its patriarch; and we have seen how it was followed by a *colónida* movement, which was the precursor of a new generation. But this does not mean that all the literature of that long period necessarily belonged to the "futurist" or to the *colónida* movement.

We have the case of the poet Domingo Martínez Luján, a bizarre specimen of the old romantic bohemian, some of whose verses will be cited in anthologies as the first to show the influence of Rubén Darío on our poetry. We have the case of Manuel Beingolea, who writes short stories of delicate humor and fantasy and who cultivates the decadence of the strange and singular. We have the case of José María Eguren, whose poetry will go down in our literary history as "pure" rather than symbolic.

Eguren, however, thanks to his exceptional influence, is a factor in the setting of trends. Although he makes his name outside of a generation, he later becomes a subject of controversy between two generations. Disdained by the "futurist" generation that acclaims Gálvez as its poet, Eguren is discovered and adopted by the *colónida* movement.

Eguren first attracts attention in the journal *Contemporáneos*, about which I should say a few words. *Contemporáneos* indisputably marks a date in our literary history. Founded by Enrique Bustamante y Ballivián together with Julio Alfonso Hernández, this journal is the voice of a group of "independents" who feel the need to assert their autonomy from the colonialist. These "independents" are more opposed to the aesthetics than the spirit of Riva Agüero's generation. *Contemporáneos* mainly represents the progress of modernism in Peru; but even as a journal of purely literary reform, it is not sufficiently aggressive or passionate. Despite the Parnassian moderation of its director, Enrique Bustamante y Ballivián, some of its attitudes sound a note of protest. The seeking out of González Prada, who at that time could find no other publisher for his articles than some obscure anarchist newspaper, is in itself a gesture of "secession." So it was that the poet of *Exóticas* and the prose writer of *Páginas libres* reappeared in 1909 in the company of "independents" whose admiration, more for the aristocrat than for the rebel, nonetheless denoted a reaction.

Contemporáneos disappeared after a few issues and Bustamante y Ballivián asked Valdelomar to join him in founding a new and more voluminous journal, *Cultura*. But before the appearance of the first issue, the codirectors fought and *Cultura* was published without Valdelomar. The first and only number gives the impression of a more eclectic, less representative journal than *Contemporáneos*. The failure of this experiment paves the way to *Colónida*.

The above and similar undertakings demonstrate that although Riva Agüero's generation never split into two antagonistic groups, it was far from uniform and unanimous. Like every other generation, Riva Agüero's had its dissidents. Spiritually and ideologically, the most significant was Pedro S. Zulen. Zulen not only disliked the academicism and the rhetoric of the "futurists," but he detested their conservative and traditionalist spirit. Confronted with a colonialist generation, Zulen declared himself pro-indigenous. The other "independents"—Enrique

Bustamante y Ballivián, Alberto J. Ureta, et cetera—were satisfied with an implicit literary succession.

Eguren

José María Eguren represents pure poetry in our literary history. This opinion is not in agreement with the thesis of Abbot
Bremond. I contend that, unlike most Peruvian poetry, the poetry of Eguren does not pretend to be historical, or philosophical, or religious, but is simply poetry.

Although the poets of the republic did not inherit from the
poets of the colony their fondness for theological poetry—
wrongly called religious or mystic—they did inherit their predilection for courtly, dithyrambic poetry. Under the republic, the
Peruvian Parnassus swells with new odes, some attenuated and
some inflated. Their point of departure was always an event or a
person, so that poetry became subordinate to chronology. Odes
were written to American heroes and events, when not to the
Spanish monarchs, and poetry commemorated a date or a ceremony rather than the feelings of an era. Satirical poetry, because of its role, was also tied to an event or a topic.

In other cases, poets cultivated the philosophical poem, which
generally was neither poetry nor philosophy. This poetry degen-
erated into an exercise in rhetoric and metaphysics.

The art of Eguren is a reaction against this garrulous, de-
clamatory art, almost exclusively composed of temporal and topical elements. As a pure poet, Eguren does not write a single
verse on order or for an occasion; he does not worry about popular or critical taste; he does not celebrate Spain, or Alfonso XIII,
or Saint Rosa of Lima; he does not even recite his verses at gatherings or parties. He is a poet who uses his verses only to trans-
mit his divine message to mankind.

How does this poet protect his personality? How does he find
and refine his writing skills in this turbid literary atmosphere?

Enrique Bustamante y Ballivián, who knows him intimately, has given us an interesting outline of his artistic development.

Two factors have been most important in the formation of this gifted poet: the impressions he received as an infant in the countryside around "Chuquitanta," his family's estate near Lima, and the Spanish classics that his brother Jorge read to him during his childhood. The former provided him not only with the landscapes that serve as background to many of his poems but also with a profound feeling for nature expressed in the symbols of the country people, who liven it with legends and fables and people it with elves, witches, monsters, and goblins. From the carefully chosen classic readings, he derived his love of literature, his rich vocabulary, and certain archaic phrases that give a special flavor to his very modern poetry. From his home, which was deeply, mystically Christian and of great moral rectitude, he obtained his purity of soul and his dreaminess. It may be added that through his sister Susana, who played the piano and sang, he became fond of music, which runs through many of his verses. As to color and descriptive powers, it should not be forgotten that Eguren is a good painter (although of lesser stature than as a poet) and that he began to paint before he wrote poetry. A critic has commented that Eguren's chief virtue is as a children's poet. Although we do not agree with the critic, he must have based his opinion on the early verses of the poet, which were written for his nieces, with childhood scenes in which they appear.[30]

Although it is wrong to describe Eguren as a children's poet, he is obviously a poet of childlike thoughts and feelings. All his poetry is an enchanted, fanciful version of life. His symbolism comes, first of all, from his childhood impressions and does not depend on literary influences or suggestions. It has its roots in the poet's very soul. The poetry of Eguren is the prolongation of his childhood. Because Eguren keeps a child's innocence and

---

[30] In the *Boletín Bibliográfico*, no. 15 (December, 1915), University of Lima. A review of a selection of Eguren's poetry made by the university librarian, Pedro S. Zulen, one of the first to appreciate the genius of the poet of *Simbólicas*.

daydreams in his verses, the vision of his poetry is virginal. The entire explanation of the miracle is found in the eyes of this spellbound child.

This feature of Eguren's art is not limited to what can be classified as children's poetry. Eguren always expresses things and nature with images that are easily recognizable as the escapades of his childhood subconscious. The image of a "red king with a beard of steel"—one of the charming notes of *Eroe*, poetry with a Rubén Darío rhythm—can be imagined only by a child. "Los reyes rojos," one of the most beautiful creations of Eguren's symbolism, betrays a similar origin in its wierd chromatic composition:

> Since daybreak
> two red kings have fought
> with golden spears.
>
> Their scowls vibrate
> through the green woods
> and on the purple hills.
>
> The falcon kings
> battle in a gold distance
> tinged with blue.
>
> Their black shapes
> are small and wrathful
> in the cadmium light.
>
> Night falls
> and the red kings fight on,
> staunch and frowning.

From his bewitched soul is also born Eguren's taste for the wondrous and fabulous. His world is the indecipherable, Aladdinesque world of "the little girl with the blue lamp." One of the characteristics of this poetry is its exoticism. *Simbólicas* has a background of Scandinavian mythology and German medievalism. The Hellenic myths are never glimpsed in his Wagnerian and grotesque landscapes.

Eguren has no forebears in either Peruvian or Spanish poetry. Bustamante y Ballivián says that González Prada "did not find the origin of Eguren's symbolism in any literature," and I too recall having heard more or less the same words from González Prada.

I classify Eguren among the precursors of the cosmopolitan period of our literature. Eguren, as I have already said, cultivates the delicate and pale flower of symbolism on unreceptive soil. But this does not mean that I agree that French symbolism contains the key to Eguren's art. It is claimed that there are traces of Rimbaud's influence in Eguren. But Rimbaud was by temperament the antithesis of Eguren. Nietzschean and anguished, Rimbaud, like Guillén in his *Deucalión*, would have cried: "I must help the Devil conquer heaven." André Rouveyre declares him "the prototype of demoniac sarcasm and scornful blasphemy." A militant of the Commune, Rimbaud had the psychology of an adventurer and revolutionary. He believed that "one must be absolutely modern," and to this end he left literature and Paris at the age of twenty to become a pioneer in Africa. He had too much vitality to accept an urban and decadent bohemian life as led by Verlaine. Rimbaud, in brief, was a rebellious angel, whereas Eguren was never satanic. Eguren's torments and nightmares were the enchanted fairytales of a child. In "Los ángeles tranquilos," he expresses his style and his soul with crystalline clarity:

> The seawind has passed, and now
> the tranquil angels
> with pearls and beryls
> sing of the dawn solitude.
>
> They strum sacred songs
> on sweet mandolins,
> gazing at the fallen plants
> in the fields and gardens.

> While the sun shakes
> its tinsel in the mist,
> they kiss white death
> in the cruel Saharas.
>
> The tranquil angels
> depart at break of day
> with pearls and beryls
> and with heaven's light in their eyes.

The poet of *Simbólicas* and *La canción de las figuras* represents symbolism in our poetry, but not *a* symbolism, and much less a symbolist school. No one can dispute his originality, for he has written lines as rigorously and absolutely original as those of "El duque":

> Duke Nut is marrying today;
> the canon comes, and the judge,
> and now, with its banners,
> the florid scarlet cavalcade;
> count to one, to two, to ten;
> the excellent Duke is marrying
> the daughter of Clove Spice.
> There they are, with bison hides,
> the horses of Wolf-of-the-Mountain,
> and that jaundiced Gaul, Rodolfo Montante,
> with a frown of triumph.
> And the beauty is in the chapel,
> but the Duke has not yet come;
> the prostrate, adulating magnates
> bow their plumes to the ground;
> the humpbacks, the leapyears,
> make their gestures, gestures, gestures;
> and the bushyhaired crowd
> sneezes, sneezes, sneezes.
> And the bride gazes with ardor
> at the porticoes and open spaces;
> her eyes are two gleaming
> topazes.

And nobles as red as scorpions
cast angry looks;
the most Herculean, taking
a deep breath, shouts out:
Who is detaining the Duke?
The mighty court is annoyed!
But the Duke does not come—
Paquita has eaten him.

Rubén Darío believed that he thought more easily in French than in Spanish, and he was probably right. His decadent, precious, Byzantine art belongs to the *fin-de-siècle* Paris of Verlaine, of which the poet felt himself to be guest and lover. His barge "came from the divine shipyard of the divine Watteau," and the gallicism of his spirit engendered the gallicism of his language. Eguren has neither of these traits. Even his style, which is Spanish in form, shows no French influence.[31] As Bustamante y Ballivián remarks, archaic phrases are frequently found in his verse. In our literature Eguren represents reaction against Spanish influence, which still consisted of baroque rhetoric and grandiloquent romanticism.

In any case, Eguren is not, like Rubén Darío, a lover of eighteenth-century, rococo France. His spirit descends from the Middle Ages rather than from the 1700's, and I find him more Gothic than Latin. I have already alluded to his fondness for Scandinavian and Germanic myths. I shall now state that in some of his early compositions like "Las bodas vienesas" and "Lis," when he was slightly influenced by Rubén Darío, the imagination of Eguren always abandons the eighteenth-century world in search of a medieval color or tone:

Ambiguous elderly
marquises begin

[31] There is no lack of Italianate words in Eguren's poetry. His taste for Italian—which does not Latinize him—springs from his acquaintance with Italian poetry, introduced to him by the readings of his brother Jorge, who lived many years in that country.

their antique dances
and their polonaises.

And archers with long
moustaches arrive
to ward off the fierce
threats of puppets.

It seems to me that some elements of his poetry, such as the
tenderness and candor of his fantasy, relate Eguren to Maeterlinck in his better days. This vague affinity is based on the mystery which Eguren reaches through a wonderland, a realm of
dreams. But Eguren interprets the mystery with the innocence
of a fanciful, visionary child, whereas in Maeterlinck the mystery is frequently the product of a literary alchemy.

In pointing out his gallicism and analyzing his symbolism, a
secret door suddenly opens onto a genealogical interpretation of
the spirit and temperament of José M. Eguren.

Eguren descends from the Middle Ages. He is a pure echo,
strayed into the American tropics, of the medieval West. He
comes not from Moorish but from Gothic Spain. With nothing
Arabic and even very little Latin in his temperament and spirit,
his tastes are rather Nordic. A pallid Van Dyck character, he
sometimes peoples his poetry with Flemish and German images
and evocations. French classicism would reproach him for his
lack of Latin order and clarity and Maurras would find him too
Teutonic and chaotic, because Eguren comes from the age of crusades and cathedrals rather than the rococo Europe of the Renaissance. Like the decorators of Gothic cathedrals, he loved the
grotesque, which he delicately stylized with pre-Renaissance
taste:

Two oblong choristers rave
and lift their rapid hands to heaven
and two blonde giantesses sigh
and ancient cretins play a prelude for the choir.

And, to the sweetness of virginal camellias,

the long-lived party follows the groom;
next, the strong, rigid Aunt Adelias;
and then, limping, limping, the bride.

("Las bodas vieneses")

The white vampires,
old and stilted
in their tight suits,
reach the shade of the stucco.

("Diosa ambarina")

The aristocratic spirit, mildewed by the centuries, survives in
Eguren. In Peru, the colonial aristocracy transformed itself into
a republican bourgeoisie, and the *encomendero* outwardly replaced his feudal and aristocratic principles with the democratic-
bourgeois principles of the war of independence. This simple
exchange enabled him to keep his privileges as *encomendero*
and *latifundista*. Thanks to this metamorphosis, the bourgeoisie
under the republic was no more authentic than the aristocracy
under the viceroyalty.

Eguren—the example would have to be a poet—is perhaps the
only descendant of the genuine medieval and Gothic Europe.
Great-grandson of the adventurous Spain that discovered America, Eguren steeped himself in the ancient aromas of legend in
his family estate on the coast. His century and his environment
did not completely stifle the medieval soul in him. (In Spain,
Eguren, like Valle Inclán, would have loved the heroes and
deeds of the Carlist Wars.) Too late to be a crusader, he is born
a poet; and the adventurer's soul is expressed in the adventurer's
fantasy.

Had he been born a half-century earlier, Eguren's poetry
would have been romantic,[32] although no less deathless because
of this. Born into the decadence of the early 1900's, he had to be

[32] Much of Eguren's writing is romantic, not only in *Simbólicas*, but also
in *Sombra* and even *Rondinelas*, his last two poetic works.

a symbolist. (Maurras is right when he sees in symbolism the end of romanticism.) Eguren would always have tried to escape the reality of his time. Art is an escape when the artist cannot accept or interpret the era and reality in which he lives. American artists of this type, within their dissimilar temperaments and epochs, have been José Asunción Silva and Julio Herrera y Reissig.

The maturing and flowering of these artists has nothing to do with and is even at variance with the painful and harsh labor involved in their country's growth. As Jorge Luis Borges would say, they are artists of a culture, not of a race. But these are the only artists that a country can possess, that a race can produce, during certain periods of its history. Valery Bryusov and Aleksandr Blok, who were symbolists as well as aristocrats, represented Russian poetry in the years preceding the revolution. With the outbreak of the revolution, the two men descended from their ancestral tower to the bloody tumult below.

In Peru, Eguren does not understand or know the people. He is remote from the Indian's history and alien to his history. He is spiritually too occidental and foreign to assimilate indigenous orientalism. But at the same time, Eguren does not understand or know capitalist, bourgeois, occidental civilization. He is interested only in its colossal playthings. Eguren may think of himself as modern because he admires the airplane, the submarine, and the automobile, the fantastic toys constructed by man to cross oceans and continents. Eguren sees man play with the machine; he does not, like Rabindranath Tagore, see the machine enslave man.

The bland, gray coast may have isolated him from the history and people of Peru. Perhaps the sierra would have made him different. A colorless, monotonous Nature is responsible, in any event, for his writing chamber poetry which, when spoken by a true poet, casts the same spell as chamber music and painting.

Alberto Hidalgo

Alberto Hidalgo signified in our literature, from 1917 to 1918, the last throes and demise of the *colónida* experiment. Hidalgo carried to their extremes the megalomania, egoism, and belligerence of the *colónida* attitude. The bacilli of this fever, without which it would have been impossible to raise the temperature of our literature, reached their highest degree of virulence in Hidalgo, who was still provincial in *Panoplia lírica*. Valdelomar was already back from his adventures in the land of D'Annunzio, where—perhaps because rustic Abruzzo and the Adriatic beach are next to Byzantine Venice in D'Annunzio—he discovered the coast of criollo-ness and glimpsed in the distance the continent of Inca-ism.

Valdelomar had kept his sense of humor throughout his most egocentric poses. Hidalgo, who was still a little stiff in his Arequipa cutaway coat, did not have the same easy smile. He was pathetically unsuited to the *colónida* manner. Hidalgo, perhaps because of a rough provincialism unsoftened by urban life, brought to our literary reform a virile taste for the machine, mechanics, skyscrapers, speed, et cetera. If our sensibility, spoiled by the thick chocolate of scholasticism, incorporated D'Annunzio thanks to Valdelomar, it assimilated the explosive, vibrant, noisy Marinetti thanks to Hidalgo. Hidalgo, writer of pamphlets and slogans, followed the lead of González Prada and More. He was too violent a person for a sedentary, rheumatic public. The centrifugal, secessionist force that drove him, swept him away from here in a whirlwind.

Today, Hidalgo, although he does not leave his home in Buenos Aires, is a poet of the Spanish language. Only as background can one speak of his adventures as a local poet. He has grown in stature until he has become a truly American poet, and his literature is circulated and sold all over the Spanish-speaking world. As always, his art is one of secession. The southern climate has tempered and strengthened his rather tropical nerves, which know all the degrees of literature and all the latitudes of imagination. But Hidalgo is, as he could not help but be, in the vanguard. In his own words, he is to the left of the left.

This means, first of all, that Hidalgo has visited the different way stations and has traveled the various roads of ultra-modern art. He is totally familiar with the vanguardist experience. This ceaseless exercise has given him a poetic technique cleansed of any suspicious leftovers. His expression is very clean, burnished, precise, and bare. The motto of his art is "simplicity."

But Hidalgo, without desiring or knowing it, is spiritually at the last station of romanticism. In many of his verses we find the confession of an absolute individualism. Of all the contemporary literary tendencies, solidarity is least present in his poetry. His lyricism is most pure when he is least egocentric; for example, when he says, "I clasp the hand of every living thing—I fully possess the nearness of the world, the world as a neighbor." With these lines he begins his poem "Envergadura del anarquista," which is the most sincere and lyrical outpouring of his individualism. And from the second line, the idea of "the nearness of the world" reveals his feeling of withdrawal and solitude.

Romanticism, understood as a literary and artistic movement linked to the bourgeois revolution, becomes individualism in concept and sentiment. Symbolism and decadence have been only romantic stages, and this is also true of modernism in artists who cannot help being extremely subjective.

There is a symptom inherent in individualist art that indicates, better than any other, a process of dissolution: the determination with which every art and even every artistic element asserts its autonomy. Hidalgo is one of those who most tenaciously adheres to this determination, if we judge by his idea of the "many-sided poem": "A poem in which each line, although subordinate to a central idea or emotion, is an independent entity." We have here his proclamation of the autonomy, the individuality, of verse. The aesthetics of an anarchist could not be otherwise.

Politically and historically, anarchism is to the extreme left of liberalism; it therefore falls, despite all protestations to the contrary, within the bourgeois ideology. The anarchist in our time can be a "rebel," but he is not historically a revolutionary.

Although he denies it, Hidalgo has not escaped the revolutionary fervor of our time in his writing of "Ubicación de Lenin" and "Biografía de la palabra revolución." Nevertheless, his subjectivity leads him to state in the preface to his last book, *Descripción del cielo*, that the former is "a poem of exaltation, of pure lyricism, and not of doctrine"; that "Lenin has served in the same way that a mountain, a river, or a machine could have served as a pretext for creating"; and that the "biography of the word 'revolution' is a eulogy of pure revolution, of revolution as such, whatever may be the cause that originated it." Pure revolution, revolution as such, my dear Hidalgo, does not exist in history and neither does it exist in poetry. Pure revolution is an abstraction. There are many revolutions, among them the liberal and the socialist. There is no pure revolution, either as a historical event or as a poetic theme.

Of the three main categories into which it is convenient, for purposes of classification and criticism, to divide contemporary poetry—pure lyricism, absolute nonsense, and revolutionary epic—Hidalgo feels the first most intensely; and therein lies the strength of his most beautiful poetry. The poem to Lenin is a lyric creation. (Hidalgo deceives himself only in his belief that he is not affected by the emotion of historical events.) This poem, which is technically perfect, is at the same time of great poetic purity. I would quote it in its entirety, but these lines are sufficient:

> In the hearts of the workers his name rises before the sun.
> The spools of thread bless him

from the high spindles
of all the sewing machines.
Typewriters, pianos of the period, play sonatas in his honor.
He is the automatic respite
that eases the peddler's rounds.
He is the General Cooperative of hopes.
His message falls in the money box of the humble,
helping them pay the installments on their houses.
He is the horizon toward which the poor open their windows.
Hanging from the bellclapper of the sun
he beats against the metals of the afternoon
so that the workers may leave at five o'clock.

His lyricism saves Hidalgo from falling into an excessively cerebral, subjective, nihilistic art. It is impossible to have any doubts about someone who can so enjoy himself as in this "Dibujo de niño":

Childhood, village of memories,
I take the streetcar to go there.
Running away from things begins with the stubbornness of
  scattered oil.
The ground is not here.
A cloud passes, and blots out the sky.
Air and light disappear and this is left empty.
Then you leap from the unreachable depths of my forgetfulness.
It was in the bend of an afternoon outlined by the light of
  your silhouette.
A nameless emotion bound our hands together.
Your glances summoned my kiss
but your laugh was a river running between us separating us, girl,
and I from my shore put you off until dreamtime.
Now thirty years are gone of those that were bestowed on me to
  give to you.
If you have died I keep this landscape of my heart, painted on
  you.

The element of nonsense, if we judge Hidalgo at present by his *Descripción del cielo*, disappears almost completely from his poetry. Although it is, in fact, one of the elements of his prose, it is never pure nonsense. It lacks hallucinatory incoherence and tends to be rational, logical nonsense. The revolutionary epic, which heralds a new romanticism untouched by the individualism of that preceding it, does not harmonize with his violently anarchical temperament and life.

His extreme individualism makes it difficult for Hidalgo to write short stories or novels, which require an extroverted author. His stories are written with introspection and his characters appear sketchy, artificial, mechanical. Even when his stories are most fanciful, they are still dominated by the intolerant, tyrannical presence of their author, who refuses to let his characters live in their own right because he puts too much of his individuality and purpose into all of them.

César Vallejo

César Vallejo's first book, *Los heraldos negros*, ushers in the dawn of a new poetry in Peru. Antenor Orrego is not speaking out of fraternal enthusiasm when he states that "this man originates an epoch of poetic liberty and autonomy, of the vernacular in writing."[33]

Vallejo is a poet of race. In Vallejo, for the first time in our history, indigenous sentiment is given pristine expression. Melgar, stunted and frustrated, is still imprisoned by classical technique and enamored of Spanish rhetoric in his *yaravíes*. Vallejo, on the other hand, creates a new style in his poetry. Indigenous sentiment has a melody of its own in his poetry and he has mastered its song. The poet, not satisfied with conveying a new message, also brings a new technique and language. His art does not tolerate the ambiguous and artificial dualism of substance and form. As Orrego observes, "to dismantle the old rhetorical scaffolding was not a caprice, but a vital necessity of the poet. When

[33] Antenor Orrego, *Panoramas*, essay on César Vallejo.

one begins to understand the writing of Vallejo, one begins to understand the need for an original and different technique."[34]

In Melgar, indigenous sentiment is glimpsed only in the background of his verses; in Vallejo, it flowers in their very structure. In Melgar, it is the intonation; in Vallejo, the word. In Melgar, it is but an erotic lament; in Vallejo, a metaphysical undertaking. Vallejo is a creator; even if *Los heraldos negros* had been his only work, it still would have inaugurated a new epoch in our literary process. These initial lines of *Los heraldos negros* probably mark the beginning of Peruvian, in the sense of indigenous, poetry:

There are such heavy blows in life . . . I don't know!
Blows like the hatred of God; as if, before them,
the backwash of everything suffered
had drained into the soul . . . I don't know!

The blows are few, but they fall . . . They open
dark furrows in the boldest face, the strongest shoulder.
Perhaps they are the ponies of barbarous Attilas,
or black heralds sent to us by Death.

They are the precipitous falls of the soul's Christs,
of some adorable faith that Destiny blasphemes.
Those bloody blows are the crepitations
of some loaf of bread that burns in the oven's door.

And man . . . Poor . . . poor man! He turns his eyes
as when somebody taps us on the shoulder;
he turns his mad eyes, and everything he lived
wells up, like a pool of guilt, in his gaze.

There are such heavy blows in life . . . I don't know!

In world literature, *Los heraldos negros* would be classified, partly because of its title, as belonging to the symbolist school. But the symbolist style is better suited than any other to interpret the indigenous spirit. Being animist and rustic, the Indian

[34] Ibid.

tends to express himself in anthropomorphic or pastoral images. Vallejo, moreover, is not entirely symbolist. Especially his early poetry contains elements of symbolism, together with elements of expressionism, dadaism, and surrealism. Vallejo is essentially a creator, always in the process of developing his technique, a process which in his art reflects a mood. In the beginning, when Vallejo borrows his method from Herrera Reissig, he adapts it to his personal lyricism.

But the Indian is the fundamental, characteristic feature of his art. In Vallejo there is a genuine Americanism, not a descriptive or local Americanism. Vallejo does not exploit folklore. Quechua words and popular expressions are not artificially introduced into his language; they are spontaneous and an integral part of his writing. It might be said that Vallejo does not choose his vocabulary. He is not deliberately autochthonous. He does not delve into tradition and history in order to extract obscure emotions from its dark substratum. His poetry and language emanate from his flesh and spirit; he embodies his message. Indigenous sentiment operates in his art perhaps without his knowledge or desire.

One of the clearest and most precise indications of Vallejo's indigenous bent is his frequent attitude of nostalgia. Valcárcel, who probably has most fully interpreted the autochthonous soul, says that the melancholy of the Indian is nothing but nostalgia. Very well, Vallejo is supremely nostalgic. He evokes the past with tenderness, but always subjectively. His nostalgia, conceived in lyric purity, should not be confused with the literary nostalgia of the *pasadistas*. Vallejo's nostalgia is not merely retrospective. He does not yearn for the Inca empire in the way that *pasadismo perricholesco* yearns for the viceroyalty. His nostalgia is a sentimental or a metaphysical protest; a nostalgia of exile, of absence.

> What might she be doing now, my sweet Andean Rita
> of rush and fruit;

now that Bizancio suffocates me and my blood
dozes like flaccid cognac within me.

> ("Idilio muerto," *Los heraldos negros*)

Brother, today I am sitting on the stone bench in
    our house,
where we miss you endlessly!
I remember how we used to play together at this
    hour, and how mamá
caressed us: "But sons . . ."

> ("A mi hermano Miguel," *Los heraldos negros*)

I have eaten alone today, and have had
no mother urging me, no "help yourself," no water,
no father who, in the talkative family rite
of eating corn, would ask for the greater
clasps of sound to make its image memorable.

> (xxviii, *Trilce*)

The stranger is finished with whom you came back,
late last night, chatting and chatting.
Now I will have no one to wait for me,
to keep my place, in good times and bad.
The hot afternoon is finished;
your great bay and your shouting;
finished, your chats with your mother,
who offered us a tea filled with afternoon.

> (xxxiv, *Trilce*)

At other times, Vallejo foresees or foretells the nostalgia that
is to come:

> Absent! The morning on which, like a mournful
> bird, I go to the shore of the sea of shadow,
> the shore of the silent empire,
> the white cemetery will be your captivity.

> > ("Ausente," *Los heraldos negros*)

Summer, I am leaving. And I am grieved
by the submissive little hands of your afternoons.

> You arrive devoutly; you arrive old;
> and now you will not meet anyone in my soul.
>
> ("Verano," *Los heraldos negros*)

Vallejo interprets the race at a moment when all its nostalgia, throbbing with a pain three centuries old, is intensified. But— and this also reveals a trait of the Indian soul—his recollections are full of that sweetness of tender corn which Vallejo savors with melancholy when he speaks to us of the "eloquent offertory of ears of corn."

Vallejo has the pessimism of the Indian in his poetry. His hesitation, his questioning, his restlessness, are summed up skeptically in a "What for!" Piety always underlies this pessimism. There is nothing satanic or morbid in him. It is the pessimism of a spirit that endures and expiates "man's affliction," as Pierre Hamp says. This pessimism is not of literary origin. It does not reflect the romantic despair of the adolescent troubled by the voice of Leopardi or Schopenhauer. He sums up the philosophical experience, he condenses the spiritual attitude, of a race and a people. There is no relationship or affinity between him and the nihilism or intellectual skepticism of the West. The pessimism of Vallejo, like the pessimism of the Indian, is not a belief or a feeling. It is tinged with an oriental fatalism that makes it closer to the Christian and mystic pessimism of the Slavs. But it can never be confused with the anguished neurosis that drove madmen like Andreyev and Artzybaskev to suicide. Therefore, in the same way that it is not a belief, it is not a neurosis.

This pessimism is full of tenderness and compassion, because it is not engendered by egocentricity and narcissism, disenchanted and exacerbated, as is the case almost throughout the romantic school. Vallejo feels all human suffering. His grief is not personal. His soul is "sad unto death" with the sorrow of all men, and with the sorrow of God, because for the poet it is not only men who are sad. In these lines he speaks to us of the grief of God:

I sense God, who walks within me
with the afternoon and with the sea.
We leave together with Him. Night falls.
We greet nightfall with Him, Orphanhood . . .

But I sense God. And it even seems
that He dictates to me I know not what good color.
He is kind and sad, like a Hospitaler;
He emanates a lover's sweet disdain:
His heart must pain Him much.

Oh, my Lord, I have recently found myself,
today when I love so much in this afternoon: today
when, in the false balance of some breasts,
I see and weep for a fragile Creation.

And You, which will You weep for . . . You,
lover of such an enormous revolving bosom . . .
I consecrate You, Lord, because You love so much;
because You never smile; because always
Your heart must pain You much.

Other lines by Vallejo deny this divine intuition. In "Los dados eternos" the poet bitterly reproaches God: "You who have always been well, You feel nothing of Your creation." But this is not the poet's true feeling, which is always expressed with piety and love. When his lyricism, exempt from any rationalist repression, flows freely and generously, it is uttered in lines like the following, which ten years ago were the first to reveal to me Vallejo's genius:

The lottery vendor who shouts "Win a thousand"
contains I know not what essence of God.

All lips pass by. The tedium
blunts his "No more" in a wrinkle.
The lottery vendor passes by, who, perhaps
nominal like God, treasures up,
among tantalizing loaves of bread, human
impotence of love.

I look at that rag of a man. And he
could give us his heart;

> but the luck he carries in his hand,
> shouting it at the top of his voice,
> will fly off, like a cruel bird, to perch—
> where, this bohemian god
> neither knows nor cares.
>
> And I say on this warm Friday
> that moves on sunlit shoulders:
> Why has the will of God
> dressed itself as a lottery vendor!

"The poet," Orrego writes, "speaks individually, he particularizes the language; but he thinks, feels, and loves individually." This great poet, lyrical and subjective, acts as an interpreter of the universe, of mankind. There is nothing in his poetry reminiscent of the egoistic, narcissistic lament of romanticism. The romanticism of the nineteenth century was basically individualistic; the romanticism of the 1900's is, on the other hand, spontaneous and logically socialist, unanimist. Vallejo, from this point of view, belongs not only to his race but also to his century, to his era.[35]

His compassion is so great that sometimes he feels responsible for part of man's suffering. And then he accuses himself. He is beset by the fear, the anguish, that he too is robbing others:

> All of my bones are alien;
> perhaps I stole them!
> I took for my own what perhaps
> was assigned to another;
> and I think that if I had not been born
> another poor man would be drinking this coffee!
> I am a bad thief . . . Where shall I go!

[35] Jorge Basadre believes that although Vallejo uses a new technique in *Trilce*, he continues to be romantic in his themes. However, as he observes in the case of Hidalgo, the newest of the "new poetry" is also romantic to the extent that it is subjective. Vallejo certainly conserves a great deal of the old romanticism and decadence up to *Trilce*, but the merit of his poetry is the way in which he transcends these residual influences. Moreover, it would be useful to come to an understanding about the meaning of the term "romanticism."

> And at this cold hour, when the earth
> transcends human dust and is so sad,
> I would like to knock on every door,
> and beg I do not know whose pardon,
> and bake him little pieces of fresh bread
> here in the oven of my heart.

This is typical of the poetry of *Los heraldos negros*. Vallejo gives his entire soul to the sufferings of the poor:

> Muledriver, you are fantastically glazed with sweat.
> The Menocucho Hacienda charges
> a thousand vexations a day in exchange for life.

This art announces the birth of a new sensitivity. It is a new, rebellious art that breaks with the courtly tradition of a literature of buffoons and lackeys. The great poet of *Los heraldos negros* and of *Trilce*—that great poet who has been ignored and disregarded in the streets of Lima, where carnival mountebanks have been welcomed and praised—appears in his art as a precursor of the new spirit, the new conscience.

In his poetry, Vallejo is always avid for the infinite, thirsty for truth. Creation in him is at the same time indescribably painful and exultant. This artist aspires only to express himself purely and innocently. Therefore, he strips himself of all rhetorical ornament and of all literary vanity. In this way, he reaches the most austere, humble, and proud simplicity. He is a mystic of poverty who removes his shoes so that his bare feet will know the hardness and cruelty of his road.

Here is what he writes to Antenor Orrego after having published *Trilce*:

This book was born in a great void. I am responsible for it. I assume all responsibility for its aesthetics. Today and perhaps more than ever, I feel the weight, unknown until now, of man's most sacred obligation: to be free! If I am not free today, I shall never be free. I feel that the curve of my forehead gathers its most heroic force. I give mself as freely as I can, and this is my greatest artistic contribution. Only God knows up to what point my freedom is sure and true. Only God knows how much I have suffered to prevent that freedom from degenerating into license. Only God knows what dreadful abysses I have gone to the edge of, filled with terror, fearful that everything is going to die so that my poor spirit may live.

This is unmistakably the voice of a true creator, an authentic artist. His confession of suffering is proof of his greatness.

Alberto Guillén

Alberto Guillén inherited the iconoclastic and egocentric spirit of the *colónida* generation. His poetry carries the paranoid exaltation of the ego to an extreme. But, in keeping with the new mood that was already developing, his poetry was virile in tone. A stranger to the poisons of the city, Guillén, like a rustic Pan, roamed the pastoral roads of the countryside. Obsessed with individualism and Nietzscheism, he felt himself to be a superman. In Guillén, Peruvian poetry repudiated, not very elegantly but emphatically, its sources.

This is the time when Guillén wrote *Belleza humilde* and *Promoteo*, but it is in *Deucalión* that the poet fulfills himself. I number *Deucalión* among the books that most nobly and purely represent the Peruvian lyricism of the early century. In *Deucalión* there is no bard who declaims from a platform, no troubador who sings a serenade. There is a man who suffers, exults, affirms, doubts, denies; a man bursting with passion, eagerness, longing; a man thirsty for truth, who knows that "our destiny is to find the road that leads to Paradise." *Deucalión* is the song of embarkation:

> Where to?
> No matter! Life hides
> germinating worlds
>
> not yet discovered:
> Heart, it is time to leave
> for the worlds that sleep!

This new knight errant does not watch over his arms in any inn. He has no horse, no squire, no armor. He walks naked and serious, like Rodin's John the Baptist.

> Yesterday I went out naked
> to challenge Fate:
> for a shield, my pride;
> for a helmet, Mambrino's.

But the tension of waiting has been too hard on his youthful nerves. And his first adventure, like Don Quixote's, has been unlucky and ridiculous. Furthermore, the poet reveals his weakness from that time on. He is not crazy enough to follow the path of Don Quixote, who was unaware of fate's mockery. He carries the ironic Sancho crouched in his soul. He is not completely deluded or altogether mad. He sees the grotesque and comic side of his wanderings. Therefore, weary and undecided, he pauses to question all the sphinxes and all the enigmas:

> For what do you give yourself, heart,
> for what do you give yourself
> if you are never to find
> your illusion?

But doubt, which gnaws at the poet's heart, still cannot conquer his hope. The poem thirsts for the infinite. His illusion may be damaged, but it is still imperious. This sonnet summarizes the whole episode:

> At the midpoint of my journey
> I asked, like Dante,
> "Traveler, do you know
> my destiny, my route?"

> Like an echo, a donkey
> gleefully answered me,
> but the good pilgrim
> gestured me onward;

> then a heroic voice
> rose up within me,
> telling me, "Keep on!"
>
> And I cast off my doubt
> and in my bare hand
> I carry my determination!

The wanderer is not always so strong. The devil tempts him at every step. In spite of himself, doubt begins to work its way into his conscience, corrupting and weakening it. Guillén agrees with the devil that "we do not know who is right, Quixote or Panza." A relativist and skeptical philosophy undermines his will. His actions become a little uncertain and mistrustful. Between Nothing and the Myth, his impulse is toward the Myth. But Guillén knows his relativity. Doubt is sterile and faith is fruitful. For this reason alone, Guillén chooses the road of faith. His quixotism has lost its candor and purity. It has become pragmatic. "Think that it is good for you not to lose hope." To hope, to believe, is a question of what is desirable and convenient. It does not matter that this intuition should be defined later in more noble terms: "And better yet, do not reason; illusions are worth more than the strongest reasoning."

But the poet still recovers, from time to time, his divine madness. His hallucination still burns. He is still capable of expressing himself with a superhuman passion:

> In the same way that old Paul
> was thrown to the ground
> I have been struck by the spear
> of infinite longing:
>
> therefore, in what I say to you,
> I put the desire for flight;
> I must help the Devil
> to conquer heaven.

And in this admirable sonnet, heavy with emotion and religious in tone, the poet states his creed:

> Strip your heart
> of all vanity
> and bring your will
> to where your illusion is;
>
> oppose with your fist,
> oppose with your freedom,
> the ancient alluvium
> of Fatality;
>
> and let your thoughts,
> like the elements,
> destroy all restraints,
>
> as the seed quickens
> into life despite
> the worm and the mire.

This poetry has roots in Nietzsche, Rodó, and Unamuno. But the flower is Guillén's and there can be no argument about its ownership. Thought is totally identified with form in *Deucalión*. Form, like thought, is bare, tense, urgent, simultaneously angry and serene. (One of the things I admire most in *Deucalión* is precisely his rejection of any ornament, his deliberate refusal to use rhetoric.) *Deucalión* is a new dawn on the horizon. In *Deucalión* man sets out, still young and pure, in search of God and to conquer the world.

But along the way, Guillén is corrupted. He becomes vain and haughty. He loses his innocence and forgets the ingenuous goal of his youth. The spectacle and emotions of an urban, cosmopolitan civilization enervate and slacken his will. His poetry is infected by the negative, corrosive humor of the West. Guillén becomes sly, mocking, and cynical. And the sin carries its expiation. After *Deucalión* everything is inferior, lacking in human intensity as well as in artistic significance. *El libro de las pará-*

bolas and *Imitación de nuestro señor yo* succeed in many ways, but they are hopelessly monotonous books. They seem to be products of an alembic in which the skepticism and egoism of Guillén are slowly distilled, drop by drop. So many drops make a page; so many drops, a preface; so many, a book.

The most interesting side of Guillén's personality is his relativism. Guillén amuses himself by denying the reality of the individual. But his testimony is suspect, because Guillén may base his reasoning on personal experience: "My personality, as I dreamed of it, as I envisaged it, has not been realized; therefore, the personality does not exist."

In *Imitación de nuestro señor yo*, Guillén's thought is Pirandellian. Here are some examples: "He, she, all exist, but in you." "I am all men in me." "Are my contradictions not proof that I bear in me many men?" "False. They do not die: as we who die in them." These lines contain strands of the philosophy of Pirandello's *One, None, and a Hundred Thousand*.

Nevertheless, I do not believe that Guillén, if he continues in this direction, will ever be classified among the authors of humorous and cosmopolitan Western literature. Guillén, basically, is a rather rural and Franciscan poet. Do not take his blasphemies literally. Deep inside, he retains a little of his provincial romanticism. His psychology has many peasant roots. Underneath, he remains strange to the quintessence of the city. When reading Guillén, one notices immediately that he is not skilled in artifice.

The title of Guillén's last book, *Laureles*, sums up the second phase of his literature and his life. In order to gain these and other laurels, which he himself secretly scorns, he has struggled, suffered, and fought. He has turned away from the road to heaven to take the road to laurels. In adolescence his ambition was more lofty; will it now be satisfied with some municipal or academic laurels?

I agree with Gabriel Alomar when he accuses Guillén of

strangling the poet of *Deucalión* with his own hands. Because of his impatience, Guillén must have laurels at all cost. But laurels do not last. Glory is made of less ephemeral materials and it is reserved for those who refuse its fallacious and fictitious advance rewards. The duty of the artist is not to break faith with his destiny. Guillén resolves his impatience in abundance, and abundance is what most damages and diminishes the merit of his work. His recent verse, although avant-garde in style, is weary and jaded and repeats his early themes.

Magda Portal

Magda Portal is important in our literary process. She is Peru's first poetess as distinguished from mere women of letters, few of whom had artistic or, more specifically, literary temperament.

The term "poetess" should be explained. In the history of Western civilization, a poetess is to some extent a contemporary phenomenon. Previous eras produced only masculine poetry; even that written by women was only a variation of men's lyric themes or philosophical ideas. There was also an asexual poetry lacking either virility or the stamp of a woman—virgin, female, mother. Today, women finally put their own flesh and spirit into their poetry. The poetess is now someone who creates a feminine poetry. And ever since women's poetry became spiritually emancipated and differentiated from men's, poetesses have occupied a high place in the catalog of all literatures.

In the poetry of Spanish America, two women, Gabriela Mistral and Juana de Ibarbourou, have for some time attracted more attention than any of their male colleagues. Delmira Agustini has founded a long and noble lineage in her country and in America. Blanca Luz Brum has brought her message to Peru. These are not solitary, exceptional cases but part of a widespread phenomenon common to all literatures. Poetry, grown old in man, is born again, rejuvenated, in woman.

A brilliantly intuitive writer, Félix del Valle, remarking on the large number of outstanding poetesses in the world, told me that the scepter of poetry had passed to women. With his natural wit, he put it this way: "Poetry is turning into a woman's occupation." This is an extreme statement; but poets certainly have a tendency to make of poetry a nihilistic, skeptical exercise, whereas poetesses tend to give it fresh roots and gleaming white flowers. Their poetry has more vitality and biological force.

Magda Portal is still not sufficiently known and appreciated either in Peru or in Spanish America. She has published only one book of prose, El derecho de matar (La Paz, 1926), and one book of verse, Una esperanza y el mar (Lima, 1927). El derecho de matar presents only one of her sides: the rebellious spirit and revolutionary messianism that in these times are indisputable evidence of an artist's historical awareness. Furthermore, the prose of Magda Portal always contains something of her magnificent lyricism. "El poema de la cárcel," "La sonrisa de Cristo," and "Círculos violeta"—three poems in this volume—have her charity, passion, and exalted tenderness. But El derecho de matar does not characterize or define her; even its title, which rings of anarchy and nihilism, does not represent her spirit.

Magda is essentially lyrical and she is compassionate in the same way Vallejo is compassionate. This is the only way she appears in the lines of "Anima absorta" and "Una esperanza y el mar," and this certainly is the way she is. She is not tainted by the decadence of the 1900's.

In her early verse, Magda Portal is almost always a poetess of tenderness. And in some of this verse may be seen her lyricism and humanity. Exempt from egoism, megalomania, or romantic narcissism, Magda Portal says to us: "I am small!"

In addition to the compassion and tenderness found in her poetry, there is the voice of a woman who lives passionately and intensely, glowing with love and longing, tormented by truth and hope.

Magda Portal has written on the frontispiece of one of her books these words by Leonardo da Vinci: "The soul, first source of life, is reflected in everything that it creates." "The true work of art is like a mirror in which the soul of the artist is seen." Magda's ardent loyalty to these creative principles reveals an artistic sense that her poetry never contradicts and always ratifies.

In her poetry she gives us, above all, a clear image of herself. She never practices sleight of hand, nor does she mystify or idealize. Her poetry is her truth. Magda does not labor to dress up her soul for us. We can enter one of her books without ceremony, confident that we shall not encounter some sham or snare. The art of this profound and pure lyricist reduces to a minimum, almost to zero, the proportion of artifice that it requires in order to be art.

This is for me the best proof of Magda's great value. In this era of social and, therefore, artistic decadence, the most urgent duty of the artist is the truth. The only works that will survive this crisis are those that constitute a confession and a testimony.

The eternal and dark contrast between the life and death principles that govern the world is always present in the poetry of Magda. At the same time that she longs for oblivion, she is eager to create and live. Magda's soul is a soul in agony. And her art is a total translation of the two forces that lacerate and inspire her. Sometimes the life principle triumphs and sometimes the death principle prevails.

This dramatic conflict gives the poetry of Magda Portal a profound metaphysics, which her spirit easily reaches through her lyricism without the aid of any philosophy. It also gives her a psychological depth that enables her to record all the contradictory voices of her dialogue, her combat, her agony. The poetess expresses herself with extraordinary strength in the following lines:

> Come, kiss me!
> What does it matter if something dark
> is gnawing at my soul
> with its teeth?
>
> I am yours and you are mine . . . kiss me! . . .
> I do not weep today . . . I am drowned in joy,
> a strange joy
> that comes from I know not where.
>
> You are mine . . . You are mine? . . .
> there is a door of ice
> between you and me:
> your thoughts!
>
> Those that beat upon your brain
> and whose hammering
> escapes me . . .
>
> Come, kiss me . . . What does it matter? . . .
> My heart called to you all night long,
> and now that you are here, your flesh and your soul,
> why should I care about what you did yesterday? . . .
>   What does it matter!
>
> Come, kiss me . . . your lips,
> your eyes, and your hands . . .
> Then . . . nothing . . .
> And your soul? And your soul!

This poetess of ours, whom we should hail as one of the foremost poetesses of Indo-America, does not descend from Ibarbourou, or Agustini, or even Mistral, whom she nonetheless resembles more than anyone else because of a certain similarity of tone. She has an original and autonomous temperament. Her secret, her word, her force were born with her and are in her.

In her poetry there is more pain than joy, more darkness than light. Magda is sad. Her life force moves her toward light and

gaiety. And Magda feels herself powerless to enjoy them. This is
her drama. But it does not embitter or worry her.

In "Vidrios de amor," a poem in eighteen emotional stanzas,
all Magda is in these lines:

> With how many tears did you shape me?
>
> I have so many times assumed
> the attitude of the suicidal trees
> along the dusty, lonesome roads—
>
> secretly, without your knowing it,
> everything must hurt you
> for having made me thus, with no sweetness
> for my acid hurts.
>
> where did I come from with my fierce
> desire to conform?
> I have never known the merry-go-round happiness
> of childhood, I have never dreamed of it.
>
> Ah!—and nevertheless
> I love happiness the way
> bitter plants will love
> a sweet fruit.
>
> Mother, alert
> and receptive,
> do not answer today because you would be drowned,
> do not answer today my almost
> tearless weeping.
>
> I bury my anguish inside me in order to watch
> the lefthand branch of my life,
> which has put only love
> into the kneading of my daughter's heart.
>
> I would like to protect her from myself
> as from a wild beast,
> from these accusing eyes,
> from this tattered voice
> in which insomnia scoops caverns,

and, for her, to be happy, ingenuous, a child,
as if all the bells of happiness
rang out their everlasting Easter in my heart.

Is all of Magda here in these lines? No, because Magda is more than a mother, more than love. Who knows out of how many dark powers, out of how many conflicting truths, a soul like hers is made?

Contemporary Literary Currents—Indigenism

The "indigenous" current typical of the new Peruvian literature is spreading and probably will intensify, but not as a result of the extrinsic or fortuitous circumstances that usually determine a literary fashion. Its significance is more profound. The fact that it coincides and intimately relates with an ideological and social current that daily gathers support among youth is sufficient evidence that literary indigenism reflects a state of mind and of conscience in the new Peru.

This indigenism, which is in germination and still needs time to flower and bear fruit, might be compared—allowing for all differences in time and space—with the "muzhikism" of prerevolutionary Russian literature. Muzhikism was bound up with the first phase of social unrest that prepared and incubated the Russian revolution. Muzhikist literature performed a historical mission by putting Russian feudalism on trial and condemning it with no possibility of appeal. The muzhikist novel and poetry were prodromes in the socialization of land as carried out by the Bolshevik revolution. It does not matter that the Russian novelist and poet had no thought of socialization when they portrayed the muzhik, nor does it matter whether they caricatured or idealized him.

In the same way, Russian "constructivism" and "futurism," which delight in representing machines, skyscrapers, airplanes, factories, et cetera, belong to a period when the urban proletariat, after creating a regime that still chiefly benefits the farmer, work to westernize Russia through industrialization.

The indigenism of our contemporary literature is linked to recent developments. If the indigenous problem is part of politics, economics, and sociology, it cannot be absent from literature and art. One would be mistaken to think of it as an artificial issue simply because many of those who advance it are novices or opportunists.

Nor should one deny its vitality because it has so far failed to produce a masterpiece. A masterpiece can only flower in soil that has been amply fertilized by an anonymous multitude of mediocre works. The genius in art is usually not a beginning but the end result of a vast experience.

There is even less reason to be alarmed by sporadic outbursts and reported excesses. They do not contain the key to historical fact. Any affirmation must be carried to extremes. To speculate on anecdotes is to remain outside history.

This current, moreover, is encouraged by the elements of cosmopolitanism that have been assimilated into our literature. I have already pointed to the interest of the American avant-garde in autonomous and local themes. In the new Argentine literature, no one feels more native to Buenos Aires than Girondo and Borges, or more gaucho than Güiraldes. On the other hand, those who, like Larreta, remain in bondage to Spanish classicism are basically incapable of interpreting their countries.

Some are stimulated by the exoticism that has invaded European literature as the symptoms of decadence in Western civilization intensify. César Moro, Jorge Seoane and other recent emigrants to Paris are expected to employ native and indigenous motifs. The art of our sculptress, Carmen Saco, has found its most valid passport in her Indian statues and designs.

This last, and external, factor has influenced such "emigrant" writers as Ventura García Calderón toward indigenism, although they are not numbered among the avant-garde or thought to have been infected by the ideals attributed to the young writers who work in their own countries.

Criollo-ism has not flourished as a nationalist current in our literature, mainly because the criollo still does not represent a nationality. It has long been accepted that our nationality is in the process of formation and now a dualism of race and spirit is observed. In any event, we have not even begun to fuse the racial elements that make up our population. The criollo is not clearly defined. Until now, the word "criollo" has been little more than a generic term to designate a many-shaded mestizo group. Our criollo lacks the distinctive character of the Argentine criollo, who, unlike the Peruvian, can be identified anywhere in the world. This confrontation proves precisely that there is an Argentine nationality, whereas there are no traits peculiar to a Peruvian nationality. Our criollo in the sierra is different from our coastal criollo. In the sierra, the mestizo is made more Indian by his terrestrial surroundings; on the coast, the spirit inherited from Spain is maintained by colonial tradition.

Nativist literature in Uruguay, born of a cosmopolitan experience like its counterpart in Argentina, has been criollo because the population of Uruguay has a unity which ours does not. Nativism in Uruguay, moreover, is essentially a literary phenomenon without the political and economic undertones of Peru's indigenism. Zum Felde, who has promoted it as a critic, states that the time has come to liquidate it.

An autonomous native feeling was needed to oppose slavish imitation of the foreign. As a movement of literary emancipation, it achieved its end. The moment was ripe. Young poets turned toward national reality and saw that, in contrast with the European, it was more authentically American. But having completed its mission, traditionalism should yield to a lyrical Americanism more in tune with life's imperative. Today's sentiments feed on different realities and ideals. Río de la Plata is no longer a gaucho domain. And gaucho folklore, having withdrawn to the most remote corners, is now being consigned to the silent cult of the museum. The advance of urban cosmopolitianism has completely transformed the customs and character of rural life in Uruguay.[36]

In Peru, criollo-ism has not only been sporadic and superficial, but it has been nourished on colonial sentiment. It has not been an affirmation of autonomy. Until very recently, it has been content to describe local customs within the surviving colonial literature. Abelardo Gamarra is probably the only exception to this domesticated criollo-ism without native pride.

Our nativism, which is also necessary for revolution and emancipation, cannot be a simple criollo-ism. The Peruvian criollo has not yet liberated himself spiritually from Spain. His Europeanization, in reaction to which he must find his own personality, has been only partly completed. Once he is Europeanized, today's criollo will become aware of the drama of Peru, recognizing in himself a bastardized Spanish and in the Indian the cement of nationality. (Valdelomar, the coastal criollo who returned from Italy imbued with the teachings of D'Annunzio and with snobbishness, had his most enlightening experience when he discovered—or imagined—the Inca.) Whereas the pure criollo generally conserves his colonial spirit, the Europeanized criollo of our times rebels against that spirit, even if only as protest against its limitations and archaism.

Undoubtedly, the criollo, diverse and numerous, can be the source of an abundance of characters and plots in our literature —narrative, descriptive, social, folkloric, et cetera. But what the genuine indigenist current subconsciously seeks in the Indian is not just character and plot, much less picturesque character and plot. Indigenism is not essentially a literary phenomenon, as is the nativism of Uruguay. It is rooted in another

[36] Alberto Zum Felde, *La cruz del sur* (Montevideo).

historical soil. The authentic indigenists, who should not be confused with those who exploit indigenous themes out of mere love of the exotic, deliberately or unknowingly collaborate in a task of redressing political and economic wrongs, not in a task of restoration or resurrection.

The Indian does not represent solely a type, a theme, a plot, a character; he represents a people, a race, a tradition, a spirit. It is impossible to consider and evaluate him from a purely literary standpoint, as though he were a national color or feature on the same plane as other ethnic elements in Peru.

On closer study, it becomes clear that the indigenist current is not based on simple literary factors, but on complex social and economic factors. Because of the conflict and contrast between his demographic predominance and his social and economic servitude, not just inferiority, the Indian deserves to be the focus of attention in present-day Peru. That three to four million people of autochthonous race occupy the mental panorama of a country of five million should not surprise anyone, especially in a period when this country is trying to find an equilibrium which to date has been denied it by history.

Indigenism in our literature, as may be gathered from my earlier statements, is basically aimed at repairing the injustices done to the Indian. Its role is not the purely sentimental one of, for example, criollo-ism. It would therefore be a mistake to judge indigenism as the equivalent of criollo-ism, which it neither replaces nor supplants.

The Indian is prominent in Peruvian literature and art, not because he is an interesting subject for a novel or a painting, but because the new forces and vital impulses of the nation are directed toward redeeming him. This tendency is more instinctive and biological than intellectual and theoretical. I repeat that the genuine indigenist does not concern himself with the Indian as a source of picturesque character and plot; if this were the case, the *zambo* would be as interesting as the Indian to the writer or artist. Moreover, the indigenist current is lyrical rather than naturalist or *costumbrista* in character, as is demonstrated in the beginnings of an Andean poetry.

In making reparation to the autochthonous race, it is necessary to separate the Indian from the Negro, mulatto, and *zambo*, who represent colonial elements in our past. The Spaniard imported the Negro when he realized that he could neither supplant nor assimilate the Indian. The slave came to Peru to serve the colonizing ambitions of Spain. The Negro race is one of the human alluvia deposited on the coast by Spain, one of the thin, weak strata of sediment that formed in the lowlands of Peru during the viceroyalty and the early period of the republic; and throughout this cycle, circumstances have conspired to maintain its solidarity with the colony. Because he has never been able to acclimatize himself physically or spiritually to the sierra, the Negro has always viewed it with distrust and hostility. When he has mixed with the Indian, he has corrupted him with his false servility and exhibitionist and morbid psychology.

Since emancipation, the Negro has become addicted to his status of liberated slave. Colonial society turned the Negro into a domestic servant, very seldom into an artisan or worker, and it absorbed and assimilated him until it became intoxicated by his hot, tropical blood. The Negro was as accessible and domesticated as the Indian was impenetrable and remote. Thus the very origin of slave importation created a subordination from which the Negro and mulatto can be redeemed only through a social and economic revolution that will turn them into workers and thereby gradually extirpate their slave mentality. The mulatto, still colonial in his attitudes, is subconsciously opposed to autochthonism. By nature he feels closer to Spain than to the Inca. Only socialism can awaken in him a class consciousness that will lead him to a definitive rupture with the last remnants of his colonial spirit.

The development of the indigenist current does not threaten or paralyze other vital elements of our literature. Indigenism does not aspire to preempt the literary scene by excluding or blocking other impulses and manifestations. It represents the trend and tone of an era because of its sympathy and close association with the spiritual orientation of new generations who, in turn, are sensitive to the imperative needs of our economic and social development.

A critic could commit no greater injustice than to condemn indigenist literature for its lack of autochthonous integrity or its use of artificial elements in interpretation and expression. Indigenist literature cannot give us a strictly authentic version of the Indian, for it must idealize and stylize him. Nor can it give us his soul. It is still a mestizo literature and as such is called indigenist rather than indigenous. If an indigenous literature finally appears, it will be when the Indians themselves are able to produce it.

The present indigenist current cannot be equated with the old colonialist current. Colonialism, which reflected the feelings of a feudal class, indulged in nostalgic idealization of the past. Indigenism, on the other hand, has its roots in the present; it finds its inspiration in the protest of millions of men. The viceroyalty was; the Indian is. And whereas getting rid of the remains of colonial feudalism is a basic condition for progress, vindication of the Indian and of his history is inserted into a revolutionary program.

It is clear that we are concerned less with what is dead than with what has survived of the Inca civilization. Peru's past interests us to the extent it can explain Peru's present. Constructive generations think of the past as an origin, never as a program.

All that survives of Tawantinsuyo is the Indian. The civilization has perished, but not the race. After four centuries, the biological material of Tawantinsuyo has proved to be indestructible and, to a degree, immutable.

Man changes more slowly than might be imagined in this century of speed, when his transformation has broken all records. But this is a phenomenon peculiar to the West, which is, above all, a dynamic civilization and the one that, logically enough, has investigated the relativity of time. In Asiatic societies, which are kindred to the Inca society, there is a certain quietism and ecstasy, periods when history seems to be suspended and a single social structure endures, petrified, for centuries. It can therefore be assumed that in four centuries the Indian has undergone very little spiritual change. Servitude has undoubtedly depressed his flesh and his spirit. But the dark depths of his soul have hardly altered. In the steep sierra and the jagged horizons still untouched by the white man's law, the Indian continues to abide by his ancestral code.

Enrique López Albújar, spokesman for the Radical generation, has written a book, *Cuentos andinos*, which is the first to explore these paths. In its harsh sketches, *Cuentos andinos* grasps the elementary emotions of life in the sierra and charts the soul of the Indian. López Albújar and Valcárcel both search in the Andes for the origin of the Quechua's cosmic consciousness. "Los tres jircas" by López Albújar and "Los hombres de piedra"[37] by Valcárcel express the same mythology. The participants and settings of López Albújar have the same backdrop as the theory and ideas of Valcárcel. This coincidence is especially interesting because it is the product of different temperaments and methods. López Albújar wants to be a naturalist and to analyze, Valcárcel to be imaginative and to synthesize. López Albújar looks at the Indian with the eyes and mind of a coastal man, Valcárcel with the eyes and mind of a sierra man. There is no

[37] Luis E. Valcárcel, *De la vida inkaica* (Lima, 1925).

spiritual kinship between the two writers, no similarity in the genre and style of the two books. Yet they listen to the same distant heartbeat of the Quechua soul.[38]

Although the Indian was formally converted by the conquest to Catholicism, he has not really surrendered his old myths. His mysticism has been modified, but his animism remains. The Indian does not understand Catholic metaphysics. His pantheist and materialist philosophy has entered into a loveless marriage with the catechism. In his concept of life, it is not Reason but

---

[38] López Albújar sounds a note in his book that concurs with that of Valcárcel's book when he speaks of the nostalgia of the Indian. The melancholy of the Indian, according to Valcárcel, is nothing but nostalgia: the nostalgia of the man who has been wrenched from his land and his home to serve the military or pacific enterprises of the state. In *Ushanam Jampi*, the hero is destroyed by his nostalgia. Conce Maille is condemned to exile by the elders of Chupán. But the longing to feel his roof overhead is stronger than his instinct for survival. He furtively steals back to his hut, although he knows that the death penalty may await him in his village.

This nostalgia defines the spirit of the people of the sun as agricultural and sedentary. The Quechuas are not and never have been adventurous or wanderers. Perhaps for this reason, their imagination is not and never has been adventurous or nomadic. Perhaps for this reason, the Indian makes his natural surroundings the object of his metaphysics. Perhaps for this reason, the *jircas* or household gods of his region govern his life. The Indian cannot be monotheist.

For four centuries the causes of indigenous nostalgia have multiplied. The Indian has frequently been an emigrant. And since he has not been able to learn to live as a nomad in those four centuries, because four centuries is very little time, his nostalgia has acquired the tone of despair that is heard in the wail of the Indian flutes.

López Albújar looks deeply into the mute abyss of the Quechua soul. In his digression on coca, he writes: "The Indian, without knowing it, is a Schopenhauerist. Schopenhauer and the Indian have a point of contact, but with this difference: the pessimism of the philosopher is theory and vanity; the pessimism of the Indian is experience and disdain. If, for the former, life is evil, for the latter it is neither evil nor good, but a sad reality that he has the profound wisdom to accept as it is."

Unamuno finds this to be a correct judgment. He also believes that the skepticism of the Indian is experience and disdain. But the historian and sociologist can perceive other things that the philosopher and the writer may scorn. Is this skepticism not partly a trait of Asiatic psychology? The Chinese, like the Indian, is materialistic and skeptical. In China, as in Tawantinsuyo, religion is more a moral code than a metaphysical concept.

Nature that is interrogated. The three *jircas*, the three hills, of Huánuco weigh more heavily on the conscience of the Huánuco Indian than the Christian hereafter.

"Las tres jircas" and "Como habla la coca" are, in my opinion, the best chapters in *Cuentos andinos*, but neither is, strictly speaking, a story. "Ushanam Jampi," on the other hand, has a strong narrative context and, moreover, is a valuable document on indigenous communism. This tale describes how popular justice operates in small Indian villages isolated from government law. Here we find an institution that survives from the autochthonous regime, an institution that categorically demonstrates that the Inca organization was a communist organization.

In an individualistist system, the administration of justice is bureaucratic and assigned to a magistrate. Liberalism, for example, fragmentizes justice and creates a caste, a bureaucracy, of judges of different hierarchies. In a communist system, the administration of justice is a function of society as a whole and, as in the Indian system, it is performed by the *vayas*, or elders.[39]

---

[39] In the prologue he wrote for *Cuentos andinos*, Ezequiel Ayllón explained indigenous popular justice in this way: "The substantive, common law, carried down from the most remote antiquity, establishes two penal substitutes that are aimed at the social rehabilitation of the delinquent and two punishments for murder and theft, which are the two crimes of greatest social significance. The Yachishum or Yachachishum is limited to warning the delinquent, making him understand the disadvantages of the crime and the advantages of mutual respect. The Alliyachishum is supposed to forestall personal vengeance by reconciling the delinquent with the injured party and his relatives, in the event that the Yachishum has not had a restraining effect. Application of the two substitutes, which are not unlike the procedures advocated by the penalists of the modern positivist school, is followed by the penalty of confinement or exile called Jitarishum, implying a definitive expatriation. It is the surgical removal of the diseased element that represents a threat to the security of people and property. If the one who has been warned, reconciled, and expelled, robs or kills again within the jurisdiction of the region, he receives the extreme penalty, with no hope of pardon, called Ushanam Jampi. This final solution is death, usually by beating, after which the body is quartered and thrown to the bottom of the river or to the dogs and birds of prey. This trial is held in a single session, orally and publicly, and it includes the accusation, defense, proof, sentence, and execution."

According to current predictions, the future of Latin America depends on the fate of *mestizaje*. In contrast to the hostile pessimism of the Le Bon school of sociology, a messianic optimism has exalted the mestizo as the hope of the continent. In the forceful words of Vasconcelos, the tropics and mestizo are the setting and the protagonist of a new civilization. But the thesis of Vasconcelos, which outlines a utopia—in the positive and philosophical meaning of the word—to the same extent that it attempts to predict the future, ignores the present. Nothing is more alien to his thought and purpose than a criticism of contemporary reality, to which he turns exclusively for elements to support his prophecy.

The *mestizaje* extolled by Vasconcelos is not precisely the mixture of Spanish, Indian, and African which has already taken place on the continent. It is a purifying fusion and refusion, from which the cosmic race will emerge centuries later. For Vasconcelos, the mestizo in his present form is not the prototype of a new race and a new culture, but only its promise. The reflections of a philosopher, of a utopian, are not bound by limitations of time or space. In his ideal construction, centuries are only moments. The work of a critic, historiographer, or politician is another matter. They must concern themselves with immediate results and be satisfied with nearby landscapes. The object of their research and the subject of their program are the real mestizo history, not the ideal of prophecy.

In Peru, because of the imprint of different environments and the combination of many racial mixtures, the meaning of "mestizo" varies. *Mestizaje* has produced a complex species rather than a solution of the dualism of Spaniard and Indian.

Dr. Uriel García discovers the neo-Indian in the mestizo. But this mestizo comes from the mixture of Spanish and indigenous races and is subject to the effects of Andean environment and ways of life. Dr. Uriel García has conducted his research in a mountain medium that has assimilated the white invader. The crossing of the two races has engendered the New Indian, strongly influenced by regional tradition and setting.

This mestizo, who in the course of several generations and under the steady pressure of a single physical and cultural environment has acquired stable characteristics, is not the mestizo produced by the same races on the coast. The coast makes less impression; the Spanish factor is more active.

The Chinese and Negro complicate *mestizaje* on the coast. Neither of these two elements has so far contributed either cultural values or progressive energies to the formation of nationality. The Chinese coolie has been driven from his country by overpopulation and poverty. He introduces into Peru his race but not his culture. Chinese immigration has not brought us any of the basic elements of Chinese civilization, perhaps because these have lost their dynamism and generating power even at home. We have become acquainted with Lao Tse and Confucius through the West. Probably the only direct importation from the Orient of an intellectual order is Chinese medicine, and its arrival is undoubtedly due to practical and mechanical reasons, stimulated by the backwardness of a people who cling to all forms of folk remedies. The skill of the small Chinese farmer has flourished only in the valleys of Lima, where the proximity of an important market makes truck gardening profitable.

The Chinese, furthermore, appears to have inoculated his descendants with the fatalism, apathy, and defects of the decrepit Orient. Gambling, which is an element of immorality and indolence and is particularly harmful to people prone to rely more on chance than on effort, is mainly encouraged by Chinese immigration. Only since the Nationalist movement, which has had wide repercussions among the expatriate Chinese of this continent, has the Chinese colony shown signs of an active interest in culture and progress. The Chinese theater, almost exclusively reserved for the nocturnal amusement of people of that nationality, has made no impression on our literature except on the exotic and artificial tastes of the decadents. Valdelomar and the *colónidas* discovered it during their opium sessions, when they were infected by the orientalism of Loti and Farrère. The Chinese, in brief, does not transfer to the mestizo his moral discipline, his cultural and philosophical tradition, or his skill as farmer and artisan. His language, his immigrant status, and the criollo's scorn for him combine to act as a barrier between his culture and the environment.

The contribution of the Negro, who came as a slave, almost as merchandise, appears to be even more worthless and negative. The Negro brought his sensualism, his superstition, and his primitivism. His condition not only did not permit him to help create culture, but the crude, vivid example of his barbarism was more likely to hamper such creation.

Racial prejudice has diminished; but the progress of sociology and history has broadened and strengthened the idea that there are differences and inequalities in the evolution of people. Although the inferiority of colored races is no longer one of the dogmas that sustain a battered white pride, all the relativism of today does not suffice to abolish cultural inferiority.

Race is only one of the elements that determine the structure of society. Vilfredo Pareto lists the following categories: (1) Soil and climate, flora and fauna, geological and mineralogical conditions, et cetera. (2) Other elements external to a given society at a given time; that is, the actions of other societies on it, which are external in space, and the consequences of the previous condition of that society, which are external in time. (3) Internal elements, of which the principal are race, the "residual" feelings that are manifested in propensities, interests, aptitudes for reasoning and observation, the state of knowledge, et cetera. Pareto argues that the structure of a society is determined by all the elements that operate on it and that once a society has been determined, it operates in turn on those elements, so that it may be said that the action is reciprocal.[40]

What is important, therefore, in a sociological study of the Indian and mestizo strata is not the degree to which the mestizo inherits the qualities or defects of the progenitor races, but his ability to evolve with more ease than the Indian toward the white man's social state or type of civilization. *Mestizaje* needs to be analyzed as a sociological rather than an ethnic question. The ethnic problem that has occupied the attention of untrained sociologists and ignorant analysts is altogether fictitious. It becomes disproportionately important to those who, abiding by the idea cherished by European civilization at its peak (and already discarded by that same civilization, which in its decline favors a relativist concept of history), attribute the achievements of Western society to the superiority of the white race. In the simplistic judgment of those who advise that the Indian be regenerated by cross-breeding, the intellectual and technical skills, the creative drive, and the moral discipline of the white race are reduced to mere zoological conditions.

Although the racial question—which has implications that lead superficial critics to improbable zoological reasoning—is artificial and does not merit the consideration of those who are engaged in a concrete and political study of the indigenous problem, the sociological question is another matter. The contrast in color will gradually disappear, but the rights of the mestizo are legitimized in his customs, feelings, and myths—the spiritual and formal elements of those phenomena that are called society and culture. In existing socio-economic conditions, *mestizaje* produces not only a new human and ethnic type but a new social type. The blurring of that type by a confused combination of races does not in itself imply any inferiority and may even presage, in certain ideal mixtures, the characteristics of the

[40] Vilfredo Pareto, *Trattato di sociologia generale*, III, 265.

cosmic race. However, because of a murky predominance of negative sediments, the undefined or hybrid nature of the social type manifests itself in a sordid and unhealthy stagnation. Chinese and Negro admixtures have almost always had a destructive and aberrant effect on this *mestizaje*. Neither European nor Indian tradition is perpetuated in the mestizo; they sterilize each other.

In an urban, industrial, and dynamic environment, the mestizo rapidly catches up with the white man and assimilates Western culture together with its customs, motivations, and consequences. Usually he does not grasp the complex beliefs, myths, and feelings that underlie the material and intellectual creations of the European or white civilization; but the mechanics and discipline of the latter automatically impose its habits and ideas on him. When he comes in contact with a mechanized civilization that is amazingly equipped to dominate nature, he finds the idea of progress, for example, irresistible. But this process of assimilation and incorporation is quickly accomplished only within a vigorous industrial culture. In the lethargy of the feudal latifundium and the backwater town, the virtues and values of racial intermixture are nullified and replaced by debilitating superstitions.

To the man of the mestizo village—portrayed by Valcárcel with a pessimism and passion tinged with sociological preoccupations—Western civilization presents a confused spectacle. Everything in this civilization that is personal, essential, intrinsic, and dynamic is alien to his way of life. Despite some external imitations and subsidiary habits, this man does not move within the orbit of modern civilization. From this point of view, the Indian in his native environment, as long as emigration does not uproot or deform him, has nothing to envy the mestizo. It is evident that he is still not incorporated into this expanding, dynamic civilization that seeks to be universal. The Indian has a social existence that preserves his customs, his understanding of life, his attitude toward the universe. The "residual" feelings and derivations described to us in the sociology of Pareto, which continue to operate in him, are those of his own history. Indian life has a style. Notwithstanding the conquest, the latifundium, and the *gamonal*, the Indian of the sierra still follows his own traditions. The *ayllu* is a social structure deeply rooted in environment and race.[41]

The Indian continues his old rural life. To this day, he keeps his native dress, his customs, and his handicrafts. The indigenous social community has not disappeared under the harshest feudalism. The indigenous society may appear to be primitive and retarded, but it is an organic type of society and culture. The experience of the Orient—in Japan, Turkey, and China itself—has proved to us that even after a long period of collapse, an autochthonous society can rapidly find its own way to modern civilization and translate into its own tongue the lessons of the West.

Alcides Spelucín

The first book of Alcides Spelucín includes the poetry that he read to me nine years ago in Lima when we were first introduced by Abraham Valdelomar in the office of the newspaper I worked on. Since then Alcides and I have seldom seen each other, but we have grown continually closer. Although outwardly dissimilar, our destinies are analogous. He and I belong not only to the same generation, but to the same time. We were born under the same sign. In our literary adolescence we were

---

[41] In this regard, the studies of Hildebrando Castro Pozo on the "indigenous community" contain extremely interesting information which I have already referred to elsewhere. This information absolutely agrees with the substance of Valcárcel's statements in *Tempestad en los Andes*, which might be thought to be overly optimistic and apologetic if they were not confirmed by objective research. Furthermore, anyone can demonstrate the unity, style, and character of indigenous life. Sociologically, the survival of what Sorel calls "spiritual elements of work" in the community are of utmost value.

both nourished on decadence, modernism, aestheticism, individualism, and skepticism. Later, we both had the painful and difficult task of liberating ourselves from their unhealthy influence. We went abroad, not to learn the secret of others, but to learn the secret of ourselves. I discuss my trip in a book on politics and Spelucín describes his in a book of poetry. But this only indicates a difference in our attitudes or temperament, not in our adventures or spirit. The two of us set sail on "the golden boat in search of a good island" and in the course of our stormy expedition we discovered God and mankind. Alcides and I have chosen the future over the past. As survivors of a literary skirmish, we feel today like troops in a historical battle.

El libro de la nave dorada is a way station in the voyage and spirit of Alcides Spelucín. In the emotional preface Orrego has written for this book, he tells the reader:

It does not represent the aesthetic present of the creator. It is a book of adolescence, and initial poetic effort that barely opens the cloister of anonymous privacy. Since them, the poet has known anguish as well as success and pleasure. His spirit is now more refined; his vision more luminous; his expression richer, more flexible, and more powerful; his thought more enlightened with wisdom; his panorama broader and more valuable because of accumulated knowledge; his heart more religious, more sensitive, and more open to the world. This should be noted so that the reader will realize the painful precocity of a poet who was little more than a child when he wrote this book.[42]

As a song of the sea and a ballad of the tropics, this book represents in the poetry of America something like an incantatory prolongation of "Sinfonía en gris mayor," a melodious echo of the music of Rubén Darío. The mark of the Uruguayan poet

---

[42] *El libro de la nave dorada* (Trujillo: Ediciones de "El Norte," 1926).

Herrera y Reissig, who had already made his influence felt in Spanish-American lyricism, is splendidly vivid in lines like the following:

> And, to the planetary awakening of the spikenard,
> the divine vespertine leopards, roaring
> sad lilacs, depart along the road to the east.
>   ("Caracol bermejo")

But the presence of Herrera y Reissig and even of Rubén Darío is noticeable only in technique and form. Spelucín has the expression but not the spirit of the decadents. He is completely healthy, with no morbid tendencies. Although Alcides has absorbed much of the poison of his epoch, his robust and fundamentally rustic soul has remained pure and wholesome. Therefore, he is more alive and personal in this prayer of immaculate lyricism:

> Will you not give me clay from the rose-colored quarry
> with which to shape my base for savoring Love?
> Will you not give me a bit of melodious earth
> with which to mould the fever of my dream, O Lord?

Like Vallejo, Alcides is compassionate, humble, and affectionate. At a time when the Byzantine egotism of D'Annunzio was fashionable, the poetry of Alcides is perfumed with the Franciscan parable. In substance, his soul is naturally Christian. His characteristic tone appears in another prayer, flavored with ears of wheat and the angelus, like some verses of Francis Jammes: "For this sweet little sister with gentle eyes."

The clear innocence of Alcides is perceptible even in the "strong stuff," derivative of Baudelaire, which, taking full responsibility for the poetry of his youth, he has included in *El libro de la nave dorada*. And this innocence may account for his socialism, which is an act of love rather than of protest.

Provisional Balance Sheet

I have not intended this very brief review of literary values to be a history or even a criticism, if criticism is understood to be limited to the field of writing techniques. My purpose has been to sketch the outlines or essential characteristics of our literature. I have tried to interpret its spirit, not to report its episodes; to present a theory, not an analysis.

This will explain the deliberate omission of certain works that undeniably would merit discussion in a history or criticism of our literature, but that are not significant to the literary process itself. In all literature, significance is measured by two criteria: the exceptional intrinsic value of the work or the historic value of its influence. The artist survives in literature either through his work or through his followers. Otherwise, he survives only in libraries and histories, where he may be of great interest to researchers and bibliographers but of almost no interest to an interpretation of the deeper meaning of literature.

The most recent generation, which is a movement well under way and still developing, cannot yet be studied in this manner.[43] National literature is put on trial in the name of the new writers; and the past, not the present, is judged. The new writers, who belong more to the future than to the present, are judge, attorney, lawyer, witness, everything but the accused. Furthermore, a table of standards that seeks to establish present or potential values would be premature and hazardous.

The new generation signifies, above all, the definitive decline of colonialism. It is now that the spiritual and sentimental prestige of the viceroyalty, jealously cultivated by its heirs, sinks into oblivion. This literary and ideological phenomenon is naturally a facet of a much vaster phenomenon. The generation of

---

[43] I also recognize that this essay has omitted some ranking contemporaries whose writing must be considered as still continuing and developing. I repeat that my study is not complete.

Riva Agüero made a last attempt in politics and literature to save the colony. But the so-called futurism, which was only a neo-*civilismo*, has been liquidated in both areas because of the flight, abdication, and dispersal of its supporters.

In the history of our literature, it is not until this generation that the colony ends and Peru finally becomes independent of the mother country. Earlier writers had laid the groundwork. González Prada was the precursor of cosmopolitan influences when forty years ago, from the platform of the Ateneo, he urged young intellectuals to rebel against Spain. In this century, the modernism of Rubén Darío, although attenuated and counteracted by the colonialism of the futurist generation, contributed innovations in style that have permeated our literature and given it a French cast. And then the *colónida* movement incited the generation of 1915, which was the first to heed the admonition of González Prada to mutiny against Spanish academicism, which had been solemnly albeit precariously restored in Lima with the installation of the appropriate Academy. But colonialism, the intellectual and sentimental prestige of the viceroyalty, remained in spirit if not in form.

Today the rupture is complete. Indigenism, as we have seen, is gradually uprooting colonialism. And this movement does not originate exclusively in the sierra. Valdelomar and Falcón, both coastal criollos, are among those who have first turned their attention to race, whatever the success of their efforts. From abroad we simultaneously receive various international influences. Our literature has entered a period of cosmopolitanism. In Lima, this cosmopolitanism is reflected in the imitation of corrosive Western decadence and in the adoption of anarchical *fin-de-siécle* styles. But under this swirling current, a new feeling and revelation are perceived. The universal, ecumenical roads we have chosen to travel, and for which we are reproached, take us ever closer to ourselves.

GLOSSARY

Aguardiente: Liquor, especially a cheap liquor distilled from sugar cane

Ayllu: A group of related Quechua families; a "community"

Caciquismo: Rule by caciques, or rural political bosses

Civilismo: A political movement that originally opposed the military through the formation of the Partido Civil (Civil party), but that later represented the joint desire of the aristocracy, big business, and the military to preserve the status quo; as a general term, extreme conservatism

Colónida: A short-lived Peruvian literary movement to which Mariátegui once belonged, anti-academic in spirit; also, the name of a literary journal

Comunero: Communal landholder

Costumbrista: A term used in Hispanic literature to describe the novel of customs and similar prose

Encomendero: The holder of an *encomienda*

Encomienda: A tract of land which, with the Indians living on it, was granted by the Spanish crown to favored individuals

Gamonal: An *hacendado*, *latifundista*, cacique, or other member of the provincial "establishment"

Greguería: A brief, poetic impression or comparison, usually in one sentence, often surrealistic; "invented" by the Spanish writer Ramón Gómez de la Serna

Hacendado: The owner of an hacienda, or landed estate

Latifundista: The owner of a latifundium, or large landed estate

Libra peruana: Ten *soles*; at the time this book was written, the *libra peruana* was worth about four U.S. dollars

Limeño: A native of Lima; as an adjective, pertaining to Lima

Lp: *Libra peruana*

Mestizaje: The mixing of races, especially of the white and the Indian

Minga: A voluntary gathering of Quechuas to work on a communal project

Mita: The colonial system of forced labor under which Indians worked the farms and mines

Montaña: As a region of Peru, the forested region east of the Andes

Pasadismo: A literary attitude that rejected the present in favor of the past, especially the colonial era

Perricholismo: A literary attitude that romanticized the colonial era; *pasadismo*

Puna: The high plateau of the Andes

Quipu: The mnemonic record-keeping device of the Incas, consisting of a main cord with from one to over a hundred colored, knotted strings pendant from it

Serrano: One who lives in a mountainous area, specifically the Peruvian sierra region

Sol: The monetary unit of Peru; SEE *Libra peruana*

Yanaconazgo: A form of tenant farming in which the farmer, or *yanacón*, in exchange for the use of a plot of land on which to raise subsistence crops for his family, works on the hacienda lands a given number of days each week and performs other services for the landowner

Yaraví: A type of plaintive Quechua song, often accompanied by the *quena*, or indigenous flute; literary *yaravíes* have been written

Zambo: A person of Negro and Indian blood

INDEX